Empirical Market Microstructure

Empirical Market Microstructure

The Institutions, Economics, and Econometrics of Securities Trading

Joel Hasbrouck

OXFORD
UNIVERSITY PRESS

2007

OXFORD
UNIVERSITY PRESS

Oxford University Press, Inc., publishes works that further
Oxford University's objective of excellence
in research, scholarship, and education.

Oxford New York
Auckland   Cape Town   Dar es Salaam   Hong Kong   Karachi
Kuala Lumpur   Madrid   Melbourne   Mexico City   Nairobi
New Delhi   Shanghai   Taipei   Toronto

With offices in

Argentina   Austria   Brazil   Chile   Czech Republic   France   Greece
Guatemala   Hungary   Italy   Japan   Poland   Portugal   Singapore
South Korea   Switzerland   Thailand   Turkey   Ukraine   Vietnam

Library of Congress Cataloging-in-Publication Data
Hasbrouck, Joel.
Empirical market microstructure: the institutions, economics, and
econometrics of securities trading/Joel Hasbrouck.
p. cm.
Includes bibliographical references and index.
ISBN-13: 978-0-19-530164-9

1. Securities. 2. Securities—Prices. 3. Investments—Mathematical models.
4. Stock exchanges—Mathematical models. I. Title.
HG4521.H353 2007
332.64—dc22   2006003935

19 18 17 16 15 14 13

Printed in the United States of America
on acid-free paper

To Lisa, who inspires these pages and much more.

Preface

This book is a study of the trading mechanisms in financial markets: the institutions, the economic principles underlying the institutions, and statistical models for analyzing the data they generate. The book is aimed at graduate and advanced undergraduate students in financial economics and practitioners who design or use order management systems. Most of the book presupposes only a basic familiarity with economics and statistics.

I began writing this book because I perceived a need for treatment of empirical market microstructure that was unified, authoritative, and comprehensive. The need still exists, and perhaps someday when the field has reached a point of perfection and stasis such a book will be written. In the meantime I simply endeavor to identify and illuminate some themes that appear, for the moment at least, to be defining the field's arc of progress.

Three of these themes are especially prominent. The first is the institution that has come to dominate many of our most important markets—the (electronic) limit order book. Much of the material here can be perceived as an attempt to understand this mechanism. The second theme is asymmetric information, an economic term that refers to the varying quality of the information that traders bring to the market. It often establishes a motive for trade by some individuals, but also frequently leads to costs borne by a larger number. The third theme is linear time-series analysis, a set of statistical tools that have proven to be robust and useful not simply in describing security market data but also in characterizing the underlying economic structure.

Although the institutional, economic, and statistical content of the book can be read separately and selectively, there is a natural ordering to these perspectives. The features of real-world trading mechanisms motivate almost everything else, so an early chapter provides an accessible summary that is largely self-contained. Once this framework has been established, the economic arguments that follow will seem more focused. The statistical time-series models are then brought in to support, refute, or calibrate the economic analyses.

The discussion of time-series analysis here is not as deep as a textbook focused solely on the subject, but it is more substantial than an applied field book would normally attempt. I weave through the book coherent and self-contained explanations of the time-series basics.

This is not done simply to save the reader the trouble of reaching for one of the texts. Coverage, sequencing, and balance in most statistics texts are driven (implicitly at least) by the nature of the data to be modeled. It is a fact that most applications and illustrations in the extant literature of time-series econometrics are drawn from macroeconomics. A theorem is a theorem, of course, irrespective of the sampling frequency. But microstructure data and models are distinctive. It is my hope that seeing time-series analysis organized from a microstructure perspective will help readers apply it to microstructure problems.

Although not presently affiliated, I have over the years served as paid or unpaid consultant or advisor to the New York Stock Exchange, NASDAQ, the Securities and Exchange Commission, and ITG. Except for a brief youthful adventure as a day trader, I lay no claim to trading experience.

One of the earliest comprehensive analyses of U.S. equity markets was the U.S. Securities and Exchange Commission *Special Study of Securities Markets* (1963). Irwin Friend was a consultant to that study and later, among many other things, my dissertation advisor. His supervision was an ongoing lesson in how to approach data with a balance of imagination and skepticism.

All students of market microstructure owe a large debt to the practitioners, who over the years have shared data, patiently described the workings of their markets, and helped us define the important and relevant problems. Jim Cochrane (then of the New York Stock Exchange) opened the door of the exchange to academics, correctly foreseeing that both groups would gain enormously. His efforts have had an enduring positive effect on the research culture of the field.

Other practitioners and regulators who have helped bring us to where we are today include Robert Colby, Michael Edleson, Robert Ferstenberg, Dean Furbush, Frank Hatheway, Rick Ketchum, Ray Killian, Martha Kramer, Tim McCormick, Annette Nazareth, Richard Olsen, Jim Shapiro, James Sinclair, George Sofianos, and David Whitcomb. To these individuals I offer my thanks in lieu of citations.

A partial list of academic researchers who have shaped my thinking and this book would include Yakov Amihud, Bruno Biais, Ian Domowitz, David Easley, Rob Engle, Larry Glosten, Yasushi Hamao, Larry Harris, Tom Ho, Charles Jones, A. S. (Pete) Kyle, Bruce Lehmann, Andrew Lo, Francis Longstaff, Richard Lyons, Ananth Madhavan, Maureen O'Hara, Christine Parlour, Lasse Pedersen, Mark Ready, Gideon Saar, Robert Schwartz, Duane Seppi, Erik Sirri, Matt Spiegel, Chester Spatt, Hans Stoll, Avanidhar (Subra) Subramanyam, S. (Vish) Viswanathan, Jiang Wang, Ingrid Werner, and many others. For encouragement and editorial assistance, I am grateful to Kim Hoag, Catherine Rae, and Terry Vaughn.

I am grateful to the Stern School of New York University for sabbatical support that sustained this work, and to Kenneth G. Langone, who endowed the professorship at Stern that I currently hold. The Business School of Columbia University graciously hosted me as a visitor during the very pleasant year in which this book was completed.

For their suffusion of curiosity, creativity and ebullience, I thank my daughters, Ariane and Siena Hasbrouck.

Contents

Empirical Market Microstructure

1
Introduction

1.1 Overview

Market microstructure is the study of the trading mechanisms used for financial securities. There is no "microstructure manifesto," and historical antecedents to the field can probably be found going back to the beginning of written language, but at some point, the field acquired a distinct identity. As good a starting point as any is the coinage of the term *market microstructure* in the paper of the same title by Garman (1976):

> We depart from the usual approaches of the theory of exchange by (1) making the assumption of asynchronous, temporally discrete market activities on the part of market agents and (2) adopting a viewpoint which treats the temporal microstructure, i.e., moment-to-moment aggregate exchange behavior, as an important descriptive aspect of such markets. (p. 257)

Microstructure analyses typically touch on one or more of the following aspects of trade.

1.1.1 Sources of Value and Reasons for Trade

We generally assume that the security value comprises private and common components. Private values are idiosyncratic to the agent and are usually known by the agent when the trading strategy is decided. Common values are the same for everyone in the market and are often known or realized only after trade has occurred. In security markets, the common value component reflects the cash flows from the security, as summarized

3

in the present value of the flows or the security's resale value. Private value components arise from differences in investment horizon, risk exposure, endowments, tax situations, and so on. Generally, common value effects dominate private value effects. A necessary condition for gains from trade within a set of agents is contingent on some sort of differentiation. In modeling, this is often introduced as heterogeneous private values.

1.1.2   Mechanisms in Economic Settings

Microstructure analyses are usually very specific about the mechanism or protocol used to accomplish trade. One common and important mechanism is the continuous limit order market. The full range, though, includes search, bargaining, auctions, dealer markets, and a variety of derivative markets. These mechanisms may operate in parallel: Many markets are hybrids.

1.1.3   Multiple Characterizations of Prices

The market-clearing price, at least at it arises in usual Walrasian tatonnement, rarely appears in microstructure analyses. At a single instant there may be many prices, depending on direction (buying or selling), the speed with which the trade must be accomplished, the agent's identity or other attribute, and the agent's relationship to the counterparty (as well as, of course, quantity). Some prices (like bids and offers) may be hypothetical and prospective.

1.2   Liquidity

Security markets are sometimes characterized by their *liquidity*. Precise definitions only exist in the contexts of particular models, but the qualities associated with the word are sufficiently widely accepted and understood that the term is useful in practical and academic discourse.

Liquidity impounds the usual economic concept of elasticity. In a liquid market, a small shift in demand or supply does not result in a large price change. Liquidity also refers to the cost of trading, something distinct from the price of the security being bought or sold. Liquid markets have low trading costs. Finally, liquidity has dynamic attributes. In a liquid market, accomplishing a purchase or sale over a short horizon does not cost appreciably more than spreading the trades over a longer interval.

Liquidity is sometimes defined as "depth, breadth, and resiliency." In a deep market if we look a little above the current market price, there is a large incremental quantity available for sale. Below the current price, there is a large incremental quantity that is sought by one or more buyers. A broad market has many participants, none of whom is presumed to exert significant market power. In a resilient market, the price effects that are associated with the trading process (as opposed to the fundamental valuations) are small and die out quickly.

It is sometimes useful to characterize agents as suppliers or demanders of liquidity. Liquidity supply has traditionally been associated with the financial services industry, that is, the brokers, dealers, and other intermediaries that are sometimes called the sell side of the market. Liquidity demanders in this view are the customers, the individual and institutional investors characterized by trading needs (and sometimes called the buy side).

From a narrower perspective, liquidity supply and demand differentiates agents who are available to trade or offer the option to trade, and those who spontaneously decide to trade. Thus, liquidity suppliers are passive, and demanders are active. In any particular trade, the active side is the party who seals the deal by accepting the terms offered by the passive side. In other words, the passive side "makes" the market and the active side "takes."

With the rise of markets that are widely, directly, and electronically accessible, the role of liquidity demander or supplier (in the sense of the preceding paragraph) is a strategic choice that can be quickly reversed. The alignment of liquidity demand and supply with particular institutions, therefore, is of diminished relevance in many modern markets.

The *liquidity externality* is a network externality. The attributes of liquidity just discussed are generally enhanced, and individual agents can trade at lower cost, when the number of participants increases. This force favors market *consolidation*, the concentration of trading activity in a single mechanism or venue. Differences in market participants (e.g., retail versus institutional investors), however, and innovations by market designers militate in favor of market segmentation (in this context, usually called *fragmentation*).

The number of participants in a security market obviously depends on features of the security, in addition to the trading mechanism. If the aggregate value of the underlying assets is high; if value-relevant information is comprehensive, uniform, and credible; or if the security is a component of an important index, there will be high interest in trading the security. Ultimately, of course, these qualities are determined endogenously with the market mechanism. But it is common, when emphasizing the exogenous aspects of these attributes to describe a *security* as being liquid or illiquid.

The sources and origins of liquidity are generally what this book and the field are about. They defy simplistic generalizations, but I have found one expression to be particularly thought-provoking: "Liquidity is created through a give and take process in which multiple counterparties selectively reveal information in exchange for information ultimately leading to a trade." The words are taken from the offering materials for the ICor Brokerage (an electronic swaps trading platform). It is a practical sentiment that resonates throughout much of what follows.

1.3 Transparency

Transparency is a market attribute that refers to how much information market participants (and potential participants) possess about the trading process. Electronic markets that communicate in real time the bids and offers of buyers and sellers and the prices of executed trades are considered highly transparent. Dealer markets, on the other hand, often have no publicly visible bids or offers, nor any trade reporting, and are therefore usually considered opaque.

1.4 Econometric Issues

Microstructure data are distinctive. Most microstructure series consist of discrete events randomly arranged in continuous time. Within the time-series taxonomy, they are formally classified as *point processes*. Point process characterizations are becomingly increasingly important, but for many purposes it suffices to treat observations as continuous variables realized at regular discrete times.

Microstructure data are often well ordered. The sequence of observations in the data set closely corresponds to the sequence in which the economic events actually happened. In contrast, most macroeconomic data are time-aggregated. This gives rise to simultaneity and uncertainty about the directions of causal effects. The fine temporal resolution, sometimes described as ultra-high frequency, often supports stronger conclusions about causality (at least in the post hoc ergo propter hoc sense).

Microstructure data samples are typically large in the sense that by most economic standards observations are exceedingly plentiful (10,000 would not be considered unusual). One would not ordinarily question the validity of asymptotic statistical approximations in samples of this size. It is worth emphasizing, though, that the usual asymptotic results apply to correctly specified models, and given the complexity of trading processes, some degree of misspecification is almost inevitable. Furthermore, despite the number of observations, the data samples are often small in terms of calendar span (on the order of days or at best months).

Microstructure data samples are new (we don't have long-term historical data for most markets). The samples may also be characterized as old, though, because market institutions are changing so rapidly that even samples a few years previous may be seriously out of date.

1.5   The Questions

Here is a partial list of significant outstanding questions in market microstructure:

- What are optimal trading strategies for typical trading problems?
- Exactly how is information impounded in prices?
- How do we enhance the information aggregation process?
- How do we avoid market failures?
- What sort of trading arrangements maximize efficiency?
- What is the trade-off between "fairness" and efficiency?
- How is market structure related to the valuation of securities?
- What can market/trading data tell us about the informational environment of the firm?
- What can market/trading data tell us about long-term risk?

Although they might have been worded differently, most of these problems have been outstanding as long as the field has been in existence.

1.6   Readings

This book draws on material from economic theory, econometrics and statistics, and descriptions of existing market institutions. Harris (2003) is a broad treatment of economic theory and trading institutions at the advanced MBA level. O'Hara (1995) is the standard reference for the economic theory of market microstructure. Brunnermeier (2001) surveys information and price formation in securities markets, treating microstructure in a broader economic context. Lyons (2001) discusses the market microstructure of the foreign exchange market, providing a useful alternative to the present treatment, which is based more on equity markets. Survey articles include Hasbrouck (1996a), Madhavan (2000), and Biais, Glosten, and Spatt (2005). Amihud, Mendelson, and Pedersen (2005) survey the rapidly growing field that links microstructure and asset pricing. Shepard (2005) is a useful collection of key readings in stochastic volatility. This research increasingly relies on high-frequency data and therefore more deeply involves microstructure issues.

Some characteristics of security price dynamics are best discussed in context of the larger environment in which the security market operates. Cochrane (2005) is a comprehensive and highly comprehensible synthesis of the economics of asset pricing. Related background readings on financial economics include Ingersoll (1987), Huang and Litzenberger (1998), and Duffie (2001).

The empirical material draws heavily on the econometrics of time-series analysis. Hamilton (1994) is the key reference here, and the present discussion often refers the reader to Hamilton for greater detail. For other econometric techniques (in particular, duration and limited dependent variable models), Greene (2002) is particularly useful. Alexander (2001), Gourieroux and Jasiak (2001) and Tsay (2002) discuss financial econometrics; Dacorogna et al. (2001) focus on high-frequency data. The econometric coverage in these excellent books partially overlaps with the present text.

It is difficult to cite authoritative sources covering institutional details of the specific markets. Markets that are recently organized or overhauled, particularly those that feature standard mechanisms, are usually well documented. The trading procedures of the Euronext markets are in this respect exemplary (Euronext (2003)). Hybrid markets that have evolved over extended periods of change and adaptation are much less straightforward. The practicalities of current trading on the New York Stock Exchange, for example, would be extremely difficult to deduce from the codified *Constitution and Rules* (New York Stock Exchange (2005)). Comerton-Forde and Rydge (2004) provide useful summaries of trading procedures in many securities markets and countries.

1.7 Supplements to the Book

My Web site (http://www.stern.nyu.edu/~jhasbrou) contains a number of links and programs that may help the reader follow, apply, emend, or extend the material in the book. Most of the mathematical derivations in the book were generated using *Mathematica*. The *Mathematica* notebooks are available on the site. Using *Mathematica* does not by any means guarantee the correctness of a derivation, but it does lessen the likelihood of a simple algebraic mistake. A *Mathematica* notebook documents a calculation in standard form. It facilitates the modification and extension of an argument, visualization, and (when necessary) the transition to numerical implementation. The solutions to most of the exercises are contained in the notebooks. The site has several SAS programs that illustrate the techniques.

2

Trading Mechanisms

This chapter surveys typical trading arrangements and establishes an institutional context for the statistical and economic models to follow. This book focuses on continuous security markets. Whatever their original mechanisms, many and the most visible of these markets presently feature an electronic limit order book. The limit order market, then, is the starting point for the survey. This is probably the most important mechanism, but there are usually at least several alternative paths to accomplishing a trade for any given security. Most security markets are actually hybrids, involving dealers, clearings, one- and two-sided auctions, and bilateral bargaining, all of which are also discussed. The survey emphasizes general features and is not specific to particular securities or a particular country. The appendix to the book contains a supplementary overview of U.S. equity markets.

Whatever the mechanism, the event that we label a trade, execution, or fill (of an order) actually only constitutes a preliminary agreement as to terms. This agreement sets in motion the clearing and settlement procedures that will ultimately result in the transfer of securities and funds. These processes are usually automatic and routine, and the traders seldom need to concern themselves with the details. It is important, though, that they require some sort of preexisting relationship, possibly one that is indirect and via intermediaries, between the parties. Establishing a brokerage account or clearing arrangement is neither costless nor instantaneous and may therefore create a short-run barrier to entry for a potential buyer or seller not previously known to the market.

Trading often involves a broker. A broker may simply provide a conduit to the market but may also act as the customer's agent. This is a more substantial role and may involve discretion about how to handle a customer's trading needs: when to trade, where to trade, what sort of orders to use, and so on. The customer–broker agency relationship gives rise to the usual problems of monitoring, contracting, and enforcement that pervade many principal–agent relationships. The broker's duty to the customer is sometimes broadly characterized as "best execution," but precise definition of what this means has proven elusive (Macey and O'Hara (1997)).

We now turn to the specific mechanisms.

2.1 Limit Order Markets

Most continuous security markets have at least one electronic limit order book. A limit order is an order that specifies a direction, quantity, and acceptable price, for example, "Buy 200 shares at $25.50 [per share]," or "Sell 300 shares at $30.00." In a limit order market, orders arrive randomly in time. The price limit of a newly arrived order is compared to those of orders already held in the system to ascertain if there is a match. For example, if the buy and sell orders just described were to enter the system (in any order), there would be no match: a price of $25.50 is not acceptable to the seller; a price of $30.00 is not acceptable to the buyer. A subsequent order to buy 100 shares at $32.00 could be matched, however, as there is an overlap in the acceptable prices. If there is a match, the trade occurs at the price set by the first order: An execution will take place (for 100 shares) at $30.

The set of unexecuted limit orders held by the system constitutes the book. Because limit orders can be canceled or modified at any time, the book is dynamic, and in active markets with automated order management it can change extremely rapidly. These markets are usually transparent, with the state of the book being widely visible to most actual and potential market participants. Short of actually trading, there is no better way to get a feel for their mechanics than by viewing the INET book (currently available at www.nasdaqtrader.com) for an actively traded stock (such as Microsoft, ticker symbol MSFT). The extraordinary level of transparency traders currently enjoy is a recent phenomenon. New York Stock Exchange (NYSE) rules historically prohibited revelation of the book. In the 1990s, this was relaxed to permit visibility of the book on the trading floor. Off-floor visibility was not available until January 2002.[1]

A market might have multiple limit order books, each managed by a different broker or other entity. Limit order books might also be used in conjunction with other mechanisms. When all trading for a security occurs through a single book, the market is said to be organized as a consolidated limit order book (CLOB). A CLOB is used for actively traded stocks in most Asian and European markets.

A mechanism's priority rules govern the sequence in which orders are executed. Price priority is basic. A limit order to buy priced at 100, for example, will be executed before an order priced at 99. Time is usually the secondary priority. At a given price level, orders are executed first-in, first-out. Although these priority rules may seem obvious and sensible, it should be noted that they usually only determine the relative standing of orders within a given book. There is rarely system-wide time priority across all books or other components of a hybrid market.

A trader may desire that an order be executed "at the market," that is, at the best available price. If the order quantity is larger than the quantity available at the single best price on book, the order will "walk the book," achieving partial executions at progressively worse prices until the order is filled. This may lead to executions at prices far worse than the trader thought possible at the time of submission. For example, at 10:47:26 on January 29, 2001, the bid side of the book for IBM on the Island ECN contained (in its entirety) bids at $112.50, $110.00, $108.00, and $2.63. The last bid was presumably entered in error, but should it have been executed, a seller would have obtained $2.63 for a share of IBM at a time when its market price was in the vicinity of $113.[2]

A provision in the Euronext system illustrates how surprises of this sort can be avoided. On Euronext, a market order is not allowed to walk the book. It will only execute for (at most) the quantity posted at the best available price. Anything remaining from the original quantity is converted into a limit order at the execution price. For example, if a market order to buy 1,000 shares arrives when the best offer is 200 shares at €100, 200 shares will be executed at €100, and the remaining 800 shares will be added to the book as a buy limit order priced at €100. If a trader in fact wants the order to walk the book, the order must be priced. Attaching a price to the order forces the trader to consider the worst acceptable price. INET requires that all orders be priced.

Markets often permit qualifications and/or variations on the basic limit order. The time-in-force (TIF) attribute of an order specifies how long the order is to be considered active. It is essentially a default cancellation time, although it does not preclude the sender from canceling before the TIF is reached. Although the precommitment associated with a TIF deprives the sender of some flexibility, it avoids the communication delays and uncertainties that sometimes arise with transmitted requests for cancellation. An immediate-or-cancel (IOC) order never goes onto the book. If it cannot be executed, it leaves no visible trace, and the sender is free to quickly try another order (or another venue). An all-or-nothing (AON) order is executed in its entirety or not at all. It avoids the possibility that a partial fill (execution) will, when reported to other traders, move the market price against the sender, leaving the remaining portion of the order to be executed at a less favorable price.

A trader seeking to buy or sell an amount that is large (relative to the quantities typically posted to the book) is unlikely to feel comfortable displaying the full extent of his or her interest. To make the situation more attractive, many markets allow hidden and/or reserve orders. Hidden orders are the simpler of the two. If an order designated as hidden cannot be executed, it is added to the book but not made visible to other market participants. The hidden order is available for execution against incoming orders, the senders of which may be (happily) surprised by fills at prices that are better than or quantities that are larger than what they might have surmised based on what was visible. Hidden orders usually lose priority to visible orders, a rule that encourages display.

Reserve ("iceberg") orders are like hidden orders, but their invisibility is only partial. Some display is required, and if the displayed quantity is executed, it is refreshed from the reserve quantity. The procedure mimics a human trader who might feed a large order to the market by splitting it up into smaller quantities (Esser and Mönch (2005)).

In a limit order market, buyers and sellers interact directly, using brokers mainly as conduits for their orders. The broker may also, however, provide credit, clearing services, information, and possibly analytics designed to implement strategies more sophisticated than those associated with the standard order types. The broker does not usually act as a counterparty to the customer trade.

The data emanating from a limit order market are usually very accurate and detailed. The real-time feeds allow traders to continuously ascertain the status of the book and condition strategies on this information. For the economist, limit order markets offer a record of agents' interactions at a level of detail that is rarely enjoyed in other settings. There are, nevertheless, some significant generic limitations. First, the sheer volume and diverse attributes of the data pose computational challenges and make parsimonious modeling very difficult. More importantly, though, the unit of observation is typically the order, and it is rarely possible to map a particular order to others submitted or canceled by the same trader. Market participants can't construct these maps either (except for their own orders), so this does not preclude us from building models that might plausibly reflect agents' common-knowledge beliefs. It does, however, constrain what we can discern about individual trading strategies.

2.2   Floor Markets

Consolidation of trading interest (actual and potential buyers and sellers) is important because it enhances the likelihood that counterparties will find each other. Before electronic markets allowed centralization of trading to be accomplished virtually, consolidation could only take place physically, on the floor of an exchange. In a floor market, the numerous and dispersed buyers and sellers are represented by a much smaller number of brokers who negotiate and strike bilateral deals face to face. These brokers are often called members, as the exchanges were historically organized as cooperatives.

The members act either as agents, representing the customer orders to others, or as principals, taking the other side of customer orders. The combination of these two functions, though, suffers from a conflict of interest. A broker who intends to act as a counterparty to his or her customer's order does not have an interest in vigorously representing the order to others on the floor (who might offer a better a price). For this reason, dual trading is either expressly forbidden or strongly regulated.

Despite behavior that may appear chaotic and noisy, floor trading is usually an orderly process. Hand signals quickly convey the key features of an order. Deceptive actions, such as bidding lower than another member's current bid (in an attempt to find a seller willing to trade at the inferior price), are forbidden. Transaction prices are quickly reported and publicly disseminated. Disputes and errors are resolved quickly.

In the nineteenth century, floor markets proliferated. In the twentieth century, they consolidated. By the dawn of the twenty-first century, they had largely evaporated.[3] The largest markets that still rely primarily on trading floors are the U.S. commodity futures markets: the Chicago Board of Trade, the New York Mercantile Exchange, and Chicago Mercantile Exchange (the Merc). The last is perhaps the easiest for an outsider to comprehend, because its trading rules (available online) are particularly straightforward and clear. The NYSE is sometimes described as a floor market. This is indeed its heritage, but the label has become less accurate as the Exchange has incorporated more electronic mechanisms.

From an empirical viewpoint, it is worth noting that the real-time data stream emanating from floor trading in futures markets is meager relative to what most electronic limit order markets provide. Futures tick data generally only convey price changes. In a sequence of trades, only those that establish new price levels are reported. Bids and offers can generally be obtained only by inquiry. Transaction volumes are not reported.

As measured by the capital generation and allocation that they facilitated, and by their historical survival and persistence, the floor markets achieved remarkable success. On the other hand, this success led to market power and political influence that sometimes worked against customers and regulators. In recent years, most floor-based trading has gone electronic. Like many paradigm shifts, the transition has been painful for the old guard. Most exchanges have nevertheless navigated the changes and survived, either by gradually automating or by building electronic markets de novo.

One event in particular seems to have starkly illuminated the costs of resisting the change. Through the mid-1990s, the market for futures based on German government debt (Bund futures) was dominated by a contract that was floor-traded on the London International Financial Futures Exchange (LIFFE). In 1997, the Deutsche Terminbörse (DTB, now Eurex) began to aggressively market an electronically traded contract. Over the course of the next year, trading shifted to the newcomer. The LIFFE eventually moved trading to an electronic platform and shut down most floor trading by the end of 1999. It did not, however, recapture significant trading volume in the Bund contract (Maguire (1998) Codding (1999)).

Despite the rapid ascendancy of electronic systems, their limitations should not be overlooked. Electronic consolidation has not rendered face-to-face interactions irrelevant. Many of the same financial institutions that rely heavily on electronic access to markets have also gone to great lengths and expense to maintain the trading operations for their diverse markets together on large, contiguous trading floors. This facilitates coordination when a deal involves multiple markets. The pricing and offering of a corporate bond, for example, might well involve the government bond, interest-rate swap, credit swap, and/or the interest rate futures desks. Thus, while no longer necessary to realize (in a single market) economies of scale, personal proximity may promote (across multiple markets) economies of scope.

2.3 Dealers

2.3.1 Dealer Markets

A dealer is simply an intermediary who is willing to act as a counterparty for the trades of his customers. A dealer, or, more commonly, a network of geographically dispersed electronically linked dealers, may be the dominant mechanism for trade. Some of the largest markets are dealer markets, including foreign exchange (FX), corporate bond and swap markets.

A trade in a dealer market, such as the FX market, typically starts with a customer calling a dealer. The dealer quotes bid and ask prices, whereupon the customer may buy at the dealer's ask, sell at the dealer's bid, or do nothing. This script presumes that the dealer and customer have a preexisting relationship. This relationship plays a more significant role (in addition to establishing the framework for clearing and settlement), because the customer's trading history and behavior may reveal his or her unexpressed trading desires or information and may therefore affect the terms of trade that the dealer offers.

The dealer–customer relationship involves reputations established and sustained by repeated interactions. The dealer's reputation is contingent on his or her willingness to always quote a reasonable bid and ask, even if the dealer would prefer not to trade in a particular direction. The customer's reputation is based on his or her frequent acceptance of the dealer's terms of trade. A customer who called the dealer repeatedly merely to check the price, never actually trading, would soon find the dealer unresponsive to his or her inquiries.

In a limit order market, a buyer who judges the book's best ask price unreasonable may place his or her own bid (buy limit order). In most dealer markets, this possibility does not exist. Dealers rarely act as an effective agent for customer limit orders. For example, prior to the Manning rules (in the mid-1990s), a NASDAQ dealer holding a customer limit order to buy was under no obligation to display the order, even when the customer's bid bettered those of all other dealers in the market (see appendix section A.3).

A large customer may have relationships with many dealers. This forms the basis for competition that mitigates the dealer's bargaining power. Small retail customers, however, often do not have such a pool and therefore have little bargaining power.

Dealer markets are also usually characterized by low transparency. The dealers provide quotes only in response to customer inquiries, and these are not publicly visible. Publication of trade prices is unusual. Unlike consolidated floor markets, dealer markets are fragmented.

For customer orders, a dealer acts as a counterparty (trading against the order), and a broker acts as agent (representing the order on behalf of the customer). These two functions are not necessarily conflicting: Both broker and dealer will profit by successful execution of the customer's order. Often, though, the broker and dealer are working at cross-purposes. An aggressive agent might survey more dealers and bargain harder to find the customer a good price, one that leaves the executing dealer with only a small profit. A lazy agent might simply take the first price quoted by the first dealer. As in floor markets, this conflict of interest is most aggravated when the broker and dealer are the same or affiliated entities.

In addition to dealer–customer interactions, interdealer trading is also important. The incoming orders that a particular dealer sees are rarely balanced (as to purchases and sales). There is usually an excess demand or supply, and accommodating these customer needs may leave the dealer with an undesired long or short position. In such cases, the dealer will attempt to sell or buy in the interdealer market. One dealer may contact another directly and nonanonymously, much as a customer might have initially contacted him or her (except that the quantity would typically be larger). Willingness to make a market and trade in these interactions is sustained by reputation and reciprocity. The dealer who is being contacted might soon need to reach out to balance his or her own position. Alternatively, a contact may be made indirectly and anonymously through an interdealer broker. Finally, interdealer trade in the FX market is typically conducted via a limit order book (such as EBS or Reuters). From the diversity of these examples, it is clear that the interdealer market is defined by its participants, not by the mechanism. Analyses of interdealer markets include Reiss and Werner (1998) and Viswanathan and Wang (2004).

Dealer markets are typically flexible. The fixed technology and infrastructure costs are low. The main barrier to entry is access to a set of customers. Dealing operations are easily scaled up or down. Certain terms of trade and security characteristics may be set to accommodate customer preferences. For example, the equity derivatives desk at a bank might sell a customer a call option for which the underlying strike price, maturity, and size differ from any other option the desk has ever bought or sold.

2.3.2 Dealers in Hybrid Markets

Dealers can make markets work where they might otherwise fail. Recall that in a limit order market, customers trade directly with only a minimal role for the broker or any other intermediary. Liquidity, in the sense of the ability to trade immediately, is often described as customer-supplied because it derives from the unexecuted customer orders in the book. The absence of an intermediary helps keep trading costs low. On the other hand, the customers' interests are driven by their immediate trading needs. They are not usually inclined to provide liquidity in an ongoing and continuous fashion. This may impair the functioning of the market because a trading venue's reputation for always accommodating trades contributes to its ability to attract order flow.

Limit order markets generally have difficulty with small stocks, securities for which trading interest is insufficient to sustain continuous trading. In many cases, continuous trading may not be necessary. That is, market participants may be satisfied with a call mechanism (described shortly) that provides for trading only at several specified times of the day. Continuous trading, though, offers more flexibility in hedging and rebalancing portfolios. A dealer may make continuous trading possible when the natural customer-supplied liquidity in the book would not suffice.

Ideally, dealers would arise endogenously, perhaps as customers who gain familiarity with the market in the course of managing their own trades and then perceive opportunities in more actively supplying bids and offers. In actively traded securities, this may well be occurring. In low-activity securities, though, the potential dealer's costs of continuously monitoring bids and offers may be too large to recover from the relatively infrequent trades. In these instances, continuous liquidity requires that a dealer be designated as such (by the market authority) and provided with additional incentives. Perhaps the best-known designated dealer is the NYSE specialist. The specialist has many roles and responsibilities, but an important one is maintaining a two-sided market when there is nothing on the limit order book and no one else on the floor bidding or offering.

Establishing the proper incentives for designated dealers, though, has proven to be difficult. The issues involve measuring the liquidity that the dealers provide, determining the beneficiaries of this liquidity, allocating the costs, and balancing the rights of dealers against the public users of limit orders (who are usually the dealers' direct competitors). The Euronext equity markets have adopted a relatively straightforward solution. Taking the position that a firm's stockholders are the most direct beneficiaries of continuous liquidity, a firm may contract with and directly compensate an agent who agrees to post continuous bids and offers. More typically, though, dealers are implicitly compensated in the form of trading profits, generated within a complex structure of privileges and obligations.

As a rough generalization, technology has weakened the competitive position of dealers (as it has, arguably, the competitive position of intermediaries in many nonsecurity markets). Electronic order management systems, in particular, now enable customers to update and revise their limit orders rapidly enough to respond to market conditions. They can quickly supply liquidity when it is profitable to do so and quickly withdraw their bids and offers when markets are volatile. The U.S. over-the-counter stock market (NASDAQ), for example, has historically been considered a dealer market. In recent years, though, trading activity has shifted onto limit order markets, and the dealer presence is considerably diminished.

Dealers also serve a useful function in facilitating large (block) trades. The block market (also called the upstairs market) is mainly institutional. When an institution contacts a dealer to fill a large order, the dealer can act as principal (taking the other side of the order and committing capital), try to locate a counterparty for the full amount, work the order over time, or some combination of these. The dealer's advantage here thus lies in access to capital, knowledge of potential counterparties, and expertise (or, nowadays, algorithmic systems) executing large orders over time. The relationship between the customer and dealer also expedites the trade. The customer implicitly warrants that his or her institution is "uninformed," specifically, not seeking to exploit a short-term informational advantage, such as prior knowledge of an earnings announcement (Seppi (1990)).

2.4   Auctions and Other Clearing Mechanisms

When there are multiple buyers and multiple sellers concentrated in one venue at one time, trade need not be coordinated. Agents will contact each other sequentially, striking bilateral bargains. Economically inefficient outcomes, however, can easily arise.[4] Another practical consideration is that if the bargaining is conducted by brokers on behalf of customers, and the trade prices are publicly reported, many customers will see their trades executed at prices worse than the best price realized over the entire set of trades. This is unlikely to promote confidence in the brokers or the mechanism.

A single-price clearing avoids these problems. It is generally implemented with a single-price double-sided auction. Supply and demand curves are constructed by ranking bids and offers. Prices, quantities, and trader identities are usually determined by maximizing the feasible trading volume.

The double-sided auction is widely used in securities markets. For securities with low natural trading interest, most trade occurs using periodic auctions (also called fixings). The Euronext markets, for example, conduct auctions once or twice per day (depending on the level of interest). Double-sided auctions are usually used to open continuous trading sessions (Euronext, Tokyo Stock Exchange, NYSE, etc.). They are also frequently used at the close of continuous trading sessions. Closing prices are widely used as reference prices in valuing margin positions, valuing mutual fund shares, determining the payoffs to cash-settled derivatives, and (occasionally) determining terms of exchange in mergers. In these situations a small change in the reference price can cause substantial gains or losses in the derivative position. With so much at stake, it is not surprising that many cases of market manipulation involve attempts to "mark the close."[5]

Although auctions may appear simple, seemingly minor details of implementation can have profound effects. Klemperer (2004) notes that "what really matters in auction design are the same issues that any industry regulator would recognize as key concerns: discouraging collusive, entry-deterring and predatory behavior" (p. 104). Although the context of the statement is a discussion of single-side auctions, it is not a bad maxim for the double-sided security variety.

Experience suggests that a particularly important aspect of design is the deadline for order submission. As any casual observer of eBay activity can attest, most bidding action occurs very shortly before the final deadline (Roth and Ockenfels (2002)). Why bid early and give competitors a lengthy interval in which to contemplate their next moves? To discourage waiting until the last instant, the Euronext markets employ random stopping times. Within a brief window (on the order of seconds), order acceptance may be terminated at any point. This introduces uncertainty into the last-instant strategy and so discourages its use.[6] The deadline may also be extended if the price at the scheduled clearing would constitute a large movement from a preceding price (such as the previous day's close).

To further minimize the noise in price determination, earlier deadlines may be imposed on large or destabilizing orders. (An order is destabilizing if it is in the same direction as the change in the likely clearing price, a buy order, for example, if the other orders cumulated to that time imply a clearing price above the previous close.) To prevent the strategy of entering orders on both sides of the market and then canceling one at the last moment, cancellations of stabilizing orders are usually subject to the same early deadline as the submission of destabilizing orders.

Although most auctions in secondary (post–initial offering) markets are double-sided, single-sided auctions are extensively used in primary (initial offering) markets. These include the U.S. Treasury debt markets, and most U.S. municipal bond offerings. Auctions are also used, though not as often, for initial issues of equity.

Single-sided auctions can sometimes arise as an ancillary mechanism in a market where most trading takes place by other means. In floor trading on the NYSE, for example, one agent, the specialist, acts as agent for customer market orders (among other responsibilities). In this role, the specialist may auction a market order by indicating quantity and direction (e.g., "2,000 shares to buy") and letting other brokers compete to offer the best price.

The economic literature on auctions is extensive. Useful texts include (in order of ascending complexity) Klemperer (2004), Krishna (2002), and Milgrom (2004). Friedman and Rust (1993) is an excellent collection of articles focusing on double auctions.

2.5   Bargaining

Some security trading interactions closely resemble the usual customer/ vendor situation in goods markets wherein a shopkeeper fixes a posted price and the passing customer can purchase (or not). Although the posted price is almost certain to be constrained by larger forces of competition (the customer's access to alternative suppliers or substitute goods), the interaction is essentially, in the microscopic view, a bargaining game. In securities trading, the retail customer and her dealer may be in a similar situation. A retail customer in the United States who wishes to buy or sell a municipal bond will contact a broker and solicit prices at which the broker (acting in a capacity as dealer) would buy or sell. The broker states the prices, and the customer can trade (or not). Faced with unfavorable terms an institutional trader might search the prices of other dealers with whom they have relationships, but individuals rarely have accounts with more than one broker. Recent work on the U.S. municipal securities markets highlights the role of bargaining power in a dealer market (Green, Hollifield, and Schuerhoff (2005)).

In economic terms, this is an ultimatum game. In the standard full-information ultimatum game, one agent (the allocator) proposes a division of the total payoff, and the other agent (the recipient) either accepts or rejects the proposal. If the recipient accepts, both players receive the proposed payoff; if the recipient rejects, both players receive zero. The main feature of this literature is the divergence between the predicted rational outcomes and those that arise in experiments (and in most individuals' experiences). The rational recipient accepts any proposal that gives any nonzero payoff, and knowing this, the rational allocator keeps for him- or herself almost all of the total payoff. In practice, recipients often reject proposals perceived as unfair, and this forces allocators to discipline their greed. The economic literature on these games in voluminous. Thaler (1988) and Camerer and Thaler (1995) are good introductions. Roth (1995) surveys experimental evidence.

When the total payoff is known to the allocator but not the recipient, the latter cannot so readily assess the fairness of a proposal. This uncertainty favors the allocator, in this case, the dealer (see, for example, Kagel, Kim, and Moser 1996). Perhaps the strongest signal about the total payoff in the dealer–customer interaction is the record of prices of recent trades. For this reason, U.S. regulators have sought to promote trade price publication through a variety of initiatives.[7]

Another standard bargaining situation arises in Liquidnet, a trading system for U.S. institutional investors. Institutions anonymously enter the quantities and directions (buy or sell) of desired trades. The Liquidnet system searches over all the entries. When it finds a match, it contacts the buyer and seller and places them in a virtual meeting room, where they can (anonymously) bargain over price. The bargaining protocol essentially allows the recipient to reject the allocator's initial proposal and suggest another, and so on, indefinitely.

When the situation allows for repeated counter proposals, the Rubinstein (1982) theorem comes into play. Briefly, the theorem sets out some reasonable sufficient conditions (most important, time preference) under which the full-information game will immediately converge to the even-split outcome. The intuition is that both sides can clearly see the consequences of a strategy (which might at first seem reasonable) of making proposals that are far from an even split and marginally improving them ("I'll sell at $1,000"; "I bid one cent"; "I'm offering at $999.99"; "I bid two cents," etc.). This will simply dissipate value through delay. In a Liquidnet negotiation, both parties know bid and ask prices from other markets (although these will typically be for smaller quantities). Usually the midpoint of the best intermarket bid and offer is proposed and accepted.

2.6 Crossing Networks and Derivative Pricing

In a crossing, the buyer and seller are paired (usually anonymously) for an agreed-on quantity. The trade is priced by reference to a price determined in and derived from some other market. Thus, though almost all of the devices considered prior to this can in principle serve as the sole market mechanism, a crossing network, in its reliance on a price determined elsewhere, is inherently a hybrid device.

In ITG's POSIT system, for example, potential buyers and sellers enter demands (quantities to buy or sell). These are not made visible. At the time of the crossing, the system matches buyers and sellers (if possible).

The execution price of the trade is the midpoint of best bid and offer in the listing market. Thirteen crossings are scheduled each day. The exact time of a cross is partially random, to discourage either side from entering a surreptitious bid or offer to obtain a more favorable price.

Instinet (an institutional brokerage) runs a cross where the match price is the average price of all trades on the day, weighted by volume. Buyers and sellers enter desired quantities and are paired off in the morning, prior to the start of regular trading. After the market closes in the afternoon, the value-weighted average price (VWAP) is computed, and the trades are executed.

In both the POSIT and Instinet VWAP crossings, quantities are matched prior to the determination of the price. A crossing can also use a price determined prior to the quantity matching. The Instinet closing cross allows institutions to submit, after the regular market close, orders that will be matched (if possible) and executed at the closing price. Instinet also conducts crossings in foreign exchange.

Crossings must be designed to discourage manipulation (if the price is determined after the quantity match) and predatory trading (if the price is determined prior to the quantity match). A strategy of the latter sort might involve submitting orders in response to news announcements made after the determination of the closing price, in the hopes of picking off unwary counterparties. In view of an after-hours announcement of a product recall, for example, the day's closing price is likely to be high relative to the following open. A sell order might trade against someone who hadn't heard the news and canceled their buy order. To prevent this, Instinet cancels crosses when there are news announcements and monitors participants, expelling those whose strategies appear to be news-driven.

Another form of derivative pricing is *price matching*. This generally refers to a dealer's strategy of precommitting to execute orders at the best visible bid or offer (posted by others). The precommitment is made selectively, to brokers representing customers, typically retail customers, whose orders are likely to be profitable for the dealer.

The pricing in crossing markets is sometimes described as *derivative*, a usage that sometimes leads to confusion. In finance, a derivative *security* has a value or payoff that is a function of some other security (the underlying). A derivative *mechanism* is a device for executing trades in a security based on a price determined for the same security in another market.

2.7   Concluding Remarks

The complexity of institutional arrangements and the rapid pace of their evolution force the modeler to exercise judgment in deciding which features are important to the task at hand. In practice, market microstructure analyses deal with the details at varying levels of abstraction.

Least demanding of fidelity to institutional details are the descriptive statistical analyses of high-frequency trade price behavior, which can be viewed as atheoretic forecasting models. At a higher level of complexity, we attempt to identify passive and active sides of trades (the bid and offer quotes and the traders who hit or lift them). For these purposes, we might view, for example, the bids of dealers and the bids representing customer limit orders as equivalent. These models often have a fair degree of economic content yet remain sufficiently tractable to estimate.

In reality, though, the agent in a limit order market is intrinsically neither active nor passive but makes a choice conditional on the state of the book. Embedding this choice in a dynamic structural model of price evolution has proven to be extremely difficult. For the most part, current models make and test predictions about the determinants of order choice.

Studies addressing regulatory issues obviously require detailed knowledge of the rules in question but also need an appreciation for how these rules are applied and interpreted in practice. Often a particular rule or feature is too difficult to model structurally, though, and we attempt to draw welfare conclusions based on comparisons of relatively crude descriptive statistics before and after the change. These conclusions must frequently be qualified due to confounding events and agents' responses to the rule changes. Although it is relatively easy to assess direct trading costs (e.g., brokerage commissions), for example, it is virtually impossible to measure indirect costs (e.g., the cost of monitoring the status of a limit order) or the cost/benefits of degraded/enhanced risk sharing.

3

The Roll Model of Trade Prices

3.1 Overview

In taking a microstructure perspective on security price dynamics, we shift focus from monthly or daily characteristics down to the features that come into play at horizons of a minute or second. Figure 3.1 illustrates this transition. For a randomly chosen stock (Premcor, symbol PCO, subsequently acquired), the figure depicts in panel A the sequence of actual trade prices over October 2003, then in panel B the prices on a particular day (October 30), and finally in panel C a particular hour on that day (11 A.M. to noon). In panel C, trade prices are augmented by plots of bid and ask quotes.

The most detailed figure hints at the extent of microstructure complexities. The three prices (bid, ask, and trade) differ. None are continuous (they all have jumps), but the bid and ask are continual in the sense that they always have values. Trades are more discrete, occurring as a sequence of well-defined points. The three prices tend to move together but certainly not in lockstep. The bid and ask sometimes change and then quickly revert. Trades usually occur at the posted bid and offer prices (but not always). And so on.

I do not attempt at the outset to build a model that can explain or even describe all of these features. Instead, I begin with a model of high-frequency trade prices originally suggested by Roll (1984). It is an excellent starting point for several reasons. It illustrates a dichotomy fundamental to many microstructure models—the distinction between price components due to fundamental security value and those attributable to the market organization and trading process. The former arise from information

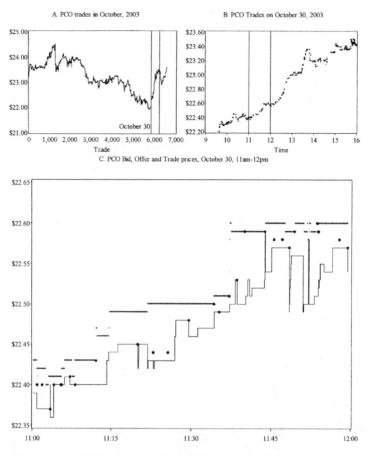

Figure 3.1. PCO price record at different time scales.

about future security cash flows and are long-lasting, whereas the latter are transient. The model possesses sensible economic and statistical representations, and it is easy to go back and forth between them. The model is useful, offering descriptions and interpretations that are, in many situations, quite satisfactory.

This chapter develops the Roll model by first presenting the random-walk model, which describes the evolution of the fundamental security value. The discussion then turns to bid and ask quotes, order arrivals, and the resulting transaction price process.

3.2   The Random-Walk Model of Security Prices

Before financial economists began to concentrate on the trading process, the standard statistical model for a security price was the random walk.

The random-walk model is no longer considered to be a complete and valid description of short-term price dynamics, but it nevertheless retains an important role as a model for the fundamental security value. Furthermore, some of the lessons learned from early statistical tests of the random-walk hypothesis have ongoing relevance in modeling market data.

Let p_t denote the transaction price at time t, where t indexes regular points of real ("calendar" or "wall-clock") time, for example, end-of-day, end-of-hour, and so on. Because it is unlikely that trades occur exactly at these times, we will approximate these observations by using the prices of the last (most recent) trade, for example, the day's closing price. The random walk model (with drift) is:

$$p_t = p_{t-1} + \mu + u_t, \tag{3.1}$$

where the u_t, $t = 0, \ldots$, are independently and identically distributed random variables. Intuitively, they arise from new information that bears on the security value. μ is the expected price change (the drift). The units of p_t are either levels (e.g., dollars per share) or logarithms. The log form is sometimes more convenient because price changes can be interpreted as continuously compounded returns. Some phenomena, however, are closely linked to a level representation. Price discreteness, for example, reflects a tick size (minimum pricing increment) that is generally set in level units.

For reasons that will be discussed shortly, the drift can be dropped in most microstructure analyses. When $\mu = 0$, p_t cannot be forecast beyond its most recent value: $E[p_{t+1} \mid p_t, p_{t-1}, \ldots] = p_t$. A process with this property is generally described as a martingale. One definition of a martingale is a discrete stochastic process $\{x_t\}$ where $E|x_t| < \infty$ for all t, and $E(x_{t+1} \mid x_t, x_{t-1}, \ldots) = x_t$ (see Karlin and Taylor (1975) or Ross (1996)). Martingale behavior of asset prices is a classic result arising in many economic models with individual optimization, absence of arbitrage, or security market equilibrium (Cochrane (2005)). The result is generally contingent, however, on assumptions of frictionless trading opportunities, which are not appropriate in most microstructure applications.

The martingale nevertheless retains a prominent role. To develop this idea, note that expectations in the last paragraph are conditioned on lagged p_t or x_t, that is, the history of the process. A more general definition involves conditioning on broader information sets. The process $\{x_t\}$ is a martingale with respect to another (possibly multidimensional) process $\{z_t\}$ if $E|x_t| < \infty$ for all t and $E(x_{t+1} \mid z_t, z_{t-1}, \ldots) = x_t$ (Karlin and Taylor (1975), definition 1.2, p. 241). In particular, suppose that at some terminal time the cash value or payoff of a security is a random variable v. Traders form a sequence of beliefs based on a sequence of information sets $\Phi_1, \Phi_2, \ldots$ This sequence does not contract: Something known at time t is known at time $\tau > t$. Then the conditional expectation

$x_t = E[v|\Phi_t]$ is a martingale with respect to the sequence of information sets $\{\Phi_k\}$.

When the conditioning information is "all public information," the conditional expectation is sometimes called the fundamental value or (with a nod to the asset pricing literature) the efficient price of the security. It is the starting point for many of the microstructure models considered here. One of the basic goals of microstructure analysis is a detailed and realistic view of how informational efficiency arises, that is, the process by which new information comes to be impounded or reflected in prices. In microstructure analyses, transaction prices are usually not martingales. Sometimes it is not even the case that the public information includes the history of transaction prices. (In dealer markets, trades are often not reported.) By imposing economic or statistical structure, though, it is often possible to identify a martingale component of the price (with respect to a particular information set). Later chapters will indicate how this can be accomplished.

A random-walk is a process constructed as the sum of independently and identically distributed (i.i.d.) zero-mean random variables (Ross (1996), p. 328). It is a special case of a martingale. The price in Equation 3.1, for example, cumulates the u_t. Because the u_t are i.i.d., the price process is time-homogenous, that is, it exhibits the same behavior whenever in time we sample it. This is only sensible if the economic process underlying the security is also time-homogenous. Stocks are claims on ongoing economic activities and are therefore plausibly approximated in the long run by random walks. Securities such as bonds, swaps, options, and so on, however, have finite maturity. Furthermore, they usually have well-defined boundary conditions at maturity that affect their values well in advance of maturity. The behavior of these securities over short samples may still be empirically well approximated by a random-walk model, but the random walk is not a valid description of the long-run behavior.

3.3 Statistical Analysis of Price Series

Statistical inference in the random-walk model appears straightforward. Suppose that we have a sample $\{p_1, p_2, \ldots, p_T\}$, generated in accordance with Equation 3.1. Because the u_t are i.i.d., the price changes $\Delta p_t = p_t - p_{t-1}$ should be i.i.d. with mean μ and variance $\mathrm{Var}(u_t) = \sigma_u^2$, for which we can compute the usual estimates. When we analyze actual data samples, however, we often encounter three features that should at the very least suggest wariness in the interpretation and subsequent use of the estimates. Short-run security price changes typically exhibit (1) means very close to zero, (2) extreme dispersion, and (3) dependence between successive observations. Each of these deserves further elaboration.

3.3.1 Near-Zero Mean Returns

In microstructure data samples μ is usually small relative to the estimation error of its usual estimate, the arithmetic mean. For this reason it is often preferable to drop the mean return from the model, implicitly setting μ to zero. Zero is, of course, a biased estimate of μ, but its estimation error will generally be lower than that of the arithmetic mean.

For example, suppose that t indexes days. Consider the properties of the annual log price change implied by the log random-walk model:

$$p_{365} - p_0 = \sum_{t=1}^{365} \Delta p_t = \mu_{\text{Annual}} + \sum_{t=1}^{365} u_t \qquad (3.2)$$

where $\mu_{\text{Annual}} = 365\,\mu$. The annual variance is $\text{Var}(p_{365} - p_0) = 365\sigma_u^2$. A typical U.S. stock might have an annual expected return of $\mu_{\text{Annual}} = 0.10$ (10%) and an annual variance of $\sigma_{\text{Annual}}^2 = 0.25^2$. The implied daily expected return is $\mu_{\text{Day}} = 0.10/365 = 0.000274$, and the implied daily variance is $\sigma_{\text{Day}}^2 = 0.25^2/365$. With $n = 365$ daily observations, the standard error of estimate for the sample average is $\sqrt{\sigma_{\text{Day}}^2/n} = \sqrt{(0.25^2/365)/365} = 0.000685$. This is about two and a half times the true mean. An estimate of zero is clearly biased downward, but the standard error of estimate is only 0.000274. At the cost of a little bias, we can greatly reduce the estimation error.

As we refine the frequency of observations from annually to monthly, to daily, and so on, the number of observations increases. More numerous observations usually enhance the precision of estimates. Here, though, the increase in observations is not accompanied by any increase in the calendar span of the sample. So do we gain or not? It depends. Merton (1980) shows that estimates of second moments (variances, covariances) are helped by more frequent sampling. Estimates of mean returns are not. For this reason, the expected return will often be dropped from our microstructure models.

3.3.2 Extreme Dispersion

Statistical analyses of speculative price changes at all horizons generally encounter sample distributions with fat tails. The incidence of extreme values is so great as to raise doubt whether population parameters like kurtosis, skewness, or even the variance of the underlying distribution are finite.

The convenient assumption that price changes are normally distributed is routinely violated. For example, from July 7, 1962, to December 31, 2004 (10,698 observations), the average daily return on the Standard &

Poor's (S&P) 500 index is about 0.0003 (0.03%), and the standard deviation is about 0.0094. Letting $\Phi(z)$ denote the standard normal distribution function, if returns are normally distributed, then the number of days with returns below 5% is expected to be $10,698 \times \Phi[(-0.05 - 0.0003)/0.0094] \approx 0.0005$, that is, considerably less than 1. In fact, there are eight such realizations (with the minimum of -20.5% occurring on October 19, 1987).

Statistical analysis of this sort of dispersion falls under the rubric of extreme value analysis (see, for example, Coles (2001) and Embrechts, Kluppelberg, and Mikosch (1997)). For a random variable X the population moment of order α is defined as EX^α. The normal density possesses finite moments of all orders. In other distributions, though, a moment may be infinite because as X goes to $\pm\infty$, X^α increases faster than the probability density declines. If EX^α is finite, then the corresponding sample estimate $\Sigma X_t^\alpha / T$, where T is the sample size, is an asymptotically consistent estimate of EX^α (using a law of large numbers). Hypothesis testing, however, often requires knowing the asymptotic variance of the sample estimate, which requires existence of the moment of order 2α. To get the standard error of the mean, for example, we need a consistent estimate of the variance.

One recent study suggests that finite moments for daily equity returns exist only up to order 3 and for daily trading volume only up to order 1.5 (Gabaix et al. 2003). These findings, if correct, impose substantive restrictions on the sorts of models that can sensibly be estimated.

Can safely we ignore this evidence? After all, why should one be concerned about convergence failures in infinite samples? The answer is that whatever one's beliefs about the properties of the distribution generating the data, the existence of extreme values in finite samples is an irrefutable fact leading to many practical consequences. Sample estimates may be dominated by a few extreme values. Increasing sample size does not increase precision as fast we'd expect. Estimated parameters are sensitive to model specification. Finally, and most disturbingly in trading applications, conclusions drawn from the model are fragile.

In some cases, it suffices to apply an ad hoc transformation to the variable. If trading volume is overdispersed, for example, one can work with the logarithm or reciprocal (as long as volume is positive). Such transformations applied to price changes or returns, however, are less attractive. We can also try to model the overdispersion. Many long-tailed distributions can be constructed as mixtures of well-behaved distributions. The question then arises as to the economic meaning of the mixing variable. One common interpretation is information intensity, that is, some measure that generally reflects the rate of information arrival and its importance for valuation. Shephard (2005) discusses the different perspectives on this important concept.

3.3.3   Dependence of Successive Observations

Time-series data are ordered, and statistical analysis must at least allow for the possibility that the ordering is associated with dependence. The most important summary measures of time-series dependence are the auto-covariances and autocorrelations. These are defined for a real-valued time series $\{x_t\}$ as $\text{Cov}(x_t, x_{t-k})$ and $\text{Corr}(x_t, x_{t-k})$ for $k = 0, 1, \ldots$. Under assumptions discussed more fully in chapter 4, these quantities depend only on k (the separation between the component terms). Accordingly they may be denoted $\gamma_k \equiv \text{Cov}(x_t, x_{t-k})$ and $\rho_k = \text{Corr}(x_t, x_{t-k})$. When the mean of the series is zero, γ_k may be estimated as the sample average cross-product, $\hat{\gamma}_k = (T - k)^{-1} \sum_{s=k+1}^{T} x_t x_{t-k}$, and the autocorrelations as $\hat{\rho}_k = \hat{\gamma}_k / \hat{\gamma}_0$ (see Fuller (1996), pp. 313–20).

The increments (changes) in a random walk are uncorrelated. So we would expect to find $\hat{\rho}_k \approx 0$ for $k \neq 0$. In actual samples, however, the first-order autocorrelations of short-run speculative price changes are usually negative. In October 2003, there were roughly 7,000 trades in PCO. The estimated first-order autocorrelation of the price changes is $\hat{\rho}_1 = -0.064$ (with an estimated standard error of 0.012). An economic explanation for this finding is the main contribution of the Roll model.

3.4   The Roll Model of Bid, Ask, and Transaction Prices

In returning to the economic perspective, we keep the random-walk assumption but now apply it to the (martingale) efficient price instead of the actual transaction price. Denoting this efficient price by m_t, we assume that $m_t = m_{t-1} + u_t$, where, as before the u_t are i.i.d. zero-mean random variables. We also suppose that all trades are conducted through dealers (section 2.3.1). The best dealer quotes are bid and ask (offer) prices, b_t and a_t. If a customer wants to buy (any quantity), he or she must pay the dealer's ask price (thereby lifting the ask). If a customer wants to sell, he or she receives the dealer's bid price (hitting the bid). Dealers incur a cost of c per trade. This charge reflects costs like clearing fees and per trade allocations of fixed costs, such as computers, telephones, and so on. These costs are noninformational, in the sense that they are not related to the dynamics of m_t. If dealers compete to the point where the costs are just covered, the bid and ask are $m_t - c$ and $m_t + c$, respectively. The bid-ask spread is $a_t - b_t = 2c$, a constant.

At time t, there is a trade at transaction price p_t, which may be expressed as

$$p_t = m_t + q_t c, \tag{3.3}$$

where q_t is a trade direction indicator set to $+1$ if the customer is buying and -1 if the customer is selling. We also assume that buys and sells are equally likely, serially independent (a buy this period does not change the probability of a buy next period), and that agents buy or sell independently of u_t (a customer buy or sell is unrelated to the evolution of m_t). This model is most clearly explicated and analyzed in Roll (1984), and will henceforth be referred to as the Roll model, but certain elements of the analysis were first discussed by Niederhoffer and Osborne (1966).

The Roll model has two parameters, c and σ_u^2. These are most conveniently estimated from the variance and first-order autocovariance of the price changes, Δp_t. The variance is

$$\gamma_0 \equiv \mathrm{Var}(\Delta p_t) = E(\Delta p_t)^2 = E\left[q_{t-1}^2 c^2 + q_t^2 c^2 - 2q_{t-1}q_t c^2 \right.$$
$$\left. -2q_{t-1}u_t c + 2q_t u_t c + u_t^2\right] = 2c^2 + \sigma_u^2. \tag{3.4}$$

The last equality follows because in expectation, all of the cross-products vanish except for those involving q_t^2, q_{t-1}^2, and u_t^2. The first-order autocovariance is

$$\gamma_1 \equiv \mathrm{Cov}(\Delta p_{t-1}, \Delta p_t) = E\Delta p_{t-1}\Delta p_t = E\left[c^2\left(q_{t-2}q_{t-1} - q_{t-1}^2 - q_{t-2}q_t\right.\right.$$
$$\left.\left. + q_{t-1}q_t\right) + c\left(q_t u_{t-1} - q_{t-1}u_{t-1} + u_t q_{t-1} - u_t q_{t-2}\right)\right] = -c^2. \tag{3.5}$$

It is easily verified that all autocovariances of order 2 or higher are zero. From the above, it is clear that $c = \sqrt{-\gamma_1}$ and $\sigma_u^2 = \gamma_0 + 2\gamma_1$. Given a sample of data, it is sensible to estimate γ_0 and γ_1 and apply these transformations to obtain estimates of the model parameters. Harris (1990) reports distributional results.

Based on all trades for PCO in October 2003, the estimated first-order autocovariance of the price changes is $\hat{\gamma}_1 = -0.0000294$. This implies $c = \$0.017$ and a spread of $2c = \$0.034$. The Roll model is often used in situations where we don't possess bid and ask data. In this sample, however, we do: the (time-weighted) average NYSE spread in the sample is $\$0.032$, so the Roll estimate is fairly close.

Although this agreement is comforting, it should be noted that the validity of the assumptions underlying the model is questionable. The plot in the one-hour segment of figure 3.1 suggests that the bid-ask spread is varying. In fact, over October it ranged between $\$0.01$ and $\$0.49$. Contrary to the assumption of serial independence, the correlation between q_t and q_{t-1} is about 0.34. That is, buys tend to follow buys, and sells tend to follow sells. Contrary to the assumption of independence between q_t and u_t, changes in the quote midpoint are positively correlated with the most recent trade direction. These are all important violations of the assumptions. In later chapters we will investigate modifications to the model that will accommodate these effects.

4

Univariate Time-Series Analysis

The Roll model described in the last chapter is a simple structural model, with a clear mapping to parameters (the variance and autocovariance of price changes) that are easily estimated. There are many interesting questions, though, that go beyond parameter estimation. We might want to forecast prices beyond the end of our data sample or to identify the series of m_t (the unobserved efficient prices) underlying our data. Furthermore, when we suspect that the structural model is misspecified, we might prefer to make assumptions about the data, rather than about the model.

To address these issues, the present chapter examines the Roll model from a different viewpoint. Whereas the previous chapter took a structural economic perspective, the present one adopts a more data-oriented statistical "reduced-form" approach. In the process of going back and forth between the structural and statistical representations, we illustrate econometric techniques that are very useful in more general situations. The chapter begins by describing some useful general properties of time series, proceeds to moving average and autoregressive models, and then discussing forecasting and estimation.

4.1   Stationarity and Ergodicity

Much statistical inference relies on the law of large numbers (LLN) and central limit theorem (CLT). These results establish the limiting properties of estimators as the sample size increases. The usual forms of these theorems apply to data samples consisting of independent observations.

Time-series data are by nature dependent. To maintain the strength of the LLN and CLT when independence doesn't hold, we rely on alternative versions of these results that assume stationarity and ergodicity. The following is an intuitive presentation of these concepts. White (2001) presents a more rigorous discussion.

A time series $\{x_t\}$ with constant mean, $Ex_t = \mu$, and autocovariances $\text{Cov}(x_t, x_{t-k}) = \gamma_k$ that do not depend on t is said to be *covariance stationary*. A time series for which all joint density functions of the form $f(x_t), f(x_t, x_{t+1}), \ldots, f(x_t, x_{t+1}, x_{t+2}), \ldots$ don't depend on t is (*strictly*) *stationary*.

The price changes implied by the Roll model, Δp_t, are covariance stationary: $E\Delta p_t = 0$ and $\text{Cov}(\Delta p_t, \Delta p_{t-k}) = \gamma_k$. The price levels are not covariance stationary. (Among other things, $\text{Var}(p_t)$ increases with t.) Covariance stationarity of the Δp_t would also be violated if we replaced the homoscedasticity assumption $Eu_t^2 = \sigma_u^2$ with something like $Eu_t^2 = 5 + \text{Cos}(t)$ or a similar time-dependent feature.[1]

We sometimes describe a sequence of independent observations by saying that an observation carries no memory of observations earlier in the sequence. This is too restrictive for time-series analysis. We typically assume instead that the effects of earlier observations decay and die out with the passage of time. A time series is *ergodic* if its local stochastic behavior is (possibly in the limit) independent of the starting point, that is, initial conditions. An ergodic process eventually "forgets" where it started. The price *level* in the Roll model is not ergodic: The randomness in the level is cumulative over time. But the price changes are ergodic: Δp_t is independent of Δp_{t-k} for $k \geq 2$. Nonergodicity could be introduced by positing $m_t = m_{t-1} + u_t + z$, where z is a zero-mean random variable drawn once at time zero.

The economic models discussed in later chapters (particularly the asymmetric information models) are often placed in settings where there is a single random draw of the security's terminal payoff and the price converges toward this value. The price changes in these models are not ergodic because everything is conditional on the value draw. Nor are they covariance stationary (due to the convergence). Empirical analyses of these models use various approaches. We sometimes assume that a sample consists of a string of these models placed end to end (for example, a sequence of trading days). In this view the sample is an *ensemble*, a collection of independent sample path realizations. Alternatively, we might view the models as stylized descriptions of effects that overlap in some unspecified fashion that results in covariance stationarity. For example, in each time period, we might have a new draw of some component of firm value.

Domowitz and El-Gamal (1999) note that ergodicity, in the sense of dependence on initial conditions, may be an important attribute of market mechanisms. In the long run, we would expect security prices to reflect fundamentals. A trade mechanism that induces persistent price components might impair this adjustment.

4.2   Moving Average Models

We will often assume that a time series like $\{\Delta p_t\}$ is covariance stationary, and now we turn to various ways in which the series can be represented. We start with a *white noise* process: a time series $\{\varepsilon_t\}$ where $E\varepsilon_t = 0$, $\text{Var}(\varepsilon_t) = \sigma_\varepsilon^2$, and $\text{Cov}(\varepsilon_t, \ \varepsilon_s) = 0$ for $s \neq t$. This is obviously covariance stationary. In many economic settings, it is convenient and plausible to assume that $\{\varepsilon_t\}$ are strictly stationary and even normally distributed, but these assumptions will be avoided here. White noise processes are convenient building blocks for constructing dependent time series. One such construction is the *moving average* (MA) model. The moving average model of order one (the MA(1) process) is:

$$x_t = \varepsilon_t + \theta\varepsilon_{t-1}. \tag{4.1}$$

The white noise driving a time-series model is variously termed the disturbance, error, or innovation series. From a statistical viewpoint, they all amount to the same thing. The economic interpretations and connotations, however, vary. When randomness is being added to a nonstochastic dynamic structural model, the term *disturbance* suggests a shock to which the system subsequently adjusts. When forecasting is the main concern, *error* conveys a sense of discrepancy between the observed value and the model prediction. *Innovation* is the word that is most loaded with economic connotations. The innovation is what the econometrician learns about the process at time t (beyond what's known from prior observations). Moving forward in time, it is the update to the econometrician's information set. In multivariate models, when x_t comprises a particularly varied, comprehensive, and economically meaningful collection of variables, the innovation series is often held to proxy the update to the *agents'* common information set as well.

The Δp_t in the Roll model have the property that the autocovariances are zero beyond lag one. The MA(1) model in (4.1) also has this property. For this process, the variance and first-order autocovariance are $\gamma_0 = (1 + \theta^2)\sigma_\varepsilon^2$, $\gamma_1 = \theta\sigma_\varepsilon^2$, and $\gamma_k = 0$ for $k > 1$. More generally, the moving average model of order K is

$$x_t = \varepsilon_t + \theta_1\varepsilon_{t-1} + \cdots + \theta_K\varepsilon_{t-K}.$$

The MA(K) process is covariance stationary and has the property that $\gamma_j = 0$ for $j > K$. If we let $K = \infty$, we arrive at the infinite-order moving average process.

Now comes a point of some subtlety. If we believe that the $\{\Delta p_t\}$ are generated by the Roll model (a *structural* economic model), can we assert that a corresponding moving average model (a *statistical* model) exists? By playing around with the θ and σ_ε^2 parameters in the MA(1) model, we can obviously match the variance and first-order autocovariance of the structural Δp_t process. But this is not quite the same thing as claiming that the full joint distribution of the Δp_t realizations generated by the structural model could also be generated by an MA(1) model. Moreover, there's a good reason for suspecting this shouldn't be possible. The structural model has two (uncorrelated) sources of randomness, u_t (the efficient price innovations) and q_t (the trade direction indicators). The MA(1) model has only one source of randomness, ε_t.

Is the existence of an MA(1) representation an important issue? Why can't we simply limit the analysis to the structural model, and avoid questions of alternative representations? There are several answers. In the first place, the full structural model involves unobserved variables. The econometrician observes neither the u_t nor q_t, so he or she doesn't know the efficient price. The moving average representation is a useful tool for constructing an estimate of the efficient price, as well as for forecasting. Moreover, a moving average representation may be valid even if the structural model is misspecified.

Fortunately, an MA(1) representation for price changes in the Roll model does exist. In this assertion, we rely on the Wold (not Wald) theorem. The Wold theorem states that any zero-mean covariance stationary process $\{x_t\}$ can be represented in the form

$$x_t = \sum_{j=0}^{\infty} \theta_j \varepsilon_{t-j} + \kappa_t$$

where $\{\varepsilon_t\}$ is a zero-mean white noise process, $\theta_0 = 1$ (a normalization), and $\sum_{j=0}^{\infty} \theta_j < \infty$. κ_t is a linearly deterministic process, which in this context means that it can be predicted arbitrarily well by a linear projection (possibly of infinite order) on past observations of x_t. For proofs, see Hamilton (1994) or Sargent (1979). For a purely stochastic series, $\kappa_t = 0$, and we are left with a moving average representation.

A related result due to Ansley, Spivey, and Wrobleski (1977) establishes that if a covariance stationary process has zero autocovariances at all orders higher than K, then it possesses a moving average representation of order K. This allows us to assert that an MA(1) representation exists for the Roll model.

Empirical market microstructure analyses often push the Wold theorem very hard. The structural models are often stylized and underidentified (we can't estimate all the parameters). The data are frequently non-Gaussian (like the trade indicator variable in the Roll model). Covariance stationarity of the observations (possibly after a transformation) is often a tenable working assumption. For many purposes, as we'll see, it is enough.

Section 3.4 derived the autocovariances of the Roll model (γ_0 and γ_1) in terms of the structural parameters (c and σ_u^2). The parameters of the corresponding MA(1) model in Equation (4.1) are θ and σ_ε^2. The MA(1) has autocovariances $\gamma_0 = (1+\theta^2)\sigma_\varepsilon^2$ and $\gamma_1 = \theta\sigma_\varepsilon^2$. From the autocovariances (or estimates thereof) we may compute the moving average parameters:

$$\theta = \frac{\gamma_0 - \sqrt{\gamma_0^2 - 4\gamma_1^2}}{2\gamma_1} \quad \text{and} \quad \sigma_\varepsilon^2 = \frac{\gamma_0 + \sqrt{\gamma_0^2 - 4\gamma_1^2}}{2} \tag{4.2}$$

This is actually one of two solutions, the so-called invertible solution. It has the property that $|\theta| < 1$, the relevance of which shortly becomes clear. The other (noninvertible) solution is $\{\theta^*, \sigma_\varepsilon^{2*}\}$. The relation between the two solutions is given by $\theta^* = 1/\theta$ and $\sigma_\varepsilon^{2*} = \theta^2\sigma_\varepsilon^2$. For the noninvertible solution, $|\theta^*| > 1$.

4.3 Autoregressive Models

A moving average model expresses the current realization in terms of current and lagged disturbances. These are not generally observable. For many purposes (particularly forecasting) it is useful to express the current realization in terms of past realizations. This leads to the autoregressive form of the model.

To develop this for the MA(1) case, note that we can rearrange $\Delta p_t = \varepsilon_t + \theta\varepsilon_{t-1}$ as $\varepsilon_t = \Delta p_t - \theta\varepsilon_{t-1}$. This gives us a backward recursion for $\varepsilon_t : \varepsilon_{t-1} = \Delta p_{t-1} - \theta\varepsilon_{t-2}, \varepsilon_{t-2} = \Delta p_{t-2} - \theta\varepsilon_{t-3}$, and so forth. Using this backward recursion gives

$$\begin{aligned} \Delta p_t &= \theta\left(\Delta p_{t-1} - \theta\left(\Delta p_{t-2} - \theta\left(\Delta p_{t-3} - \theta\varepsilon_{t-4}\right)\right)\right) + \varepsilon_t \\ &= \theta\Delta p_{t-1} - \theta^2\Delta p_{t-2} + \theta^3\Delta p_{t-3} - \theta^4\varepsilon_{t-4} + \varepsilon_t; \end{aligned} \tag{4.3}$$

or, with infinite recursion:

$$\Delta p_t = \theta\Delta p_{t-1} - \theta^2\Delta p_{t-2} + \theta^3\Delta p_{t-3} + \cdots + \varepsilon_t. \tag{4.4}$$

This is the autoregressive form: Δp_t is expressed as a linear function of its own lagged values and the current disturbance. Although the moving average representation is of order one, the autoregressive representation is of infinite order.

If $|\theta| < 1$, then the autoregressive representation is convergent: the coefficients of the lagged Δp_t converge to zero. Intuitively, the effects of lagged realizations eventually die out. When a convergent autoregressive representation exists, the moving average representation is said to be invertible. Convergence is determined by the magnitude of θ. The condition $|\theta| < 1$ thus defines the invertible solution for the MA(1) parameters (compare equation (4.2) and the related discussion). Hamilton (1994, p. 64) discusses general criteria for invertibility.

To move between moving average and autoregressive representations, it's often convenient to use the lag operator, L (sometimes written as the backshift operator, B). It is defined by the relation $Lx_t = x_{t-1}$. Multiple applications work in a straightforward fashion ($L^2 x_t = x_{t-2}$, etc.). The operator can also generate "leads" (e.g., $L^{-3}x_t = x_{t+3}$). Using the lag operator, the moving average representation for Δp_t is $\Delta p_t = \varepsilon_t + \theta L \varepsilon_t = (1 + \theta L)\varepsilon_t$. The autoregressive representation is:

$$\Delta p_t = \left(\theta L - \theta^2 L^2 + \theta^3 L^3 + \cdots\right)\Delta p_t + \varepsilon_t. \qquad (4.5)$$

We derived this by recursive substitution. But there is an alternative construction that is particularly useful when the model is complicated. Starting from the moving average representation, we may write $(1 + \theta L)^{-1}\Delta p_t = \varepsilon_t$, where we've essentially treated the lag operator term as an algebraic quantity. If L were a variable and $|\theta| < 1$, we could construct a series expansion of the left-hand side around $L = 0$. This expansion, through the third order, is $[1 - \theta L + \theta^2 L^2 - \theta^3 L^3 + O(L^4)]\Delta p_t = \varepsilon_t$, where $O(L^4)$ represents the higher order terms. This can be rearranged to obtain the autoregressive representation given in equations (4.4) or (4.5).

In summary, we have modeled a time series by assuming covariance stationarity, proceeding to a moving average representation (via the Wold theorem), and finally to the autoregressive representation. The last two representations are equivalent, but in any particular problem, one might be considerably simpler than the other. For example, the Roll model is a moving average of order one, but the autoregressive representation is of infinite order.

Sometimes, though, the autoregressive representation is the simpler one. An autoregressive representation of order one has the form $x_t = \phi x_{t-1} + \varepsilon_t$, or in terms of the lag operator, $(1 - \phi L)x_t = \varepsilon_t$. The moving average form is:

$$x_t = (1 - \phi L)^{-1}\varepsilon_t = \left(1 + \phi L + \phi^2 L^2 + \cdots\right)\varepsilon_t$$
$$= \varepsilon_t + \phi \varepsilon_{t-1} + \phi^2 \varepsilon_{t-2} + \cdots$$

Here, we have used a power series expansion of $(1 - \phi L)^{-1}$. Recursive substitution would give the same result. The moving average representation is of infinite order.

The following exercise develops an autoregressive representation for a persistent discretely valued series. It demonstrates the generality of the Wold theorem by showing that such a process can be modeled using zero-mean uncorrelated disturbances. It also illustrates the limitations of the theorem by showing that the disturbances are dependent.

Exercise 4.1. For the trade direction indicator q_t in the Roll model, Madhavan, Richardson, and Roomans (1997) allow for serial dependence. Suppose that $q_t \in \{-1, +1\}$, and that $\Pr(q_{t+1} = +1 | q_t = +1) = \Pr(q_{t+1} = -1 | q_t = -1) = \alpha$ (and, of course, $\Pr(q_{t+1} = +1 | q_t = -1) = \Pr(q_{t+1} = -1 | q_t = +1) = (1 - \alpha)$. α is called the continuation probability. If $\alpha = 1/2$, trade directions are uncorrelated. If $1/2 < \alpha < 1$, trade directions are persistent (buys tend to follow buys, etc.). With this structure, q_t may be expressed as the AR(1) process $q_t = \phi q_{t-1} + v_t$ where $Ev_t = 0$, $Ev_t^2 = \sigma_v^2$, and $Ev_t v_{t-k} = 0$ for $k \neq 0$. The model may be analyzed by constructing a table of the eight possible realizations (paths) of (q_t, q_{t+1}, q_{t+2}).

a. Assuming that q_t is equally likely to be ± 1, compute the probabilities of each path. Show that $\phi = 2\alpha - 1$.
b. Compute v_{t+1} and v_{t+2}. Verify that $Ev_{t+1} = Ev_{t+2} = 0$ and $\text{Cov}(v_{t+1}, v_{t+2}) = Ev_{t+1}v_{t+2} = 0$.
c. Demonstrate that the v_t values are not serially independent by verifying that $\text{Cov}(v_{t+1}, v_{t+2}^2) \neq 0$.

4.4   Forecasting

A crucial calculation in agents' trading decisions is their forecast of the security's future value. It is convenient to construct these forecasts by taking expectations of MA and AR representations, but there is an important qualification. The assumption of covariance stationarity suffices only to characterize a restricted form of the expectation. An expectation (e.g., $E[x_t | x_{t-1}, x_{t-2}, \ldots]$) generally involves the full joint distribution $f(x_t, x_{t-1}, x_{t-2}, \ldots)$, not just the means and covariances. Considerable simplification results, however, if we approximate the true expectation by a linear function of the conditioning arguments, that is, $E[x_t | x_{t-1}, x_{t-2}, \ldots] \approx \alpha_0 + \alpha_1 x_{t-1} + \alpha_2 x_{t-2} + \cdots$. This approximate expectation is technically a linear projection. When the difference is important, it will be denoted E^* to distinguish it from the true expectation. The following material summarizes results on linear forecasting discussed at greater length in Hamilton (1994, pp. 72–116).

The technique of linear projection is especially compatible with AR and MA representations because the AR and MA representations have no more and no less information than is needed to compute the projection. It is quite conceivable that a more complicated forecasting scheme, for example, one involving nonlinear transformations of $\{x_{t-1}, x_{t-2}, \ldots\}$, might be better (have smaller forecasting errors) than the linear projection, but such a forecast could not be computed directly from the AR or MA representation. More structure would be needed.

We'll first consider the price forecast in the Roll model. Suppose that we know θ and have a full (infinite) price history up the time t,

$\{p_t, p_{t-1}, p_{t-2}, \ldots\}$. Using the autoregressive representation, we can recover the innovation series $\{\varepsilon_t, \varepsilon_{t-1}, \varepsilon_{t-2}, \ldots\}$. Then:

$$E^* \left[\Delta p_{t+1} | p_t, p_{t-1}, \ldots \right] = E^* \left[\varepsilon_{t+1} + \theta \varepsilon_t | p_t, p_{t-1}, \ldots \right] = \theta \varepsilon_t. \qquad (4.6)$$

Therefore, the forecast of next period's price is: $f_t \equiv E^*[p_{t+1} | p_t, p_{t-1}, \ldots] = p_t + \theta \varepsilon_t$. How does f_t evolve?

$$\begin{aligned} \Delta f_t = f_t - f_{t-1} &= p_t + \theta \varepsilon_t - \left(p_{t-1} + \theta \varepsilon_{t-1} \right) \\ &= (\varepsilon_t + \theta \varepsilon_{t-1}) + \theta \varepsilon_t - \theta \varepsilon_{t-1} = (1 + \theta)\, \varepsilon_t. \end{aligned} \qquad (4.7)$$

That is, the forecast revision is a constant multiple of the innovation. The innovations process is uncorrelated, so the forecast revision is as well.

Now we raise a more difficult question. A martingale has uncorrelated increments, so f_t might be a martingale. Can we assert that $f_t = m_t$, that is, have we identified the true implicit efficient price? It turns out that there is a bit of problem. If $f_t = m_t$, then $p_t = f_t + c q_t$ and $\Delta p_t = \Delta f_t + c \Delta q_t$. But this implies

$$\Delta p_t = \varepsilon_t + \theta \varepsilon_{t-1} = (1 + \theta) \varepsilon_t + c \Delta q_t \Leftrightarrow -\theta (\varepsilon_t - \varepsilon_{t-1}) = c \Delta q_t. \qquad (4.8)$$

In other words, all of the randomness in the model is attributable to the q_t. But this is structurally incorrect: We know that changes in the efficient price, u_t, also contribute to the ε_t. Thus, we have not identified m_t. It will later be shown that $f_t = E^*[m_t | p_t, p_{t-1}, \ldots]$, that is, that f_t is the projection of m_t on the conditioning variables.

Exercise 4.2 The Roll model assumes that trade directions are serially uncorrelated: $\mathrm{Corr}(q_t, q_s) = 0$ for $t \neq s$. In practice, one often finds positive autocorrelation (see Hasbrouck and Ho (1987) Choi, Salandro, and Shastri (1988)). Suppose that $\mathrm{Corr}(q_t, q_{t-1}) = \rho > 0$ and $\mathrm{Corr}(q_t, q_{t-k}) = 0$ for $k > 1$. Suppose that ρ is known.

a. Show that $\mathrm{Var}(\Delta p_t) = 2c^2(1 - \rho) + \sigma_u^2$, $\mathrm{Cov}(\Delta p_t, \Delta p_{t-1}) = -c^2(1 - 2\rho)$, $\mathrm{Cov}(\Delta p_t, \Delta p_{t-2}) = -c^2 \rho$, and $\mathrm{Cov}(\Delta p_t, \Delta p_{t-k}) = 0$ for $k > 2$.
b. Suppose that $0 < \rho < 1$ describes the true structural model. We compute an estimate of c, denoted $\hat{c}$, assuming that the orginal Roll model is correct. Show that $\hat{c} < c$, that is, that $\hat{c}$ is biased downward.

Exercise 4.3 The basic Roll model assumes that trade directions are uncorrelated with changes in the efficient price: $\mathrm{Corr}(q_t, u_t) = 0$. Suppose that $\mathrm{Corr}(q_t, u_t) = \rho$, where ρ is known, $0 < \rho < 1$. The idea here is that a buy order is associated with an increase in the security value, a connection that will be developed in the models of asymmetric information. Suppose that ρ is known.

a. Show that $\text{Var}(\Delta p_t) = 2c^2 + \sigma_u^2 + 2c\rho\sigma_u, \text{Cov}(\Delta p_t, \Delta p_{t-1}) = -c(c + \rho\sigma_u)$, and $\text{Cov}(\Delta p_t, \Delta p_{t-k}) = 0$ for $k > 1$.
b. Suppose that $0 < \rho < 1$ describes the true structural model. We compute an estimate of c, denoted $\hat{c}$, assuming that the orginal Roll model is correct. Show that $\hat{c} > c$, that is, that $\hat{c}$ is biased upward.

4.5   Estimation

In practice, the Roll model parameters are usually estimated as transformations of the estimated variance and first-order autocovariance of the price changes (see section 3.4). It is not uncommon, however, for the estimated first-order autocovariance to be positive. Harris (1990) shows that this can easily happen due to estimation error, even though the model is correctly specified. In these cases, Hasbrouck (2005) suggests a Bayesian approach.

More generally, MA and AR representations can be estimated using a wide variety of approaches. The MA parameters can be obtained from the autocovariances (by solving the set of equations and requiring that the solution be invertible). MA models can be estimated via maximum likelihood (assuming a particular distribution for the disturbances). The MA representation can also be obtained by numerically inverting the AR representation.

The autoregressive representation can often be conveniently estimated using ordinary least squares (OLS). The basic requirement for consistency of OLS estimation is that the residuals are uncorrelated with the regressors. This is true in equation (4.4) because the $\{\varepsilon_t\}$ are serially uncorrelated, and the regressors (lagged price changes) are linear functions of prior realizations of ε_t. For example, $\Delta p_{t-1} = \varepsilon_{t-1} + \theta\varepsilon_{t-2}$ is uncorrelated with ε_t.

Microstructure data often present particular challenges to statistical software. Samples often contain embedded breaks. In a sample of intra-day trade prices that spans multiple days, for example, the closing price on one day and the opening price on the following day will appear successively. The overnight price change between these observations, though, will almost certainly have different properties than the intraday price changes. If the goal is modeling the latter, the overnight price changes should be dropped. This is often accomplished by inserting missing values into the series at the day breaks.

A related issue concerns lagged values realized before the start of the sample. In an autoregression like equation (4.4), if t is the first observation of the sample, none of the lagged values on the right-hand side are known. Most non-microstructure applications take the perspective that the start of sample simply represents the beginning of the record for a process that was already unfolding. For example, when a sample of GDP data begins in 1900, one would assume that the economy had been up and running prior to that date, and that 1900 merely represented the start of the record. In other words, prior to 1900 the process was evolving unobserved. The correct estimation approach is then unconditional, that is, the lagged missing values are viewed as unknown but distributed in accordance with the model. In many microstructure situations, though, the data begin right at the start of trading process. There is no prior unobserved evolution of the trading process. In these cases, conditional estimation, wherein the missing lagged disturbances are set to zero, is more defensible.

4.6   Strengths and Weaknesses of Linear Time-Series Models

This chapter reviews the elements of linear time-series analysis. The development begins with covariance stationarity, which is a plausible and minimal working assumption in many modeling situations. Using the Wold theorem, this leads to a moving average model, then to a vector autoregression, and finally to a forecasting procedure. These are powerful results, but to maintain a balanced perspective, it is now necessary to dwell on some of the framework's limitations.

The characterization of a time series offered by the linear models is not complete. The models do not fully describe the data-generating process. They do not specify how we should computationally simulate the process. Exercise 4.2, for example, posits first-order autocorrelation in the trade directions. We might simulate this as follows. Let $a_t = u_t + \beta u_{t-1}$ where $u_t \sim N(0, \sigma_u^2)$ and $0 < \beta < 1$. Then let $q_t = Sign(a_t)$, where $Sign(x) = +1$ if $x > 0$; -1 if $x < 0$; and 0 if $x = 0$. The resulting $\{q_t\}$ process is covariance stationary; we can specify AR and MA models, identify their parameters, compute forecasts $E^*[q_t|q_{t-1}, q_{t-2}, \ldots]$, and so on. We can't, however, completely reverse the inference and recover the generating mechanism.

As demonstrated in exercise 4.1, the disturbances in MA and AR models are not serially correlated, but may be serially dependent (as manifested by nonzero serial moments of order greater than two). This bears directly on the structural interpretations of these models. The MA and AR representations of a discretely valued process such as q_t are essentially linear models of limited dependent variables. The usual econometric guidelines discourage such specifications on the grounds that the disturbances must possess complicated and nonintuitive properties (see, for example, Greene (2002) p. 665).

These concerns are not misplaced in the present situation if our goal is a fully specified structural model. For example, if we believe that the a_t in the generating process summarize attributes of arriving individual traders, the higher order serial dependencies will generally imply complicated higher order dependencies in the attributes of successively arriving individuals. Rather than model this behavior, it is usually easier to specify a statistical model (such as a logit or probit) for which these features are not needed.

Logit and probit models are certainly part of the microstructure toolbox. We do not, however, use them reflexively simply because some variables of interest happen to be discrete. They are more complicated than linear specifications, and so are more demanding in programming and computation. A larger consideration is that there may be other structural features that are more important than discreteness. Probably paramount among these other concerns is time-varying and persistent volatility.

Even in light of those remarks, linear time-series analysis nevertheless retains strength and utility. It provides logically coherent and computationally simple tools for describing first-order dynamics, forecasting, and forming expectations. The underlying assumptions are minimal (chiefly covariance stationarity), so the analyses may be more robust to misspecification than more refined models. The representations are compatible with a wide range of structural models and so are relatively easy to illustrate and interpret. In short, they are useful aids in developing intuitions of how financial markets work.

5

Sequential Trade Models

5.1 Overview

In the Roll framework, everyone possesses the same information. New public information can cause the quotes to change, but trades have no impact. Because trades are not informative, there's no particular need for them to be reported and disseminated in a timely fashion. Trading is not a strategic problem because agents always face the same spread. The costs reflected in dealers' spreads reflect only expenditures for computers, communications, salaries, business fees, and so on, the sort of expenses that a wholesaler of any good or service might incur.

Although some securities markets might function this way some of the time, most work very differently. Trade reports are valuable information. Orders appear to move prices. Spreads vary across markets and with market conditions. Of course, trading strategies must reflect these realities. It turns out that dropping the assumption of uniform information opens the door for sensible economic explanations for these features of market behavior. The asymmetric information models described in this and following chapters take this direction.

These models have the following general features. The security payoff is usually of a common value nature. The primary benefit derived from ownership of the security is the resale value or terminal liquidating dividend that is the same for all holders. But for trade to exist, we also need private value components, that is, diversification or risk exposure needs that are idiosyncratic to each agent. The private values are often modeled in an ad hoc fashion. Sometimes we simply assert the existence of unspecified private values that generate the assumed behavior.

Generally, public information initially consists of common knowledge concerning the probability structure of the economy, in particular the unconditional distribution of terminal security value and the distribution of types of agents. As trading unfolds, the most important updates to the public information set are market data, such as bids, asks, and the prices and volumes of trades. Many of the models make no provision for the arrival of nontrade public information (e.g., news announcements) during trading. Private information may consist of a signal about terminal security value, or more commonly, perfect knowledge of the terminal security value.

When all agents are ex ante identical, they are said to be symmetric. This does not rule out private values or private information. It simply means that all individual-specific variables (e.g., the coefficient of risk aversion, a value signal) are identically distributed across all participants. In an asymmetric information model, some subset of the agents has superior private information.

The majority of the asymmetric information models in microstructure examine market dynamics subject to a single source of uncertainty, that is, a single information event. At the end of trading, the security payoff (terminal value) is realized and known. Thus, the trading process is an adjustment from one well-defined information set to another. From a statistical perspective, the dynamics of this adjustment are neither stationary nor ergodic. The dynamics are not time-homogenous, although path realizations can be sequentially stacked to provide a semblance of ongoing trading.

Theoretical market microstructure has two main sorts of asymmetric information models. In the sequential trade models, randomly selected traders arrive at the market singly, sequentially, and independently. Key early references along this line of inquiry include Copeland and Galai (1983) and Glosten and Milgrom (1985). The other class of models usually features a single informed agent who can trade at multiple times. Following O'Hara (1995), we'll describe these as strategic trader models. When an individual trader only participates in the market once (as in the sequential trade models), there is no need for her to take into account the effect her actions might have on subsequent decisions of others. A trader who revisits the market, however, must make such calculations, and they involve considerations of strategy. This second class of models is also sometimes described as continuous auction, but the continuity of the market is not really an essential feature. This line of thought begins with Kyle (1985).

The essential feature of both models is that a trade reveals something about the agent's private information. A "buy" from the dealer might result from a trader who has private positive information, but it won't originate from a trader who has private negative information. Rational, competitive market makers will set their bid and ask quotes accordingly. All else equal, more extreme information asymmetries lead to wider quotes. Trades will also engender a "permanent" impact on subsequent prices. The spread and trade-impact effects are the principal empirical implications of these models. We begin with the sequential trade models.

5.2   A Simple Sequential Trade Model

The essential sequential trade model is a simple construct. The model presented here is a special case of Glosten and Milgrom (1985). It is also contained as a special case in many other analyses. There is one security with a value (payoff) V that is either high or low, $\overline{V}$ or $\underline{V}$. The probability of the low outcome is δ. The value is revealed after the market closes. It is not, however, affected by trading. It is determined, by a random draw of nature, prior to the market open. The trading population (the customers) comprises informed and uninformed traders. Informed traders (insiders) know the value outcome. The proportion of informed traders in the population is μ.

A dealer posts bid and ask quotes, B and A. A trader is drawn at random from the population. If the trader is informed, she buys if $V = \overline{V}$ and sells if $V = \underline{V}$. If the trader is uninformed, he buys or sells randomly and with equal probability. The dealer does not know whether the trader is informed. The event tree for the first trade is given in figure 5.1.

In the figure, I and U denote the arrivals of informed and uninformed traders. A buy is a purchase by the customer at the dealer's ask price, A; a sell is a customer sale at the bid. The value attached to the arrow is the probability of the indicated transition. Total probabilities are obtained

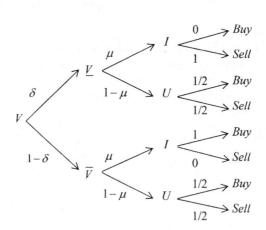

Figure 5.1.   The event tree for the basic sequential trade model.

by multiplying along a path. For example, the probability of a low real-ization for V, followed by the arrival of an uninformed trader who buys is $\delta(1-\mu)/2$. The sum of the total probabilities over terminal *Buy* nodes gives the unconditional probability of a buy: $\Pr(Buy) = (1 + \mu(1 - 2\delta))/2$. Similarly, $\Pr(Sell) = (1 - \mu)(1 - 2\delta))/2$. In the case where $\delta = 1/2$ (equal probabilities of good and bad outcomes), the buy and sell probabilities are also equal.

Now consider the dealer's situation. The purchases and sales of the uninformed traders are not sensitive to the quoted bid or ask. So if the dealer is a monopolist, expected profits are maximized by setting the bid infinitely low and the ask infinitely high. Obviously, at these prices, only the uninformed trade. In practice, the dealer's market power is constrained by competition and regulation. Competition arises from other dealers, but also and more generally from anyone who is setting a visible quote, such as a public customer using a limit order. In some venues, regulation limits the dealers' power. For example, NASD's Rules of Fair Practice (Article III, Section IV) generally prohibit markups (sale price over purchase price) in excess of 5%.

We'll assume that competition among dealers drives expected profits to zero. Furthermore, for the usual reasons, the dealer can't cross-subsidize buys with sells or vice versa. (If he were making a profit selling to cus-tomers, for example, another dealer would undercut his ask.) It thus suffices to consider buys and sells separately.

The dealer's inference given that the first trade is a buy or sell can be summarized by her revised beliefs about the probability of a low outcome, denoted $\delta_1(\cdot)$. Given that the customer buys, this probability is

$$\delta_1(Buy) = \Pr(\underline{V}|Buy) = \frac{\Pr(\underline{V}, Buy)}{\Pr(Buy)} = \frac{\delta(1-\mu)}{1 + \mu(1 - 2\delta)}. \tag{5.1}$$

Because μ and δ are between zero and one, $\partial\delta_1(Buy)/\partial\mu < 0$: The revision in beliefs is stronger when there are more informed traders in the population.

At the end of the day, the dealer's realized profit on the transaction is $\pi = A - V$. Immediately after the trade, the dealer's expectation of this profit is $E[\pi|Buy] = A - E[V|Buy]$, where $E[V|Buy] = \delta_1(Buy)\underline{V} + (1 - \delta_1(Buy))\overline{V}$. If competition drives this expected profit to zero, then

$$A = E[V|Buy] = \frac{\underline{V}(1-\mu)\delta + \overline{V}(1-\delta)(1+\mu)}{1 + \mu(1 - 2\delta)}. \tag{5.2}$$

A dealer's quote is essentially a proposal of terms of trade. When the bid is hit or the offer is lifted, this proposal has been accepted. In some trading situations, such an acceptance induces dismay. Depending on the context, this is variously termed the winner's curse, ex post regret, or (in the real estate market) buyer's remorse. In the present model, however, the ask is simply what the dealer believes the security to be worth. Ex post regret does not arise. The quote is regret-free.

The ask quote strikes a balance between informed and uninformed traders. The conditional expectation of value can be decomposed as

$$E[V|Buy] = E[V|U, Buy]\Pr(U|Buy) + E[V|I, Buy]\Pr(I|Buy). \quad (5.3)$$

Substituting this into the zero-expected profit condition $A = E[V|Buy]$ and rearranging gives:

$$\underbrace{(A - E[V|U, Buy])}_{\substack{\text{Gain from an} \\ \text{uninformed trader}}} \Pr(U|Buy) = -\underbrace{(A - E[V|I, Buy])}_{\substack{\text{Loss to an} \\ \text{informed trader}}} \Pr(I|Buy) \quad (5.4)$$

The expected gains from uninformed traders are balanced by the losses to informed traders. In this model, therefore, there is a net wealth transfer from uninformed to informed traders.

The analysis for the dealer's bid is similar. Following a sale to the dealer,

$$\delta_1(Sell) = \Pr(\underline{V}|Sell) = \frac{\Pr(\underline{V}, Sell)}{\Pr(Sell)} = \frac{\delta(1 + \mu)}{1 - (1 - 2\delta)\mu}. \quad (5.5)$$

For δ and μ between zero and one, $\delta_1(Sell) > \delta_1(Buy)$. $\underline{V}$ is less likely if the customer bought, reasons the dealer, because an informed customer who knew $V = \underline{V}$ would have sold. Furthermore $\partial\delta_1(Sell)/\partial\mu > 0$. The dealer's bid is set as

$$B = E[V|Sell] = \frac{\underline{V}(1 + \mu)\delta + \overline{V}(1 - \mu)(1 - \delta)}{1 - \mu(1 - 2\delta)}. \quad (5.6)$$

The bid-ask spread is

$$A - B = \frac{4(1 - \delta)\delta\mu(\overline{V} - \underline{V})}{1 - (1 - 2\delta)^2\mu^2}. \quad (5.7)$$

In the symmetric case of $\delta = 1/2$, $A - B = (\overline{V} - \underline{V})\mu$.

In many situations the midpoint of the bid and ask is taken as a proxy for what the security is worth absent transaction costs. Here, the midpoint is equal to the unconditional expectation EV only in the symmetric case ($\delta = 1/2$). More generally, the bid and ask are not set symmetrically about the efficient price.

Exercise 5.1 As a modification to the basic model, take $\delta = 1/2$ and suppose that immediately after V is drawn (as either $\underline{V}$ or $\overline{V}$), a broker is randomly drawn. The probability of an informed trader within broker b's customer set is μ_b. Other brokers have proportion

$\mu_{\sim b}$, with $\mu_b < \mu_{\sim b}$. Quote setters post bids and asks. If the order comes into broker b, however, he has option to trade against the customer by matching the bid or ask set by the other dealers. Show that broker b's expected profits on a customer buy order are $(\overline{V} - \underline{V})(\mu_{\sim b} - \mu_b)/2 > 0$.

Exercise 5.2 Consider a variant of the model in which there is informed trading only in the low state $(V = \underline{V})$. Verify that

$$\delta_1(Buy) = \frac{\delta(1-\mu)}{1-\delta\mu}; \quad \delta_1(Sell) = \frac{\delta(1+\mu)}{1+\delta\mu}$$

$$Ask = \frac{\overline{V}(1-\delta) + \underline{V}\delta(1-\mu)}{1-\delta\mu}; \quad Bid = \frac{\overline{V}(1-\delta) + \underline{V}\delta(1+\mu)}{1+\delta\mu}.$$

Exercise 5.3 Consider a variant of the model in which informed traders only receive a signal S about V. The signal can be either low or high: $S \in \{\underline{S}, \overline{S}\}$. The accuracy of the signal is $\gamma : Pr[\underline{S}|\underline{V}] = Pr[\overline{S}|\overline{V}] = \gamma$. Informed traders always trade in the direction of their signal. Show that $\delta(Buy) = [\delta_1(1-(2\gamma-1)\mu)]/[1-(2\gamma-1)(2\delta-1)\mu]$.

5.3 Market Dynamics: Bid and Ask Quotes over Time

After the initial trade, the dealer updates his beliefs and posts new quotes. The next trader arrives, and the process repeats. This recurrence is clearest in the expressions for $\delta(Buy)$ and $\delta(Sell)$ in Eqs. (5.1) and (5.5). These equations map a prior probability (the δ in the right-hand side) into a posterior probability based on the direction of the trade. Let δ_k denote the probability of a low outcome given δ_{k-1} and the direction of the kth trade, with the original (unconditional) probability being $\delta_0 \equiv \delta$. Then Eqs. (5.1) and (5.5) can be generalized as

$$\delta_k(Buy_k; \delta_{k-1}) = \frac{\delta_{k-1}(1-\mu)}{1+\mu(1-2\delta_{k-1})} \text{ and}$$

$$\delta_k(Sell_k; \delta_{k-1}) = \frac{\delta_{k-1}(1+\mu)}{1-(1-2\delta_{k-1})\mu}. \tag{5.8}$$

The updating recursion can be expressed in general form because all probabilities in the event tree except δ are constant over time.

Exercise 5.4 The δ_k following a sequence of orders can be expressed recursively as $\delta_k(Order_1, Order_2, \ldots, Order_k) = \delta_k(Order_k; \delta_{k-1}(Order_{k-1}; \delta_{k-2}(Order_{k-2}; \ldots)))$. Verify that $\delta_2(Sell_1, Buy_2) = \delta$. That is, offsetting trades are uninformative.

Market dynamics have the following features:

- The trade price series is a martingale. Recall from the foregoing analysis that $B_k = E[V|Sell_k]$ and $A_k = E[V|Buy_k]$. Because the trade occurs at one or the other of these prices, the sequence of trade prices $\{P_k\}$ is a sequence of conditional expectations $E[V|\Phi_k]$ where Φ_k is the information set consisting of the history (including the kth trade) of the buy/sell directions. A sequence of expectations conditioned on expanding information sets is a martingale.
- The order flow is not symmetric. Using q_k to denote the trade direction as we did in the Roll model (+1 for a buy, −1 for a sell), $E[q_k|\Phi_{k-1}]$ is in general nonzero.
- The spread declines over time. Knowing the long-run proportion of buys and sells in the order flow is tantamount to knowing the outcome. With each trade, the dealer can estimate this proportion more precisely, and hence uncertainty is reduced.
- The orders are serially correlated. Although the agents are drawn independently, one subset of the population (the informed traders) always trades in the same direction.
- There is a price impact of trades. For any given pattern of buys and sells through trade k, a buy on the $k+1$ trade causes a downward revision in the conditional probability of a low outcome, and a consequent increase in the bid and ask. The trade price impact is a particularly useful empirical implication of the model. It can be estimated from market data and is plausibly a useful proxy for information asymmetries.

5.4   Extensions

The sequential trade framework is a modeling platform that is easily extended to accommodate various features of trading. The following subsections describe some of these developments.

5.4.1   Quote Matching

To this point the information asymmetries in the model have centered on fundamental value. Superior information concerning a security's payoffs certainly bestows an economic advantage. But this is not the only sort of information differential that can arise. En route to the market nexus, most orders pass through brokers or other intermediaries, whose relationships with the order submitters may convey advantage. Brokers, for example, usually possess trading history, credit scores and other sorts of client data. If their assessment of the likelihood that the customer is informed, conditional on customer identity, is lower than the likelihood for other brokers, they may profitably trade against their own customers if this is permitted. Exercise 5.1 describes a stylized model of this behavior.

This model can be considered at best a partial equilibrium. Why do broker b's customers include more sheep and fewer wolves? Why can't other brokers attract a similar customer base? The model nevertheless illustrates a nonfundamental informational advantage. This is an important point because although information asymmetries related to value are quite plausible in some markets, they are more dubious in others. In equity markets, for example, advance knowledge of an earnings surprise, takeover announcement, or similar event confers an obvious advantage. Similar events do not, however, characterize the government bond and foreign exchange markets. Models of these markets, therefore, must rely on a broader concept of private information. This important point has been stressed by Lyons (2001).

5.4.2   Fixed Transaction Costs

Suppose that in addition to asymmetric information considerations, the dealer must pay a transaction cost c on each trade (as in the Roll model). The modification is straightforward. The ask and bid now are set to recover c as well as the information costs: $A = E[V|Buy] + c$ and $B = E[V|Sell] - c$. The ask quote sequence may still be expressed as a sequence of conditional expectations: $A_k = E[V|\Phi_k] + c$, where Φ_k is the information set that includes the direction of the kth trade. Therefore the ask sequence is a martingale. So, too, is the bid sequence. Because trades can occur at either the bid or the ask, however, the sequence of trade prices is not a martingale (due to the $\pm c$ asymmetry in the problem). In terms of the original Roll model, the effect of asymmetric information is to break the independence between trade direction q_t and the innovation to the efficient price u_t. Developments along these lines are discussed in Glosten and Milgrom (1985, p. 83).

5.4.3   Price-Sensitive Liquidity Traders and Market Failures

The uninformed traders in the basic model are, if not necessarily stupid, then at least rather simple. They aren't price sensitive: Their trading demands are inelastic. If they have to buy, they'll pay the ask without reservation. Such desperation does exist, but it is not the rule. Most traders, even if driven by private value considerations, are somewhat price sensitive.

The traders (both informed and uninformed) in Glosten and Milgrom (1985) are actually modeled as agents subject to a random utility, $U = \rho x V + C$, in their notation. Here, ρ is the rate of substitution between current and future (terminal date) consumption, x is the number of shares held at the payoff date, and C is current consumption. ρ is random across traders, and its distribution is common knowledge. High ρ implies a strong preference for future consumption and therefore (other things equal), a tendency to buy the security. The dealer's ρ is normalized to unity. The price of current consumption may also be normalized to unity.

Initially for an uninformed trader $EU = \rho x EV + C$. He will buy (paying the dealer's ask price A) if $\rho EV > A$. He will sell (at the dealer's bid price B) if $\rho EV < B$. If $B < \rho EV < A$, the agent won't trade. (In the present model, a nontrade event is uninformative. When there is event uncertainty, a nontrade may be informative. This point is developed shortly.)

With inelastic uninformed trading demands, the dealer can set the bid and ask as wide as necessary to cover her losses to the informed traders. With elastic demands, though, there will generally be fewer uninformed agents willing to trade at these prices. The zero-expected-profit equilibrium will generally therefore exhibit a wider spread than in the inelastic case.

It is also possible that there exist no bid and ask values (other than $B = \underline{V}$ and $A = \overline{V}$) at which the dealer's expected profit is nonnegative. That is, the uninformed traders are so price sensitive that they are unwilling to participate in sufficient number to cover the dealer's losses to the informed traders (Glosten and Milgrom 1985, p. 84). Agents trying to access the market bid and ask quotes see a blank screen. This is a market failure.

The market failure can be repaired by information dissemination that removes the asymmetry or requiring the dealer to trade at a loss (presumably to be offset by some other benefit or concession). In fact, both do occur. Trading often stops (or is officially halted) pending a major news announcement. Exchanges, dealer associations, and simple considerations of reputation often effectively force a dealer to maintain a market presence when he would prefer to withdraw.

This is a point of considerable social and regulatory importance. Though coverage and enforcement varies widely, most countries now have laws that prohibit insider trading. These prohibitions are grounded in considerations of fairness and economic efficiency. The economic efficiency argument holds that market failures are extremely costly for the uninformed traders, who are denied the gains from trade (such as improved risk sharing, etc.).

5.4.4 Event Uncertainty

In actual security markets, information and information asymmetries often arrive in a lumpy fashion. Long periods with no new information and steady or sluggish trading are punctuated by periods of extremely active trading before, during, and after major news announcements.

Easley and O'Hara (1992) model this variation using event uncertainty. Taking the basic model as the starting point, a random step is placed at the beginning of the day: whether an information event has occurred.

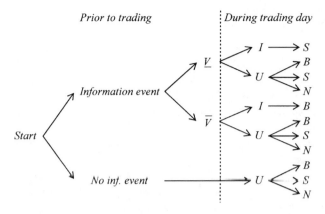

Figure 5.2. Event tree at the start of the day.

Figure 5.2 depicts the new event tree. Besides the random occurrence of information events, the tree also features an additional type of trader action: no trade. For "no trade" to convey useful information, it must be observable. In the empirical implementation discussed in the next chapter, "no trade" will be reinterpreted as something more akin to "slow trade." In the present context, though, it is most straightforward to envision a market where agents physically approach the dealer and then decide whether to trade.

The updating of dealers beliefs is fairly intuitive. A customer buy might arise from an informed buyer, and so increases the conditional probability of $\overline{V}$; a customer sale increases the perceived likelihood of $\underline{V}$. A no-trade event decreases the dealer's conditional belief that an information event has occurred. Because information asymmetries can only arise subsequent to an information event, the dealer's perceived cost of informed trading drops after a no-trade event, and the spread narrows. This implication of the model has influenced empirical work.

An informed trader always trades (in the direction of her knowledge). An uninformed trader might not trade. The no-trade probabilities for uninformed agents are the same whether an information event has occured or not, but the proportion of uninformed traders in the customer mix is higher in the absence of an information event. To the dealer, therefore, absence of trade suggests a decreased likelihood of an information event.

5.4.5   Orders of Different Sizes

The basic sequential trade model has one trade quantity. Trades in real markets, of course, occur in varying quantities. Easley and O'Hara (1987) present a framework similar to that used in the last section. Their model features event uncertainty and two possible order sizes. The market maker posts one set of bid and ask quotes for small trades and another set for large trades.

The most challenging aspect of model construction is the requirement that the zero-expected-profit condition must hold for all quantities and directions. Expected losses on large buy orders, for example, can't be cross-subsidized by expected profits on small sell orders.

In the models considered to this point, all trades in which the market maker might participate have some nonzero probability of involving an uninformed trader. This is a pooling feature of the trade mix. Were some class of trades to involve only informed traders (and therefore certain losses), no bid and ask prices (except $\underline{V}$ and $\overline{V}$) would be possible. Such outcomes are "separating." Informed traders maximize their profits by trading in the largest possible size. For a pooling equilibrium to exist, large orders must have some chance of originating from uninformed traders. A pooling equilibrium is also contingent on the existence of event uncertainty.

5.4.6   Orders of Different Types

The only orders permissible to this point have been marketable ones—orders that would result in an immediate execution. Real-world security markets admit a much wider range. Many of the variations arise when a customer has a trading strategy that can be codified in a simple rule, that when communicated with the order avoids the necessity for further monitoring or modification on the customer's part.

One common variant is the price-contingent order. When used to sell, these are called stop-loss orders. When the trade price hits or drops through a preset barrier, the order becomes marketable. For example, consider a stop-loss order to sell triggered ("elected") at a price of 50. When the trade price reaches 50, this is converted into a market order. Note that actual execution price for this order may well be below 50 if the market is moving quickly. There are also buy-stop orders, which become marketable when the price rises through a preset barrier.

Easley and O'Hara (1991) analyze a sequential trade model where the market accepts stop orders. The main implications of the model are as follows. Informed traders will never use stop orders. The information content of prices declines (the market becomes less informationally efficient). There is a greater probability of large price changes. In the model (and in real markets), a trade can trigger a wave of elections.

5.5   Empirical Implications

This book's presentation of information asymmetry focuses on its role in trading situations. More broadly, though, asymmetric information figures prominently in many models of corporate finance and asset pricing. The sequential trade models (and others to follow) establish a connection between information asymmetries and observable market phenomena. The construction of proxies for the former via empirical analysis of the latter ranks as one of the most important goals of empirical microstructure research.

In the model of section 5.2, the structural asymmetric information parameter is μ (the proportion of informed traders in the population). μ is positively related to both the bid-ask spread and the revision in beliefs (compare Eqs. (5.7) and (5.1)). These results suggest use of the bid-ask spread or the impact an order has on subsequent prices as proxies for asymmetric information. Although it is often most convenient to measure the spread, the spread impounds noninformational costs (c in the Roll model) and inventory effects (discussed in chapter 11). Price impact, on the other hand, must be estimated from models of the joint dynamics of orders and prices. These specifications are discussed in later chapters, but the general character of the effect is sufficiently important to warrant immediate elaboration.

5.6   Price Impact

Price impact refers to the effect of an incoming order on subsequent prices. The term carries connotations of a mechanism that is forceful and direct. In fact, the process is complex and subtle. It involves signal extraction mediated through the forces of economic competition.

Signal extraction entails learning about an unknown (in this case, value) from conditioning information consisting of indirect or noisy observations (the trades). Put another way, the dealer's key inference is a prediction of the closing revelation of true value based on the order flow. This prediction per se does not fully account for the revision of the bid and ask, however. For the prediction to be fully reflected in the quotes, there must be other dealers, who also observe the trade, and who will compete away any attempt by any other dealer to extract a profit by setting an inferior bid or ask. To take an extreme example, a monopolist dealer could possibly set $B = \underline{V} + \varepsilon$ and $A = \overline{V} - \varepsilon$ for some trivial $\varepsilon > 0$, irrespective of prior orders. The order flow and (therefore) the dealer's beliefs about V would evolve exactly as in the competitive case, but with no price changes.

In this light, orders do not "impact" prices. It is more accurate to say the orders *forecast* prices. The distinction is important, but empirical resolution is difficult. "Functional" causality and forecast enhancement are generally indistinguishable. The usual (Granger-Sims) test for causality is implemented as a test of forecasting ability (Hamilton (1994) p. 302).

Focusing on the signal extraction process leads to interesting implications. Most important, market dynamics reflect the beliefs of market participants, not necessarily the reality. In particular, μ is the dealers' belief about the likelihood of an informed trader. If we subsequently determine that on a particular day a corporate insider had been illegally trading in the market, we are in a position to assert that the actual likelihood of an informed trade on that day was higher than what the dealers believed. It is the latter beliefs, however, that determine the price reaction. Absent any changes in these beliefs, we should not expect an empirical analysis to detect any elevation in the price impact.

A trade causes a revision in the expectation of V for all agents in the market, with the important exception of the agent who actually traded. This customer has no better information than he did before the trade. This is clearly the case for an informed trader, who possesses perfect knowledge. But it is also true of an uninformed trader. The uninformed trader who completes transaction k knows that the probability of informed trade on that trade is not μ but zero. For this trader, then, $\delta_k = \delta_{k-1}$. Whether informed or uninformed, the agent's ultimate effect of his trades is succinctly summarized in the aphorism, "The stock doesn't know that you own it" (Goodman 1967).

Alternatively the expectation of terminal value conditional on one's own contemplated trades does not depend on whether the trades are actually completed. For example, if the incoming order is a purchase by an unidentified agent, everyone in the market will revise upward their expectation of the terminal security value, *except* for the agent who actually sent in the order.[1]

In a sense, the trading process creates superior information for uninformed traders. From the perspective of an uninformed agent who has just made the kth trade, the dealers' subsequent quote revisions are erroneous. Once the trade is completed, any uninformed trader possesses information superior to the dealers.

Does this create a manipulation opportunity? It is difficult to generally characterize market manipulations, but one strategy that might be offered up in example involves buying, moving the price upward in the process, and selling at the higher price. Traders in the basic model have only one chance to buy or sell, so there is no possibility of any such round-trip. But suppose that this limitation is removed, and we let an uninformed buyer immediately return to the market. Can he reverse his trade at a profit? (As an exercise, verify that the answer is "no.")

It is clear, however, that a sequence of uninformed trades in the same direction will move the market's conditional assessment of δ. This may create a profit opportunity for an agent who knows that the trades were uninformed, even though the agent is ignorant of the fundamental value information. Suppose that the first two trades are uninformed sells. The ask quote preceding the third trade is set to reflect the updated δ:

$$\delta_3(Sell_1, Sell_2, Buy_3) = \delta(1+\mu)/[1+(2\delta-1)\mu] > \delta_0.$$

It therefore follows that $EV - Ask_3 > 0$, where $EV = \delta_0 \underline{V} + (1 + \delta_0)\overline{V}$, the unconditional expectation. Knowing that all trades to this point (including his own) have been uninformed (ignorant of the true V), EV is also the buyer's conditional expectation. In buying at the ask, he is paying less than the security is worth.

What sort of agent might have the information required to behave in this fashion? Orders typically reach a market through agents (brokers). Brokers typically know something about their customers, and so may be in a good position to judge if someone is uninformed. Trading ahead of your customer is generally prohibited, but the strategy described only requires trading *after* the customer.

6

Order Flow and the Probability of Informed Trading

Though the richest implications of the sequential trade models involve the joint dynamics of trades and prices, inference can also be based solely on the order arrival process. This chapter describes the procedure. First, to illustrate the general features of the problem, we examine the statistical properties of the numbers of buys and sells from the basic sequential trade model. We next turn to a more flexible model that allows for event uncertainty. The analysis is based on Easley, Kiefer, and O'Hara (1997) and Easley, Hvidkjaer, and O'Hara (2002).

6.1 The Distribution of Buys and Sells

For the model described in section 5.2 the probabilities of a buy order conditional on low and high outcomes are $\Pr(Buy|\underline{V})=(1-\mu)/2$ and $\Pr(Buy|\overline{V})=(1+\mu)/2$. These probabilities are constant over successive trades. Also, conditional on V, order directions are serially independent: The probability of a buy does not depend on the direction of the last or any prior orders. If we observe n trades, the conditional distributions of b buys, $\Pr(b|n,\underline{V})$ and $\Pr(b|n,\overline{V})$, are binomial:

$$\Pr(b|n, V) = p^b (1-p)^{n-b} \binom{n}{b} \quad \text{where } p = \begin{cases} (1-\mu)/2 & \text{if } V = \underline{V} \\ (1+\mu)/2 & \text{if } V = \overline{V}. \end{cases}$$

$$(6.1)$$

The number of buys conditional only on n, then, is a mixture of binomials:

$$\Pr(b|n) = \delta \Pr(b|n,\underline{V}) + (1-\delta)\Pr(b|n,\overline{V}).$$

$$(6.2)$$

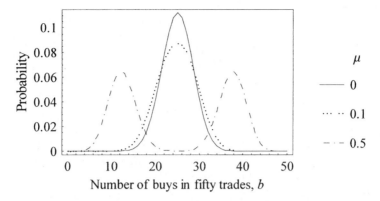

Figure 6.1. Distribution of the number of buy orders.

With no informed trading, the distribution is approximately normal. As it increases, the component distributions become more distinct. With $\mu = 0.1$, the distribution is broader but still unimodal. With $\mu = 0.5$, the distribution is bimodal (see figure 6.1).

This suggests the properties of the data that will identify an estimate of μ. With high μ, all days will tend to have one-sided order flow, a preponderance of buys or sells, depending on the outcome of the value draw. Although this model could be estimated by maximum likelihood, actual applications are based on a modified version, described in the next section.

6.2 Event Uncertainty and Poisson Arrivals

This model is a variation of the sequential trade model with event uncertainty (section 5.4.4). The principal difference is that agents are not sequentially drawn in discrete time but arrive randomly in continuous time.

These events are modeled as a Poisson arrival process. Specifically, suppose that the traders arrive randomly in time such that the probability of an arrival in a time interval of length Δt is $\lambda \Delta t$ where λ is the arrival intensity per unit time, and the probability of two traders arriving in the same interval goes to zero in the limit as $\Delta t \to 0$. Then,

- The number of trades in any finite interval of length Δt is Poisson with parameter $\theta = \lambda \Delta t$. (The Poisson distribution for a random variable n with parameter θ has the form $\Pr(n) = e^{-\theta}\theta^n/n!$ for $n = 0, 1, \ldots$ The mean and variance of this distribution are $En = \mathrm{Var}(n) = \theta$.)
- The duration τ between two successive arrivals is exponentially distributed: $f(\tau) = \tau e^{-\lambda \tau}$.

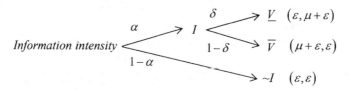

Figure 6.2. Sequential trade model with event uncertainty and Poisson arrivals.

- If two types of traders arrive independently with intensities λ_1 and λ_2, then the arrival intensity for undifferentiated traders, that is, traders of any type, is $\lambda_1 + \lambda_2$.

See Ross (1996, pp. 59–65).

The arrival intensities for informed and uninformed traders are μ and ε. The effect of these parameters on the arrival intensities of buyers and sellers depends on the information state of the market. Figure 6.2 depicts this dependence. In all states, uninformed buyers and sellers arrive with intensity ε. If there is an information event that results in a low value realization, for example, informed sellers appear, the total arrival intensity of sellers is $\varepsilon + \mu$.

On any day the unconditional numbers of buys and sells are jointly distributed as a Poisson mixture:

$$\Pr(b, s) = (1 - \alpha)\Pr(b; \varepsilon)\Pr(s; \varepsilon)$$
$$+ \alpha \left[\delta \Pr(b; \varepsilon)\Pr(s; \mu + \varepsilon) + (1 - \delta)\Pr(b; \mu + \varepsilon)\Pr(s; \varepsilon) \right], \quad (6.3)$$

where $\Pr(n; \lambda)$ denotes the probability of n arrivals when λ is the intensity parameter. Figure 6.3 depicts this distribution for parameter values $\alpha = 0.4$, $\mu = \varepsilon = 10$, (per day). The figure depicts the distribution both as a contour map (with elevation corresponding to probability) and in three dimensions (with probability on the vertical axis). In both depictions it is clear that the dominant features are two lobes, corresponding to the days when the order flow tends to be one-sided.

$\Pr(b, s)$ from equation (6.3) can be used to construct a sample likelihood function. (Note that the buys and sells do not enter individually. The only thing that matters is the total number on a given day.) All parameters may be estimated by maximum likelihood. Most interest, however, centers on a transformation of the parameters that corresponds to the probability of informed trading (*PIN*). This may be developed as follows.

The expected total order arrival intensity is $2\varepsilon + \alpha\mu$, consisting of uninformed buyers, uninformed sellers, and (with probability α) informed traders. *PIN* is the unconditional probability that a randomly chosen trader on a randomly chosen day is informed. Thus,

$$PIN = \alpha\mu/(\alpha\mu + 2\varepsilon). \quad (6.4)$$

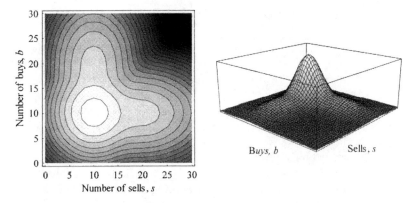

Figure 6.3. Joint probability density for the number of buy and sell orders.

In the basic model, the probability of an informed trader is μ. This can be obtained as a special case of the present model.[1] When μ increases in the basic model, daily order flows became increasingly one-sided (compare figure 6.1). This is also true in the present model: An increase in *PIN* will lead to more pronounced lobes in figure 6.3.

The interplay between α and μ in this model is interesting. These parameters enter into *PIN* only as the product $\alpha\mu$, and so can offset each other. We can obtain similar probability distributions for buys and sells whether informed traders are many (high μ) and information events are infrequent (low α) or informed traders are few (low μ) and information events are frequent (high α). This is important for estimation. Order one-sidedness in a sample may yield a relatively precise estimate for *PIN*. Samples are typically less informative about μ and α individually. Estimation errors in these two parameters are usually strongly negatively correlated. If we are primarily interested in *PIN*, though, this imprecision in the component parameters is a lesser concern. Moreover, *PIN* can be constant over days even when there is variation in μ and α, as long as it is offsetting. Thus, *PIN* might be stable even when high-μ/low-α days are interspersed with low-μ/high-α days.

6.3   Discussion

Although the expanded model is more realistic than the simple version, it remains highly stylized. Information events that can occur at most once per day, events that always occur at the beginning of the day, two possible value realizations, etc., seem to push this model far away from anything that might be found in reality. As a result, it is probably a mistake to take the model's estimates too literally. The details of *PIN*'s construction, though, suggest that it is a meaningful measure of order flow one-sidedness. There are certainly situations in securities markets where this is sensibly related to information. If public news announcements, for example, diffuse slowly, traders who can react before others may send in orders to hit or lift quotes that are, given the new information, stale. Until the stale quotes are eliminated, order flow will be one-sided. More broadly, order flow may be one-sided in a stock with poor liquidity due to order fragmentation. *PIN* may well pick up cross-sectional variation in these mechanisms.

Although we have described the computation of *PIN* as an estimate that falls out of a sequential trade model, its origins are somewhat more modest. The economic content of a sequential trade model lies in its predictions about the joint dynamics of orders and prices, for example, the effect of the orders on the quote midpoint and the spread, neither of which directly affects *PIN*. *PIN* is determined solely by the order arrival processes. These processes, though certainly reasonable, are model assumptions rather than model predictions.

The obvious difference between the Roll and the sequential trade models is that the former focuses on price and the latter on orders. There is also, however, a profound difference in how the time series are viewed. The Roll model exists in a covariance stationary framework, where information arrives uniformly and all relevant probability distributions are time-invariant.

The setup in the sequential trade models, though, is neither stationary nor ergodic. Stationarity is violated, for example, because even before the day begins, we know that the distribution of the spread immediately prior to the tenth trade differs from that prior to the ninth trade. Ergodicity is violated because successive probabilities of buys, for example, always depend on the outcome of the initial value draw.

The dynamics of the sequential trade model resemble an adjustment process subsequent to a shock. This might be most accurate, for example, in modeling trading leading up to a significant prescheduled corporate news announcement. The covariance stationary framework of the Roll model, on the other hand, would conform more closely to an average trading day in which diverse information arrives continually during the day.

These differences also arise in estimation. The maximum likelihood estimate of *PIN* relies on a sample consisting of independent path realizations. We assume that an initial draw is made at the beginning of the day (literally) and that the process starts anew each day. Then the sample proportions of buys on different days are independent and inference can proceed.

7

Strategic Trade Models

In the sequential trade framework, there are many informed agents, but each can trade only once and only if he or she is "drawn" as the arriving trader. Furthermore, if order size is a choice variable, the informed agent will always trade the largest quantity. The Kyle (1985) model, discussed in this chapter, differs in both respects. In the Kyle model, there is a single informed trader who behaves strategically. She sets her trade size taking into account the adverse price concession associated with larger quantities. Furthermore, she can, in the multiple-period version of the model, return to the market, spreading out her trades over time.

The practice of distributing orders over time to minimize trade impact is perhaps one of the most common strategies used in practice. With decimalization and increased fragmentation of trading activity, market participants have fewer opportunities to easily trade large quantities. In the present environment, therefore, order-splitting strategies are widely used by all sorts of traders (uninformed as well as informed). Although the Kyle model allows for strategic trade, whereas the sequential trade models do not, it is more stylized in some other respects. There is no bid and ask, for example; all trades clear at an informationally efficient price.

7.1 The Single-Period Model

The terminal security value is $v \sim N(p_0, \Sigma_0)$. There is one informed trader who knows v and enters a demand x. Liquidity ("noise") traders submit a not order flow $u \sim N(0, \sigma_u^2)$, independent of v. The market maker (MM) observes the total demand $y = x + u$ and then sets a price, p. All of the trades are cleared at p. If there is an imbalance between buyers and sellers, the MM makes up the difference.

Nobody knows the market clearing price when they submit their orders. Because the liquidity trader order flow is exogenous, there are really only two players we need to concentrate on: the informed trader and the MM. The informed trader wants to trade aggressively, for example, buying a large quantity if her information is positive. But the MM knows that if he sells into a large net customer buy, he his likely to be on the wrong side of the trade. He protects himself by setting a price that is increasing in the net order flow. This acts as a brake on the informed trader's desires: If she wishes to buy a lot, she'll have to pay a high price. The solution to the model is a formal expression of this trade-off.

We first consider the informed trader's problem (given a conjectured MM price function) and then show that the conjectured price function is consistent with the informed trader's optimal strategy. The informed trader conjectures that the MM uses a linear price adjustment rule $p = \lambda y + \mu$ where y is the total order flow: $y = u + x$. λ is an inverse measure of liquidity. The informed trader's profits are $\pi = (v - p)x$. Substituting in for the price conjecture and y yields $\pi = x[v - \lambda(u + x) - \mu]$. The expected profits are $E\pi = x(v - \lambda x - \mu)$. In the sequential trade models, an informed trader always makes money. This is not true here. For example, if the informed trader is buying ($x > 0$), it is possible that a large surge of uninformed buying ($u \gg 0$) drives the $\lambda(u + x) + \mu$ above v. The informed trader chooses x to maximize $E\pi$, yielding $x = (v - \mu)/2\lambda$. The second-order condition is $\lambda > 0$.

The MM conjectures that the informed trader's demand is linear in v: $x = \alpha + \beta v$. Knowing the optimization process that the informed trader followed, the MM can solve for α and β: $(v - \mu)/2\lambda = \alpha + \beta v$ for all v. This implies

$$\alpha = -\mu/2\lambda \quad \text{and} \quad \beta = 1/2\lambda. \tag{7.1}$$

The inverse relation between β and λ is particularly important. As liquidity drops (i.e., as λ rises) the informed agent trades less. Now the MM must figure out $E[v|y]$. This computation relies on the following result, which are also used later in other contexts.

Bivariate normal projection. Suppose that X and Y are bivariate normal random variables with means μ_X and μ_Y, variances σ_X^2 and σ_Y^2, and covariance σ_{XY}. The conditional expectation of Y given X is $E[Y|X = x] = \mu_Y + (\sigma_{XY}/\sigma_X^2)(x - \mu_X)$. Because this is linear in X, conditional expectation is equivalent to projection. The variance of the projection error is $\text{Var}[Y|X = x] = \sigma_Y^2 - \sigma_{XY}^2/\sigma_X^2$. Note that this does not depend on x.

Here, given the definition of the order flow variable and the MM's conjecture about the informed traders behavior, $y = u + \alpha + \beta v$, we have $Ey = \alpha + \beta Ev = \alpha + \beta p_0$, $\text{Var}(y) = \sigma_u^2 + \beta^2 \Sigma_0$, and $\text{Cov}(y, v) = \beta \Sigma_0$.

Using these in the projection results gives

$$E\left[v\left|y\right.\right] = p_0 + \frac{\beta\left(y - \alpha - \beta p_0\right)\Sigma_0}{\sigma_u^2 + \beta^2\Sigma_0} \quad \text{and}$$

$$\text{Var}\left[v\left|y\right.\right] = \frac{\sigma_u^2\Sigma_0}{\sigma_u^2 + \beta^2\Sigma_0}. \tag{7.2}$$

This must equal $p = \lambda y + \mu$ for all values of y, so

$$\mu = \frac{-\alpha\beta\,\Sigma_0 + \sigma_u^2 p_0}{\sigma_u^2 + \beta^2\Sigma_0} \quad \text{and} \quad \lambda = \frac{\beta\,\Sigma_0}{\sigma_u^2 + \beta^2\Sigma_0}. \tag{7.3}$$

Solving Eqs. (7.1) and (7.3) yields:

$$\alpha = p_0\sqrt{\frac{\sigma_u^2}{\Sigma_0}}; \quad \mu = p_0; \quad \lambda = \frac{1}{2}\sqrt{\frac{\Sigma_0}{\sigma_u^2}}; \quad \text{and} \quad \beta = \sqrt{\frac{\sigma_u^2}{\Sigma_0}}. \tag{7.4}$$

7.1.1 Discussion

Both the liquidity parameter λ and the informed trader's order coefficient β depend only on the value uncertainty Σ_0 relative to the intensity of noise trading σ_u^2.

The informed trader's expected profit is:

$$E\pi = \frac{(v - p_0)^2}{2}\sqrt{\frac{\sigma_u^2}{\Sigma_0}}. \tag{7.5}$$

This is increasing in the divergence between the true value and the unconditional mean. It is also increasing in the variance of noise trading. We can think of the noise trading as providing camouflage for the informed trader. This is of practical importance. All else equal, an agent trading on inside information will be able to make more money in a widely held and frequently traded stock (at least, prior to apprehension). How much of the private information is impounded in the price? Using the expression for β in equation (7.2) gives $\text{Var}[v|p] = \text{Var}[v|y] = \Sigma_0/2$. That is, half of the insider's information gets into the price. This does not depend on the intensity of noise trading.

The essential properties of the Kyle model that make it tractable arise from the multivariate normality (which gives linear conditional expectations) and a quadratic objective function (which has a linear first-order condition). The multivariate normality can accommodate a range of modifications. The following exercises explore modifications to the model that still fit comfortably within the framework.

Exercise 7.1 (Partially informed noise traders) The noise traders in the original model are pure noise traders: u is independent of v.

Consider the case where the "uninformed" order flow is positively related to the value: $\text{Cov}(u, v) = \sigma_{uv} > 0$. We might think of u as arising from partially informed traders who do not behave strategically. Proceed as before. Solve the informed trader's problem; solve the MM's problem; solve for the model parameters $\{\alpha, \beta, \mu, \lambda\}$ in terms of the inputs $\{\sigma_u^2, \Sigma_0, \sigma_{uv}\}$. Interpret your results. Show that when $\text{Corr}(u, v) = 1$, the price becomes perfectly informative.

Exercise 7.2 (Informed trader gets a signal instead of complete revelation) The informed trader in the basic model has perfect information about v. Consider the case where she only gets a signal s. That is, she observes $s = v + \varepsilon$ where $\varepsilon \sim N(0, \sigma_\varepsilon^2)$, independent of v. Solve for the model parameters $\{\alpha, \beta, \mu, \lambda\}$ in terms of the inputs, σ_u^2, Σ_0, and σ_ε^2. Interpret your results. Verify that when $\sigma_\varepsilon^2 = 0$, you get the original model solutions.

Exercise 7.3 Around 1985, a Merrill Lynch broker noticed a pattern of profitable trades originating from a Bahamas branch of Bank Leu and began to piggyback his own orders on the Bank Leu flow. Suppose that when the informed trader in the basic model puts in an order x, her broker simultaneously puts in an order x, with γx, with $\gamma > 0$. Solve for the model parameters $(\alpha, \beta, \mu, \lambda)$ in terms of the inputs, σ_u^2, Σ_0, and γ. It turned out that the Bank Leu orders originated from a New York investment banker, Dennis Levine, who subsequently pleaded guilty to insider trading (see Stewart (1992)).

7.2 Multiple Rounds of Trading

A practical issue in market design is the determination of when trading should occur. Some firms on the Paris Bourse, for example, trade in twice-per-day call auctions, others continuously within a trading session. What happens in the Kyle model as we increase the number of auctions, ultimately converging to continuous trading?

We will consider the case of N auctions that are equally spaced over a unit interval of time. The time between auctions is $\Delta t = 1/N$. The auctions are indexed by $n = 1, \ldots N$. The noise order flow arriving at the nth auction is defined as Δu_n. This is distributed normally, $\Delta u_n \sim N(0, \sigma_u^2 \Delta t)$ where σ_u^2 has the units of variance per unit time. The use of the difference notation facilitates the passage to continuous time. The equilibrium has the following properties.

- The informed trader's demand is $\Delta x_n = \beta_n(v - p_{n-1})\Delta t_n$, where β_n is trading intensity per unit time.
- The price change at the nth auction is $p_n = p_{n-1} + \lambda_n(\Delta x_n + \Delta u_n)$.
- Market efficiency requires $p_n = E[v|y_n]$ where y_n is the cumulative order flow over time.

In equilibrium the informed trader "slices and dices" her order flow, distributing it over the N auctions. This corresponds to the real-world practice of splitting orders, which is used by traders of all stripes, not just informed ones.

Recall that in the sequential trade models, orders are positively auto-correlated (buys tend to follow buys). Does a similar result hold here? Is autocorrelation a consequence of the informed trader's strategic behavior? There is an argument supporting this conjecture that is intuitive and compelling at first glance. The informed trader splits her orders over time, and so tends to trade on the same side of the market. If her information is favorable $v > p_0$, she will be buying on average; with negative information, she'll be selling. This establishes a pattern of continuation in her orders, and as a result $Corr(\Delta x_i, \Delta x_j) > 0$ for any pair of auctions i and j we might care to examine. Total order flow, being the sum of her demand and that of the uninformed, is thus the sum of one series that is positively autocorrelated and one that is uncorrelated. We'd expect the positive auto-correlation to persist in the total, diluted perhaps by the uncorrelated noise, but present nonetheless.

In fact, however, total order flow is uncorrelated. Correlation would imply that order flow is at least partially predictable. Since order flow and price changes are linearly related (the λ_n are known at the start of the day), predictability in the former is equivalent to predictability in the latter. Autocorrelation in price changes is ruled out by market efficiency. More formally, the conditional expectation of the incremental order flow is:

$$E[\Delta y_n | y_{n-1}] = E[\Delta u_n + \Delta x_n | y_{n-1}] = E[\beta_n(v - p_{n-1})\Delta t | y_{n-1}] = 0.$$

The first equality is definitional; the second holds because the noise order flow has zero expectation. The third equality reflects the market efficiency condition that $E[v | y_{n-1}] = p_{n-1}$. From a strategic viewpoint, the informed trader hides behind the uninformed order flow. This means that she trades so that the MM can't predict (on the basis of the net order flow) what she will do next.

Figure 7.1 depicts the market depth parameter over time as a function of the number of auctions. In the sequential trade models, manipulation by an uninformed trader is not generally profitable (section 5.6). A similar result holds here. Huberman and Stanzl (2004) show that the linear price schedules of the Kyle model do not allow manipulation and also that *only* linear price schedules have this property.

7.3 Extensions and Related Work

The Kyle model lies near the center of a large family of theoretical analyses. The following list is suggestive of the directions, but far from comprehensive. Back (1992) develops continuous time properties. Back and

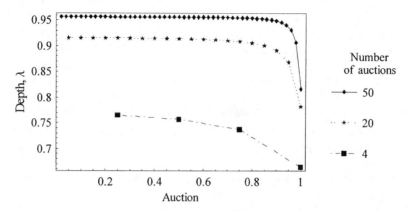

Figure 7.1. Market impact and number of auctions.

Baruch (2004) explore the links between the strategic and sequential trade models. Notably, in their common framework, the informed agent trades randomly in continuous time. Admati and Pfleiderer (1988) incorporate strategic uninformed traders (also see Foster and Viswanathan 1990). Subrahmanyam (1991a) considers risk-averse market makers and informed traders. Spiegel and Subrahmanyam (1992) model the uninformed agents as rational risk-averse hedgers. Analyses that feature multiple securities include Caballe and Krishnan (1994) and Subrahmanyam (1991b) (also see Admati (1985)). Subrahmanyam considers the case of a multiple security market that includes a basket security, for example, a stock index futures contract or an index exchange traded fund. The diversification in an index greatly mitigates firm-specific information asymmetries, making index securities generally cheaper to trade. Holden and Subrahmanyam (1992, 1994), Foster and Viswanathan (1996), and Back, Cao, and Willard (2000) consider multiperiod models with multiple informed traders.

8

A Generalized Roll Model

8.1 Overview

Following the economic analysis, we now turn to empirical examination of asymmetric information by developing a generalization of the Roll model. One sensible first step is to allow the efficient price to be partially driven by the trade direction indicator variable. A number of models along these lines have been proposed. The developments in this chapter are compatible with and can be viewed as special cases of most of these models. The phrase "generalized Roll model" is not in common use. It is used here to emphasize the roots of the present developments in the Roll model.

Although many of these models are estimated jointly over prices and trades (the q_t), the present chapter discusses only univariate specifications for price changes, deferring the multivariate models to the next chapter. One reason for this is that some general features of these models are best encountered in a univariate setting. In particular, it is easier to see from the univariate representation of a bivariate model the specification problems that almost certainly plague (but in a more subtle fashion) the multivariate analyses. A second consideration is that although we have good recent data on U.S. equity markets that allow us to infer q_t, this is not universally the case. In many data samples and markets, only trade prices are recorded.

8.2 The Structural Model

The efficient price still behaves as a random walk, but the increments have two components.

$$m_t = m_{t-1} + w_t$$
$$w_t = \lambda q_t + u_t. \tag{8.1}$$

Here, λq_t reflects the information content of the time-t trade ($\lambda_t > 0$), and u_t impounds public information, with $\text{Corr}(q_t, u_t) = 0$. More precisely, because trades are often reported, u_t is better described as reflecting non-trade public information. We follow the earlier convention that the actual trade price is $p_t = m_t + c q_t$, that is, the dealer recovers costs of c. In this context, c is interpreted as noninformational costs.

The trade is at the ask if $q_t = +1$, and at the bid if $q_t = -1$, which imply that the ask and bid are $m_{t-1} + c + \lambda + u_t$ and $m_{t-1} - c - \lambda + u_t$. Thus, the bid and ask are set symmetrically about $m_{t-1} + u_t$. The spread is $2(c + \lambda)$, where c reflects the noninformational fixed costs of the trade (clearing costs, clerical costs, etc.) and λ reflects the adverse selection cost. In the spirit of the asymmetric information models, λ is the price impact necessary to balance expected gains from trading against uninformed agents with expected losses to informed agents.

These conventions suggest the following timing. Immediately after the trade at $t - 1$, the efficient price is m_{t-1}. Then public information arrives as the realization of u_t. The dealer sets the bid and ask symmetrically about $m_{t-1} + u_t$. Then a trade arrives (a realization of q_t), and the efficient price is updated to m_t.

8.3   Statistical Representations

We now turn to reduced-form representations of the model. The model has three parameters $\{\lambda, c, \sigma_u^2\}$, and two sources of randomness: u_t and q_t. Inference is based on the properties of the observed price changes. In terms of the structural model:

$$\Delta p_t = p_t - p_{t-1} = c(q_t - q_{t-1}) + \lambda q_t + u_t. \tag{8.2}$$

The price change autocovariances are:

$$\gamma_0 = E(\Delta p_t)^2 = c^2 + (c + \lambda)^2 + \sigma_u^2$$
$$\gamma_1 = E(\Delta p_t \Delta p_{t-1}) = -c(c + \lambda). \tag{8.3}$$

All autocovariances of order two or more are zero. This implies (via the Wold theorem and the Ansley et al. (1977) result) that the price changes can be represented as the MA(1) process $\Delta p_t = \varepsilon_t + \theta \varepsilon_{t-1}$. Section 4.2 discussed determination of the moving average parameters from the autocovariances.

Neither the two autocovariances $\{\gamma_0, \gamma_1\}$ nor the two MA parameters $\{\theta, \sigma_\varepsilon^2\}$ suffice to identify the three structural parameters of the model

$\{\lambda, c, \sigma_u^2\}$. One option is to fix one of the structural parameters. Setting $\lambda = 0$ returns us to the original Roll model (no asymmetric information). If $\sigma_u^2 = 0$, then we are left with only asymmetric information (no public information). Setting $c = 0$ eliminates noninformational costs. It is sometimes useful to consider these special cases, but from an economic perspective they are quite restrictive.

One important parameter of the structural model can be identified without further restrictions. From (8.1) the variance of the efficient price changes is $\text{Var}(w_t) = \sigma_w^2 = \lambda^2 + \sigma_u^2$. Using (8.3), this same quantity can be computed as $\gamma_0 + 2\gamma_1$. It will later be shown that the identification of σ_w^2 is a general result, extending to multiple lags and multivariate and/or multiple-price models.

The intuition for this property lies in the behavior of long-term returns. σ_w^2 is the variance per unit time of the random-walk component of the security price. This variance is time-scaled: If we use a longer interval to compute the change, the variance is simply multiplied by the length of the interval: $\text{Var}(m_t - m_{t-k}) = k\sigma_w^2$. But over long periods, microstructure effects become relatively less important. Most of the long-term dynamics in p_t are attributable to m_t. That is, as k gets large,

$$\sigma_w^2 = \frac{\text{Var}[m_t - m_{t-k}]}{k} \approx \frac{\text{Var}[p_t - p_{t-k}]}{k},$$

irrespective of microstructure effects. Identification of parameters other than σ_w^2, however, requires more structure or more data.

8.4   Forecasting and Filtering

In the basic Roll model the price forecast (based on a linear projection) was shown to be

$$f_t \equiv \lim_{k \to \infty} E^*[p_{t+k}|p_t, p_{t-1}, \ldots] = E^*[p_{t+1}| p_t, p_{t-1}, \ldots] = p_t + \theta\varepsilon_t. \quad (8.4)$$

This is the price forecast for the generalized Roll model as well, because it has the same MA(1) representation. The earlier discussion emphasized that although f_t has uncorrelated increments (like a martingale), it is *not* generally equal to m_t from the structural model. Instead, it is what is usually called a filtered state estimate, the expectation of an unobserved variable conditional on the history of observations. In the present case, $f_t = E^*[m_t|p_t, p_{t-1}, \ldots]$.

We can demonstrate this by using the structural model to compute f_t and then showing that this is equal to $p_t + \theta\varepsilon_t$. First, because $m_t = p_t - cq$, $f_t = p_t - cE[q_t|p_t, p_{t-1}, \ldots]$. Next, because the price history is equivalent to the innovation history, $f_t = p_t - cE[q_t|\varepsilon_t, \varepsilon_{t-1}, \ldots]$. We will consider projections of the form $E^*[q_t|\varepsilon_t, \varepsilon_{t-1}, \ldots] = \beta_0\varepsilon_t + \beta_1\varepsilon_{t-1} + \beta_2\varepsilon_{t-2} + \ldots$

Because the ε_t values are uncorrelated, $\beta_i = \text{Cov}(q_t, \varepsilon_{t-i})/\sigma_\varepsilon^2$. The $\text{Cov}(q_t, \varepsilon_{t-i})$ can be computed as follows. There are two ways of representing Δp_t, the statistical and the structural, and they must agree:

$$\varepsilon_t + \theta\varepsilon_{t-1} = (c + \lambda)q_t - cq_{t-1} + u_t. \tag{8.5}$$

Rearranging this to isolate ε_t gives $\varepsilon_t = (c + \lambda)q_t - cq_{t-1} + u_t - \theta\varepsilon_{t-1}$. From this it is clear that $\text{Cov}(q_t, \varepsilon_t) = c + \lambda$ and $\text{Cov}(q_t, \varepsilon_{t-k}) = 0$ for $k \geq 1$. The expectation then reduces to $E^*[q_t|\varepsilon_t, \varepsilon_{t-1}, \ldots] = [(c + \lambda)/\sigma_\varepsilon^2]\varepsilon_t$. Using this,

$$E^*[m_t|p_t, p_{t-1}, \ldots] = p_t - c\left(\frac{c+\lambda}{\sigma_\varepsilon^2}\right)\varepsilon_t = p_t + \theta\varepsilon_t.$$

The second equality follows from equating the first-order autocovariance implied by the structural model in (8.3) to that implied by the statistical model: $-c(c + \lambda) = \theta\sigma_\varepsilon^2$.

8.5   The Pricing Error: How Closely Does p_t Track m_t?

We've motivated the c parameter in the model as a cost variable. If customers come in and trade against dealer bids and asks, then c is the amount by which a customer buyer overpays relative to the efficient price (and similarly for a customer seller). This does not imply that terms of trade are unfair, or that dealers make profits after their costs, but it does imply a clear distinction between those who supply liquidity and those who demand it.

Many markets, though, don't have such a clean dichotomy between dealers and customers. In limit order markets, bids and asks are set by other customers. Sometimes we consider the customers who supply liquidity as quasi-dealers, that is, dealers in all but name. More generally, though, a customer in such a market has a choice between using a market or a limit order and (if a limit order) how it is to be priced. In such markets, the dealer/customer or liquidity supplier/demand roles become blurry. Even when we can't directly impute a cost to either side in trade, though, it is still of interest to know how closely the trade prices track the efficient price. This is measured by $\text{Var}(s_t) \equiv \sigma_s^2$ where $s_t = p_t - m_t$. The structural model here implies $s = cq_t$, so $\sigma_s^2 = c^2$.

Unfortunately, because c is not identified by the data, σ_s^2 is not identified either. However, it does possess a lower bound. To see this, note first that $s_t = p_t - m_t = (p_t - f_t) - (m_t - f_t)$. Because f_t is a linear projection of m_t on $\{p_t, p_{t-1}, \ldots\}$, the filtering error $m_t - f_t$ is uncorrelated with $p_t - f_t$. Therefore

$$\sigma_s^2 = \text{Var}(p_t - f_t) + \text{Var}(m_t - f_t). \tag{8.6}$$

The first term on the right-hand side does not depend on the structural identification and is easily computed as $\text{Var}(p_t - f_t) = \text{Var}(-\theta\varepsilon_t) = \theta^2\sigma_\varepsilon^2$.

Now we turn to the second term, essentially seeking the structural identification for which it is minimized.

Consider the reduced-form and structural models under the restriction $\sigma_u^2 = 0$, or equivalently that $u_t = 0$ for all t. In this case, the only randomness in the structural model arises from q_t, and equation (8.5) establishes an exact correspondence between the two representations and their disturbances. That is, if $\varepsilon_t + \theta\varepsilon_{t-1} = (c + \lambda)q_t - cq_{t-1}$, then we can set $\varepsilon_t = (c + \lambda)q_t$ for all t and $\theta = -c/(c + \lambda)$. The filtered estimate of m_t then becomes $f_t = p_t + \theta\varepsilon_t = p_t - cq_t = m_t$. So under the restriction $\sigma_u^2 = 0$, the filtered estimate is exact, and $\text{Var}(m_t - f_t) = 0$. As a variance cannot be negative, this establishes that under any structural identification, σ_s^2 cannot fall below $\underline{\sigma}_s^2 = \theta^2\sigma_\varepsilon^2$. In terms of the structural parameters, this is

$$\underline{\sigma}_s^2 = \frac{1}{2}\left[c^2 + (c + \lambda)^2 + \sigma_u^2 - \sqrt{(\lambda^2 + \sigma_u^2)\left[(2c + \lambda)^2 + \sigma_u^2\right]}\right]. \tag{8.7}$$

It is easy to exceed this lower bound, that is, to find a set of structural parameters for which $\sigma_s^2 \geq \underline{\sigma}_s^2$. For the generalized Roll model, the lower bound is attained when all information is trade-related. In the original model, all information is public, and $\sigma_s^2 = -\gamma_1 = -\theta\sigma_\varepsilon^2 > \underline{\sigma}_s^2 = \theta^2\sigma_\varepsilon^2$, because $-1 < \theta < 0$.

There does not exist an upper bound for σ_s^2. The problem is that there are many alternative structural models that are observationally equivalent (have the same θ and σ_ε^2). For example, consider $p_t = m_{t-2} + cq_t$. Here, trade price is driven by an efficient price that is two periods "stale." Then $s_t = p_t - m_t = -w_t - w_{t-1} + cq_t$. Relative to the original model, σ_s^2 is inflated by $2\sigma_w^2$. One can make economic arguments that it is unlikely that the price is extremely lagged relative to beliefs. Were quotes set relative to yesterday's efficient price, customers would be unwilling to trade on one side of the market. Arguments like this might justify at least a provisional assumption about how stale the price is likely to be, but they must be based on economics rather than statistics. Statistical analysis does not provide an upper bound.

Finally, σ_w^2 is the random-walk variance per unit time. For example, if the model is estimated over one-minute intervals, then σ_w^2 is variance per minute. It may be rescaled, of course, to give an implied hourly or daily random-walk variance (see exercise 8.3). The pricing error variance σ_s^2, on the other hand, is the variance of a difference between two level variables at a point in time. It does not have a time dimension.

8.6   General Univariate Random-Walk Decompositions

Up to now, the chapter has explored the correspondence between a known structural model and its statistical representations. This was useful for illuminating what we could (and could not) learn about the former from the latter. Here we ask what can be inferred starting from a moving average representation of price changes that is not of order one but is instead of arbitrary order: $\Delta p_t = \theta(L)\varepsilon_t$. The only economic structure we impose on the prices is $p_t = m_t + s_t$ where m_t follows a random walk $(m_t = m_{t-1} + w_t)$ and s_t is (as in the preceding section) a tracking error that may be serially correlated and partially or completely correlated with w_t.

The observable variable, p_t, is thus decomposed into a random-walk and a covariance-stationary error. Random-walk decompositions were originally developed and applied in macroeconomic settings, where the random-walk component is considered the long-term trend and the stationary component impounds transient business cycle effects. This literature mostly employs the trend/cycle terminology. The treatment here follows the historical development of this literature. I begin with Beveridge and Nelson (1981) and follow with the more general case described in Watson (1986). Later chapters explore multivariate extensions and cointegration.

In macroeconomics applications, random-walk decompositions are usually called permanent/transitory. The random-walk terminology is used here to stress the financial economics connection to the random-walk efficient prices. The permanent/transitory distinction is in some respects more descriptive, however, of the attributions that we're actually making.

From a microstructure perspective, the key results expand on those demonstrated for the generalized Roll model: The moving average representation for the price changes suffices to identify the variance of the implicit efficient price σ_w^2, the projection of the efficient price on past price changes, and a lower bound on the variance of the difference between the transaction price and the efficient price. The development in this section is heuristic and intuitive. The appendix gives a more formal development.

The starting point is the price forecast f_t:

$$f_t \equiv \lim_{k \to \infty} E^*[p_{t+k} \mid p_t, p_{t-1}, \ldots]$$

$$= p_t + E^*[\Delta p_{t+1} \mid \varepsilon_t, \varepsilon_{t-1}, \ldots] + E^*[\Delta p_{t+2} \mid \varepsilon_t, \varepsilon_{t-1}, \ldots] + \cdots$$

$$= p_t + \sum_{k=0}^{\infty} \theta_{k+1}\varepsilon_{t-k} + \sum_{k=0}^{\infty} \theta_{k+2}\varepsilon_{t-k} + \sum_{k=0}^{\infty} \theta_{k+3}\varepsilon_{t-k} + \cdots \qquad (8.8)$$

$$= p_t + \left(\sum_{j=0}^{\infty} \theta_{j+1}\right)\varepsilon_t + \left(\sum_{j=0}^{\infty} \theta_{j+2}\right)\varepsilon_{t-1} + \left(\sum_{j=0}^{\infty} \theta_{j+3}\right)\varepsilon_{t-2} + \cdots$$

With this construction, the first-difference of f_t is

$$\Delta f_t = \Delta p_t + \left(\sum_{j=0}^{\infty} \theta_{j+1}\right)\varepsilon_t - \theta_1\varepsilon_{t-1} - \theta_2\varepsilon_{t-2} - \cdots$$

$$= \sum_{j=0}^{\infty} \theta_j \varepsilon_{t-j} + \left(\sum_{j=0}^{\infty} \theta_{j+1} \right) \varepsilon_t - \theta_1 \varepsilon_{t-1} - \theta_2 \varepsilon_{t-2} - \cdots \qquad (8.9)$$

$$= \left(\sum_{j=0}^{\infty} \theta_j \right) \varepsilon_t = \theta(1) \varepsilon_t.$$

So the increments to f_t, being a constant multiple of an uncorrelated series, are themselves uncorrelated. Although this is not a sufficient condition for f_t to be a martingale, it is a necessary one. Is it reasonable, then, to simply assert that f_t *is* the efficient price?

If $f_t = m_t$ then writing $m_t = m_{t-1} + w_t$ establishes a correspondence: $w_t = \theta(1) \varepsilon_t$. Its variance is

$$\sigma_w^2 = \theta(1)^2 \sigma_\varepsilon^2. \qquad (8.10)$$

This particular result is invariant to identification. The discrepancy between efficient and transaction prices is $s_t = p_t - m_t$. Using equation (8.8),

$$s_t = C_0 \varepsilon_t + C_1 \varepsilon_{t-1} + C_2 \varepsilon_{t-2} + \cdots \quad \text{where } C_i = -\sum_{j=i+1}^{\infty} \theta_j. \qquad (8.11)$$

From this,

$$\sigma_s^2 = \sum_{i=0}^{\infty} C_i^2 \sigma_\varepsilon^2. \qquad (8.12)$$

Equivalently, we may express s_t in terms of the w_t: $s_t = A_0 w_t + A_1 w_{t-1} + A_2 w_{t-2} + \cdots$, where $A_k = -\theta(1)^{-1} \sum_{j=k+1}^{\infty} \theta_j$.

This has all followed from assuming that $f_t = m_t$, in which case s_t is a function of current and past w_t. But suppose that s_t, while still zero-mean and covariance stationary, is uncorrelated with w_t:

$$s_t = \eta_t + B_1 \eta_{t-1} + B_2 \eta_{t-2} + \cdots,$$

where $\{\eta_t\}$ is a white-noise process uncorrelated with $\{w_t\}$. This is more complicated than the previous case. If the moving averages are finite, it is still possible to solve for the Bs and σ_η^2 in terms of the θs and σ_ε^2, but the computation involves solving a polynomial equation. Rather than pursue this case further, though, we will move right on to the general case where s_t contains terms in w_t and terms uncorrelated with w_t:

$$s_t = (A_0 w_t + A_1 w_{t-1} + \cdots) + (\eta_t + B_1 \eta_{t-1} + \cdots). \qquad (8.13)$$

This model is now unidentified, but as with the generalized Roll model, we have two substantive results. First, the variance of the efficient price increments, σ_w^2, is the same for all feasible sets of parameters. We have already determined this for one particular set, the case where s_t involves only terms in w_t. Second, σ_s^2 computed under this restriction is a lower bound. The chapter appendix develops these results in greater depth. Hasbrouck (1993) establishes the lower bound result in a microstructure setting. Independently, Eckbo and Liu (1993) arrive at the result in a macroeconomic context.

This discussion has proceeded from the starting point of a MA model for price changes $\Delta p_t = \theta(L)\varepsilon_t$. Starting from an autoregressive representation, $\phi(L)\Delta p_t = \varepsilon_t$, we can invert to obtain the moving average (by computing $\phi(L) = \theta(L)^{-1}$). This is not, however, necessary if we're simply interested in σ_w^2. Because $\phi(1) = \theta(1)^{-1}, \sigma_w^2 = \phi(1)^{-2}\sigma_\varepsilon^2$ (see exercise 8.2). Similarly, with a mixed ARMA like $\phi(L)\Delta p_t = \theta(L)\varepsilon_t$, $\sigma_w^2 = \phi(1)^{-2}\theta(1)^2\sigma_\varepsilon^2$.

Exercise 8.1 (The Roll model with stale prices) The beliefs of market participants at time t are summarized in m_t, where $m_t = m_{t-1} + w_t$. But due to operational delays, trades actually occur relative to a lagged value: $p_t = m_{t-1} + cq_t$. What are the autocovariances of Δp_t? What is its moving average representation?

Exercise 8.2 (Lagged price adjustment, without a bid-ask spread) Delays may also lead to price adjustments that do not instantaneously correct. Suppose $m_t = m_{t-1} + w_t$, but $p_t = p_{t-1} + \alpha(m_t - p_{t-1})$, with $0 < \alpha < 1$. Show that the autoregressive representation for price changes is $\phi(L)\Delta p_t = \varepsilon_t$ where $\phi(L) = (1 - (1 - \alpha)L)$ and $\varepsilon_t = \alpha w_t$. Verify that $\phi(1)^{-2}\sigma_\varepsilon^2 = \sigma_w^2$.

Exercise 8.3 For log price changes over five-minute intervals, we estimate a second-order moving average model: $\Delta p_t = \varepsilon_t - 0.3\varepsilon_{t-1} + 0.1\varepsilon_{t-2}$, where $\sigma_\varepsilon^2 = 0.00001$.

a. What is the random-walk standard deviation per five-minute interval?
b. Assuming a six-hour trading day, what is the implied random-walk standard deviation over the day?
c. Compute the lower bound for the standard deviation of the pricing error.

8.7   Other Approaches

There is a long tradition in empirical finance of measuring market efficiency (informational and operational) by measuring or assessing how closely security prices follow a random walk. Statistical measures commonly focus on autocovariances, autocorrelations, or variance ratios.

The autocovariances and autocorrelations of a random-walk are zero at all nonzero leads and lags. This makes for a clean null hypothesis, and there exists a large number of tests to evaluate this null. But if a random walk is rejected (and in microstructure data, it usually is), how should we proceed? Statistical significance (rejecting the null) does not imply economic significance. It is difficult to reduce a set of autocovariances and autocorrelations to a single meaningful number.

One approach is to compare the variances of returns computed at different intervals or endpoints. It was noted before that transaction price returns computed over long horizons are dominated by the random-walk component. A variance ratio compares the variance per unit time implied by a long horizon with a variance per unit time computed from a short horizon:

$$V_{M,N} = \frac{\text{Var}(p_t - p_{t-M})/M}{\text{Var}(p_t - p_{t-N})/N},\tag{8.14}$$

where $M, N > 0$. If p_t follows a random walk, $V_{M,N} = 1$ for all M and N. Usually, though if microstructure effects dominate short-horizon returns, then typically, with $M < N$, $V_{M,N} > 1$. That is, microstructure effects inflate the variance per unit time in the short run. If we set N large, $V_{M,N}$ generally declines as M approaches N from below. In a sense, then, this can summarize how quickly (in terms of return interval) the prices come to resemble a random walk.

As a single summary statistic, though, $V_{M,N}$ is problematic. There are few principles to apply in choosing M and N. Furthermore, negative auto-correlation at some lags can be offset by positive correlation at others, resulting in Vs near unity, even though the process exhibits complicated dependent behavior.

Variance ratios are also computed when the horizons are the same, but endpoints differ. In some markets, for example, the first and last trades of the day occur using different mechanisms, Typically, the opening price (first trade) is determined using a single-price call, and the closing price is that last trade in a continuous session. The relative efficiencies of the two mechanisms are sometimes assessed by variance ratios like $\text{Var}(p_t^{Open} - p_{t-1}^{Open})/\text{Var}(p_t^{Close} - p_{t-1}^{Close})$. Studies along these lines include Amihud and Mendelson (1987, 1991), Amihud, Mendelson, and Murgia (1990), and Ronen (1998).

Appendix: Identification in Random-Walk Decompositions

This discussion provides more detail on the results described in section 8.6. Let $p_t = m_t + s_t$ where $m_t = m_{t-1} + w_t$ and $s_t = A(L)w_t + B(L)\eta_t$, where w_t and η_t are uncorrelated. Using the lag operator, the price changes are:

$$\Delta p_t = (1 - L)p_t = (1 - L)m_t + (1 - L)s_t$$
$$= [1 + (1 - L)A(L)]w_t + (1 - L)B(L)\eta_t.\tag{8.15}$$

The corresponding MA model is $\Delta p_t = \theta(L)\varepsilon_t$.

Subsequent developments rely on a device called the autocovariance generating function (AGF). For a covariance-stationary univariate time series $\{x_t\}$ with autocovariances $\gamma_k = \text{Cov}(x_t, x_{t-k})$ for $k = \cdots -2, -1, 0, 1, 2, \ldots$ the AGF is:

$$\gamma_x(z) = \cdots + \gamma_{-2}z^{-2} + \gamma_{-1}z^{-1} + \gamma_0 + \gamma_1 z + \gamma_2 z^2 + \cdots \qquad (8.16)$$

For a univariate time series there is a symmetry $\gamma_k = \gamma_{-k}$. Furthermore, if $\{x_t\}$ and $\{y_t\}$ are mutually uncorrelated at all leads and lags, the autocovariance function of the series $\{x_t + y_t\}$ is given by $g_{x+y}(z) = g_x(z) + g_y(z)$. Although the AGF may initially seem like nothing more than a way to tabulate autocovariances, it can also be used to compute the autocovariances. Specifically, if $\{x_t\}$ possesses a moving average representation $x_t = \theta(L)\varepsilon_t$, then $g_x(z) = \theta(z^{-1})\theta(z)\sigma_\varepsilon^2$. Hamilton (1994, section 3.6) discusses the AGF in greater depth.

Returning to the problem at hand, from the moving average representation for price changes, $g_{\Delta p}(z) = \theta(z^{-1})\theta(z)\sigma_\varepsilon^2$. From the structural representation

$$g_{\Delta p}(z) = \left[1 - (1 - z^{-1})A(z^{-1})\right]\left[1 - (1-z)A(z)\right]\sigma_w^2$$
$$+ \left[(1 - z^{-1})B(z^{-1})\right]\left[(1-z)B(z)\right]\sigma_\eta^2. \qquad (8.17)$$

Equating these two expressions and evaluating both sides at $z = 1$ gives $\sigma_w^2 = [\theta(1)]^2\sigma_\varepsilon^2$, where $\theta(1) = 1 + \theta_1 + \theta_2 + \cdots$ If price changes are originally expressed in autoregressive form, we don't need to compute the full moving average. From $\phi(L)\Delta p_t = \varepsilon_t$, we can go right to $\sigma_w^2 = [\phi(1)]^{-2}\sigma_\varepsilon^2$, where $\phi(1)$ is the sum of the *autoregressive* coefficients.

If the pricing error is driven entirely by the information innovation w_t, $s_t = A(L)w_t$. Equating the structural and statistical representations for Δp_t gives

$$\theta(L)\varepsilon_t = [1 - (1 - L)A(L)]w_t. \qquad (8.18)$$

Both ε_t and w_t are white-noise processes. The correspondence suggests that $w_t = \theta(1)\varepsilon_t$. Using this and solving for $A(L)$ gives $A(L) = (1 - L)^{-1}[\theta(L) - \theta(1)]\theta(1)^{-1}$. Expanding $(1 - L)^{-1}$ about $L = 0$ and multiplying through gives:

$$A(L) = \theta(1)^{-1}(-\theta_1 - \theta_2 - \theta_3 - \cdots) + \theta(1)^{-1}(-\theta_2 - \theta_3 - \cdots)L$$
$$+ \theta(1)^{-1}(-\theta_2 - \theta_3 - \cdots)L^2 + \cdots \qquad (8.19)$$

The implied $A(L)$ coefficients are identical to those given in equation (8.11) and the related discussion.

If the pricing error is uncorrelated with w_t at all leads and lags, $s_t = B(L)\eta_t$. The equivalence of the autocovariance generating functions in this case implies $\theta(z^{-1})\theta(z)\sigma_\varepsilon^2 = \sigma_w^2 + (1 - z^{-1})B(z^{-1})(1 - z)B(z)\sigma_\varepsilon^2$. If the order of $\theta(L)$ is n and the coefficients (or estimates) are known, then the B coefficients may be determined by solving the nth-order polynomial equation.

9

Multivariate Linear Microstructure Models

Although the trade price is usually the single most important variable in a microstructure analysis, other variables can help explain its dynamics. These include orders, trades, prices of the same security in other markets, prices of related securities, and so on. Inclusion of these variables can enhance the forecasting power of a model. Under certain assumptions, the multivariate models support an attribution of this forecasting power, essentially identifying price changes with particular sources of information. This chapter discusses models where there is one price and one or more supplementary variables. The principal qualification on these variables is that they should not be cointegrated with ("very closely related to") the price under consideration. Models with cointegrated prices are discussed in the following chapter. For the present material, Hamilton (1994, Ch. 10 and 11) discusses general modeling aspects; Hasbrouck (1988, 1991a, 1991b and 1993) describes microstructure applications.

We are interested in analyzing the dynamics of an $n \times 1$ vector-valued time series $y_t = [\Delta p_t \quad x'_t]'$ where the first element is the price change, x_t is an $(n-1) \times 1$ vector of additional variables, and $[\,]'$ denotes matrix transposition. Placing the price change first is simply an expositional simplification and carries no implications that this variable is first in any causal sense. The chapter treats the general case but uses a particular structural model for purposes of illustration. The structural model is a bivariate model of price changes and trade directions: $y_t = [\Delta p_t \quad q_t]'$.

9.1 Modeling Vector Time Series

The basic descriptive statistics of a vector stochastic process $\{y_t\}$ are the process mean $\mu = E[y_t]$ and the vector autocovariances. The vector autocovariances are defined as the matrices

$$\Gamma_k = E(y_t - E[y_t])(y_{t-k} - E[y_t])' \quad \text{for } k = \ldots -2, -1, 0, +1, +2, \ldots \quad (9.1)$$

In suppressing the dependence of μ and Γ_k on t, we have implicitly invoked an assumption of covariance stationarity. Note that although a univariate autocorrelation has the property that $\gamma_k = \gamma_{-k}$, the corresponding property in the multivariate case is $\Gamma_k = \Gamma'_{-k}$.

If $\mu = 0$, or equivalently if the y_t have been de-meaned, then by a multivariate version of the Wold theorem, there exists a vector moving average (VMA) representation of the process:

$$y_t = \varepsilon_t + \theta_1 \varepsilon_{t-1} + \theta_2 \varepsilon_{t-2} + \cdots = (I + \theta_1 L + \theta_2 L^2 + \cdots)\varepsilon_t = \theta(L)\varepsilon_t, \quad (9.2)$$

where ε_t is a vector white-noise process with $E\varepsilon_t = 0$, $\text{Var}(\varepsilon_t) = E\varepsilon_t \varepsilon'_t = \Omega$, and $E\varepsilon_t \varepsilon'_{t-k} = 0$ for $k \neq 0$. The θ_i are the $n \times n$ coefficient matrices, and $\theta(L)$ is a matrix lag polynomial.

As in the univariate case, for purposes of forecasting and estimation it is often useful to express a multivariate process in terms of its own lagged values. The vector autoregression (VAR) corresponding to (9.2) is:

$$y_t = \phi_1 y_{t-1} + \phi_2 y_{t-2} + \cdots + \varepsilon_t, \quad (9.3)$$

where the ϕ_i are the $n \times n$ coefficient matrices. This representation exists if the VMA is invertible. In principle, invertibility can be verified by examining the roots of the VMA determinantal equation (Fuller (1996), theorem 2.8.2, p. 78). In practice, the VMA representation is constructed from the VAR, that is, we're usually going in the other direction. Nevertheless, we will see in later chapters structural models that are clearly noninvertible. To compute the VAR representation from the VMA, we note that from equation (9.2), $\theta(L)^{-1} y_t = \varepsilon_t$, and from (9.3), $(I - \phi_1 L - \phi_2 L^2 - \cdots)y_t = \varepsilon_t$. So we can determine the ϕ_i by taking a series expansion of $\theta(L)^{-1}$.

We now describe a particular structural model.

9.2 A Structural Model of Prices and Trades

The univariate models discussed earlier focused on price changes. The model described here also includes order dynamics. In the earlier models, the trade directions (the q_t) are generally assumed to be serially uncorrelated. In reality trades in most markets are positively autocorrelated, for example, buys tend to follow buys. One way of modeling this is to allow q_t to follow the MA(1) process:

$$q_t = v_t + \beta v_{t-1}, \quad (9.4)$$

where $\beta > 0$ and v_t is a white-noise process. Note that because $q_t = \pm 1$, the v_t will be serially uncorrelated, but not independent (see section 4.6).

In the generalized Roll model, q_t appears in two roles. First, it simply determines whether the trade occurs at the bid or ask. Second, it drives the revision in the efficient price due to inferred private information. Although the point was not emphasized in the discussion of the original model, q_t was unforecastable: $E[q_t|q_{t-1}, q_{t-2}, \ldots] = 0$. This is not true in the present case. Here, the update to traders' beliefs accompanying the realization of q_t is the innovation $q_t - E[q_t|q_{t-1}, q_{t-2}, \ldots] = v_t$. The increment to the efficient price is therefore driven by the order innovation:

$$m_t = m_{t-1} + w_t \quad \text{where} \quad w_t = u_t + \lambda v_t. \tag{9.5}$$

Using $p_t = m_t + cq_t$ and equation (9.4), the price changes may be written:

$$\Delta p_t = u_t + \lambda v_t + c[(v_t + \beta v_{t-1}) - (v_{t-1} + \beta v_{t-2})]. \tag{9.6}$$

By stacking equations (9.4) and (9.6) to form a matrix equation:

$$\begin{bmatrix} \Delta p_t \\ q_t \end{bmatrix} = \begin{bmatrix} 1 & c+\lambda \\ 0 & 1 \end{bmatrix} \begin{bmatrix} u_t \\ v_t \end{bmatrix} + \begin{bmatrix} 0 & c(\beta-1) \\ 0 & \beta \end{bmatrix}$$
$$\times \begin{bmatrix} u_{t-1} \\ v_{t-1} \end{bmatrix} + \begin{bmatrix} 0 & -c\beta \\ 0 & 0 \end{bmatrix} \begin{bmatrix} u_{t-2} \\ v_{t-2} \end{bmatrix}. \tag{9.7}$$

Equation (9.7) is a VMA, but it is not in a form like equation (9.2) where the coefficient of the current disturbance is the identity matrix. To accomplish this normalization, define

$$\varepsilon_t = B \begin{bmatrix} u_t \\ v_t \end{bmatrix} \quad \text{where} \quad B = \begin{bmatrix} 1 & c+\lambda \\ 0 & 1 \end{bmatrix}$$

Then using $[u_t \ v_t]' = B^{-1}\varepsilon_t$, the model may be put in the form of equation (9.2) with

$$\theta_1 = \begin{bmatrix} 0 & c(\beta-1) \\ 0 & \beta \end{bmatrix}; \quad \theta_2 = \begin{bmatrix} 0 & -c\beta \\ 0 & 0 \end{bmatrix}; \quad \theta_k = 0 \quad \text{for } k > 2. \tag{9.8}$$

Finally,

$$\Omega \equiv \text{Var}(\varepsilon_t) = \begin{bmatrix} \sigma_u^2 + (c+\lambda)^2 \sigma_v^2 & (c+\lambda)\sigma_v^2 \\ (c+\lambda)\sigma_v^2 & \sigma_v^2 \end{bmatrix}. \tag{9.9}$$

The VAR representation (equation (9.3)) may be computed by series expansion of $\theta(L)^{-1}$. It is of infinite order. The leading coefficients are:

$$\phi_1 = \begin{bmatrix} 0 & -c(1-\beta) \\ 0 & \beta \end{bmatrix}; \quad \phi_2 = \begin{bmatrix} 0 & -c\beta^2 \\ 0 & -\beta^2 \end{bmatrix};$$
$$\phi_3 = \begin{bmatrix} 0 & c\beta^3 \\ 0 & \beta^3 \end{bmatrix}; \quad \phi_4 = \begin{bmatrix} 0 & -c\beta^4 \\ 0 & -\beta^4 \end{bmatrix}; \ \ldots \tag{9.10}$$

Because $|\beta| < 1$, the coefficients are decreasing in magnitude.

If $\beta = 0$, the structural model is identical to the generalized Roll model discussed in chapter 8. Even in this case, though, the multivariate statistical models discussed in the present section will differ from the univariate models considered earlier.

The structural model does not exhibit the full range of dynamic interactions that VAR models can accommodate. Causality in this model is one-way: from trades to prices. Other mechanisms, however, might transmit effects in the opposite direction. A strong price movement due to public information, for example, might draw in momentum traders buying on what they perceive to be an emerging price trend.

9.3   Forecasts and Impulse Response Functions

As in the univariate case, the forecasts implied by the model are interesting as descriptive tools but also as estimates of market participants' beliefs. Forecasts are usually computed from autoregressive representations, but to stress the latter interpretation, we will work initially from the moving average form. From equation (9.2),

$$
E^*[y_{t+k}|y_t, y_{t-1}, \ldots] = E^*[y_{t+k}|\varepsilon_t, \varepsilon_{t-1}, \ldots]
$$
$$
= \theta_k \varepsilon_t + \theta_{k-1}\varepsilon_{t-1} + \theta_{k-2}\varepsilon_{t-2} + \cdots \quad \text{for } k \geq 0
$$
$$(9.11)$$

The first equality reflects our ability to recover the disturbances recursively from the VAR form of the model (using equation (9.3)). The second equality is a consequence of the fact that $E[\varepsilon_{t+k}|\varepsilon_t, \varepsilon_{t-1}, \ldots] = 0$ for $k \geq 1$.

The price forecast is of particular interest:

$$
f_t \equiv \lim_{k \to \infty} E^*[p_{t+k}|p_t, p_{t-1}]
$$
$$
= p_t + \sum_{k=1}^{\infty} E^*\left[\Delta p_{t+k}|p_t, p_{t-1}\right]
$$
$$
= p_t + \left(\sum_{j=0}^{\infty} [\theta_{j+1}]_1\right)\varepsilon_t + \left(\sum_{j=0}^{\infty} [\theta_{j+2}]_1\right)\varepsilon_{t-1} + \left(\sum_{j=0}^{\infty} [\theta_{j+3}]_1\right)\varepsilon_{t-2} + \cdots
$$
$$(9.12)$$

where $[\theta_{j+1}]_1$ denotes the first row of matrix θ_{j+1}. As in the univariate case, it can be verified that

$$
\Delta f_t = \left(\sum_{j=0}^{\infty} [\theta_j]_1\right)\varepsilon_t.
$$

Thus, f_t has uncorrelated increments. In general, $f_t = E^*[m_t|y_t, y_{t-1}, \ldots]$, the projection of m_t on the history of the model variables, but except in special cases $f_t \neq m_t$.

This forecast procedure involves stepping the model ahead beyond its current (actual, observable) state. We may also be interested in forecasting subsequent to a hypothetical innovation, for example, a typical trade (or a trade that we may be contemplating). The timing convention here is that we are forecasting conditional on $y_{t-1}, y_{t-2}, \ldots$ (or, equivalently, $\varepsilon_{t-1}, \varepsilon_{t-2}$), and an ε_t that we specify.

This sort of forecast can also be used as a descriptive tool for illustrating the behavior of an estimated model. The dynamic structure usually emerges most clearly when we examine an innovation at time zero and also set to zero all prior innovations. The resulting forecast is called the impulse response function:

$$\psi_s(\varepsilon_0) \equiv E^*[y_s|\varepsilon_0, \varepsilon_{-1} = \varepsilon_{-2} = \cdots = 0] \quad \text{for } s \geq 0. \tag{9.13}$$

$\psi_s(\varepsilon_0)$ summarizes the effect of an innovation ε_0 after s periods have elapsed.

From the VMA representation (equation (9.2)), we have $\psi_s(\varepsilon_0) = \theta_s \varepsilon_0$. (In fact, the impulse response calculation is often used to obtain the VMA coefficients.) For some variables (notably price changes), the cumulative impulse response function may be more useful:

$$\Psi_s(\varepsilon_0) \equiv \sum_{k=0}^{s} \psi_s(\varepsilon_0). \tag{9.14}$$

Whether computing the impulse response function as a descriptive tool or forecasting the effects of a contemplated action, we need to give some thought to the specification of ε_0. As a realistic example, we might wish to examine a buy order ($q_t = +1$), either to illustrate how the market responds to a typical buy order or to forecast what will happen (at least in the short run) if we actually place such an order.

If we know that the structural model is the particular one described in section 9.2, we simply set v_t so that $q_t = +1$, set $u_t = 0$ and forecast using equation (9.7). We do not usually know the structural model, however. Typically we're working from estimates of a statistical model (a VAR or VMA). This complicates specification of ε_0. From the perspective of the VAR or VMA model of the trade and price data, the innovation vector and its variance are:

$$\varepsilon_t = \begin{bmatrix} \varepsilon_{\Delta p,t} \\ \varepsilon_{q,t} \end{bmatrix} \quad \text{and} \quad \Omega = \begin{bmatrix} \sigma_{\Delta p}^2 & \sigma_{\Delta p,q} \\ \sigma_{\Delta p,q} & \sigma_q^2 \end{bmatrix}. \tag{9.15}$$

The innovations in the statistical model are simply associated with the observed variables, and have no necessary structural interpretation. We can still set $\varepsilon_{q,t}$ according to our contemplated trade ($\varepsilon_{q,t} = +1$), but how should we set $\varepsilon_{\Delta p,t}$?

The answer to this specific problem depends on the immediate (time t) relation between the trade and price-change innovations. The broader issue in time-series analysis concerns contemporaneous effects among the model variables. It turns out that although there is no single reliable answer, the structure of the covariance matrix Ω tells us something about the range of possibilities. The next section shows how to determine this.

9.4   Resolution of Contemporaneous Effects

The uncertainty surrounding contemporaneous effects in VAR/VMA specifications can be resolved by imposing a causal ordering, essentially a restriction that the innovation in one variable may affect that of another but not the reverse. Alternative orderings generally lead to different forecasts and impulse response functions, so consideration of these alternatives suggests bounds on these functions.

The main tool for imposing a causal ordering is the Cholesky factorization (also called the Cholesky decomposition). For a nonsingular covariance matrix (more generally, a symmetric positive definite matrix) Ω, the Cholesky factorization is given by $\Omega = F'F$ where F is an upper triangular matrix (i.e., has zeros below the main diagonal.)

Suppose that Ω is the covariance matrix of a vector random variable ε. We can view ε as being constructed as $\varepsilon = F'z$ where $\text{Var}(z) = I$. Because F is upper triangular, F' is lower triangular:

$$\begin{bmatrix} \varepsilon_1 \\ \varepsilon_2 \\ \vdots \\ \varepsilon_n \end{bmatrix} = \begin{bmatrix} f_{11} & 0 & \cdots & 0 \\ f_{21} & f_{22} & \cdots & 0 \\ \vdots & \vdots & \ddots & 0 \\ f_{n,1} & f_{n,2} & \cdots & f_{n,n} \end{bmatrix} \begin{bmatrix} z_1 \\ z_2 \\ \vdots \\ z_n \end{bmatrix}. \tag{9.16}$$

In this representation, it is natural to think of z_1 as the ε_1 factor. In turn, ε_2 is driven by z_1 and by a second residual ε_2 factor, and so on. Essentially, we are taking ε_1 as the first driver, projecting ε_2 on ε_1, projecting ε_3 on ε_1 and ε_2, and so on.

The Cholesky factorization of a covariance matrix for two zero-mean random variables x_1 and x_2 is given by:

$$\begin{bmatrix} \sigma_1^2 & \sigma_{12} \\ \sigma_{12} & \sigma_2^2 \end{bmatrix} = F'F$$

$$\text{where } F' = \begin{bmatrix} \sigma_1 & 0 \\ \sigma_{12}/\sigma_1 & \sqrt{\sigma_2^2 - \sigma_{12}^2/\sigma_1^2} \end{bmatrix}. \tag{9.17}$$

The intuition is that x_1 can be "generated" as the product of σ_1 and z_1 (a random variable with unit variance), and x_2 as the product of z_1 and a projection coefficient (σ_{12}/σ_1), plus a multiple of z_2 (a second factor that is uncorrelated with z_1). Thus, x_1 is placed first in the causal ordering.

The causal ordering imposed by the decomposition is the same order in which the variables appear in the covariance matrix. Although we often arrange variables so that the most interesting ones are first or nearly so, there are no statistical reasons for preferring one ordering over another.

Ordering effects may be illustrated using the sample structural model. We start from the statistical representation of the model and see how close we can come to recovering the true structure. Using (9.17) to compute the Cholesky decomposition for the Ω given in equation (9.9), letting $\sigma_1^2 = \sigma_{\Delta p}^2 = \sigma_u^2 + (c+\lambda)^2\sigma_v^2$, and so on, do we recover the structure of ε_t in (9.9)? We do not. As the model is specified, Δp_t is the first variable and q_t the last. With this ordering, the Cholesky decomposition will imply a structure in which the price change drives the contemporaneous trade. This is the reverse of how the structural model actually works.

To investigate the alternative ordering ("q_t first"), we could go back to the beginning and specify all equations in terms of a reordered variable set (with $y_t = [q_t \quad \Delta p_t]'$), but it is easier to permute $\mathrm{Var}(\varepsilon_t)$, compute the Cholesky factorization, and then reverse the permutation to restore the original order. The permuted innovation term is:

$$\varepsilon_t^* = \begin{bmatrix} \varepsilon_{q,t} \\ \varepsilon_{\Delta p,t} \end{bmatrix} = \begin{bmatrix} v_t \\ u_t + (c+\lambda)v_t \end{bmatrix}. \tag{9.18}$$

The corresponding variance and Cholesky decomposition are:

$$\Omega^* = \begin{bmatrix} \sigma_v^2 & (c+\lambda)\sigma_v^2 \\ (c+\lambda)\sigma_v^2 & \sigma_u^2 + (c+\lambda)^2\sigma_v^2 \end{bmatrix}$$

$$= F^{*\prime}F^* \quad \text{where } F^* = \begin{bmatrix} \sigma_v & (c+\lambda)\sigma_v \\ 0 & \sigma_u \end{bmatrix}. \tag{9.19}$$

Rearranging to restore the starting order, the original $\mathrm{Var}(\varepsilon_t)$ can be expressed as:

$$\Omega = F'F \quad \text{where } F = \begin{bmatrix} \sigma_u & (c+\lambda)\sigma_v \\ 0 & \sigma_v \end{bmatrix}. \tag{9.20}$$

For example, a factor interpretation $\varepsilon_t = F'z_t$ with a "one-unit" shock to the trade factor then gives:

$$\varepsilon_t = F' \begin{bmatrix} 0 \\ 1 \end{bmatrix} = \begin{bmatrix} (c+\lambda)\sigma_v \\ \sigma_v \end{bmatrix}. \tag{9.21}$$

This implies that a one-σ_v shock to q_t causes an immediate shock of $(c+\lambda)\sigma_v$ to Δp_t. Thus, imposing this ordering in the statistical model identifies the correct ordering in the structural model.

9.5 Random-Walk Decompositions
in Multivariate Models

We consider the general case where $y_t = [\Delta p_t \quad x_t']'$ possesses a VMA representation $y_t = \theta(L)\varepsilon_t$ where $\text{Cov}(\varepsilon_t) = \Omega$. The random-walk decomposition is still expressed as $p_t = m_t + s_t$, where $m_t = m_{t-1} + w_t$, and s_t is a zero-mean covariance stationary process. s_t may be partially driven by current and lagged w_t, and may also have components uncorrelated with these disturbances.

9.5.1 The Random-Walk Variance

The variance of the random-walk innovation is

$$\sigma_w^2 = [\theta(1)]_1 \Omega [\theta(1)]_1', \tag{9.22}$$

where $[\theta(1)]_1$ denotes the first row of $\theta(1)$, that is, the row corresponding to Δp_t. If Ω is diagonal, the right-hand side of equation (9.22) consists of n distinct terms, each of which represents the corresponding variable's contribution to σ_w^2.

If Ω is nondiagonal, these contributions can be described using Cholesky factorizations. Letting $d = [\theta(1)]_1 F'$, where F is the upper triangular Cholesky factor, $\sigma_w^2 = \sum d_i^2$. The vector d can be computed from the VMA representation of the model, and its squares represent the individual variance contributions. The magnitudes of the d_i are, of course, dependent on the ordering used to construct the Cholesky factorization. For the illustration model, the VMA coefficients are given in equation (9.8) and the Cholesky factorization (permuted, with trades "first") is given by equation (9.20). This implies

$$\sigma_w^2 = \begin{bmatrix} 1 & -c \end{bmatrix} \begin{bmatrix} \sigma_u & (c+\lambda)\sigma_v \\ 0 & \sigma_v \end{bmatrix} \begin{bmatrix} \sigma_u & 0 \\ (c+\lambda)\sigma_v & \sigma_v \end{bmatrix} \begin{bmatrix} 1 \\ c \end{bmatrix}$$

$$= \begin{bmatrix} \sigma_u & \lambda\sigma_v \end{bmatrix} \begin{bmatrix} \sigma_u \\ \lambda\sigma_v \end{bmatrix} = \sigma_u^2 + \lambda^2 \sigma_v^2. \tag{9.23}$$

This recovers the public information and trade-related ("private information") components.

From the perspective of the sequential and strategic trade models, the effects of trades on prices arise from asymmetric information. The foregoing decomposition therefore suggests proxies for the latter. $\lambda^2 \sigma_v^2$ is an absolute measure. If the prices are measured in logs, $\lambda\sigma_v$ is approximately the standard deviation of the trade-drive return component. The quantity

$\lambda^2 \sigma_v^2 / \sigma_w^2$ is a relative measure, essentially the coefficient of determination in a project of price changes on trades.

More generally, decomposition of the random-walk variance provides a basis for measuring the importance of different sources of market information. The x_t variable set can potentially include order characteristics, coarse identification information about order submitters, and (subject to the qualifications of the following chapter) prices of other securities (e.g., of a stock index futures contract). The decompositions can often support refined attributions of where value-relevant information first arises.

9.5.2 The Pricing Error

If we provisionally assume that $f_t = m_t$, then the pricing error is $s_t = p_t - f_t$. Using the moving average representations for p_t and f_t, we can show that equation (8.11) holds in the multivariate setting when each scalar θ_i in (8.11) is replaced by $[\theta_i]_1$, the first row of the matrix θ_i. The pricing error variance is

$$\sigma_s^2 = \sum_{k=0}^{\infty} C_k \Omega C_k'$$

$$\text{where} \quad C_k = - \sum_{j=k+1}^{\infty} [\theta_j]_1. \tag{9.24}$$

This expression gives the variance exactly only in the case where $f_t = m_t$. More generally it establishes a lower bound.

In the structural model, $s_t = cq_t = c(v_t + \beta v_{t-1})$, which implies $\sigma_s^2 = c^2 (1 + \beta)^2 \sigma_v^2$. Applying equation (9.24), using (9.8) and (9.9),

$$\sigma_s^2 = [\theta_1 + \theta_2]_1 \, \Omega \, [\theta_1 + \theta_2]_1' + [\theta_2]_1 \, \Omega \, [\theta_2]_1' \tag{9.25}$$

$$= c^2 \left(1 + \beta^2\right) \sigma_v^2.$$

Thus, for this particular structural model, the lower bound is exact.

Recall that if $\beta = 0$, trades are uncorrelated, and the structural model is equivalent to the generalized Roll model. For that model, the lower bound was exact only in the special case where all information was trade related. The present result is therefore stronger. Including trades in the model gives us additional explanatory power.

9.6 Informational Attributions

We now turn to the general case of $y_t = [\Delta p_t \quad x_t']'$, where x_t is a set of supplementary explanatory variables. The first point is that holding constant the time span of the sample, σ_w^2 is in principle invariant to the choice of x_t. The same value should be obtained if x_t is a large and comprehensive set of market data, or if $y_t = \Delta p_t$ (a univariate analysis). In finite samples, of course, the computed values of σ_w^2 will differ numerically, but these differences should not generally be attributed to economic features of the problem. It should not be asserted, for example, that a particular set of conditioning information implies a more or less volatile efficient price. This is a consequence of the covariance stationary framework assumed for the analysis. If $\text{Var}(\Delta p_t)$ is unconditionally constant over time, then the long-run price change variance $(\text{Var}(\sum_{i=1}^{n} \Delta p_{t+i})$, for large $n)$ will also be constant (see section 8.3).

In contrast, the filtered price estimate f_t does depend on x_t. Among other things, the precision of the filter is likely to be enhanced by richer conditioning information. As an illustration, consider the bivariate structural model under the restriction that $\beta = 0$ (in which case the structural model is identical to the generalized Roll model). When $y_t = [\Delta p_t \quad q_t]$, $f_t = m_t$, that is, the projection is exact. When we don't condition on trades $(y_t = \Delta p_t)$, however, $f_t \neq m_t$ generally.

The information attributions implied by decompositions of σ_w^2 depend on the choice of x_t. A specification of x_t that is significantly coarser than the true public information set may generate misleading implications. The price changes of individual stocks, for example, exhibit common factors. This suggests that analysis of Δp_t for an individual stock should include in the x_t variable such as the price change in a stock index. A coarse variable, for example, the return on the cash index over the previous day, is likely to contribute little in a decomposition of σ_w^2. A more current (yet still widely disseminated) series, for example, recent 10-second returns on the corresponding stock index futures contract, will almost certainly imply (and correctly so) a larger informational attribution. The estimated total informational contribution of the remaining variables will drop, but some individual contributions might in fact rise (depending on their correlations with each other and the futures returns).

What if x_t represents an information set that is in some respects *finer* than the true public information collection? Although it would be unusual to include variables that are known to no market participants, analyses sometimes include data available to only a few. Hasbrouck (1996b) estimates specifications that differentiate New York Stock Exchange (NYSE) program orders. Program orders involve multiple stocks, and would therefore presumably convey different information than an order for a single stock. Although the NYSE specialist could identify program orders, traders off the floor generally could not. Kurov and Lasser (2004) examine the impact of futures trades classified by whether or not they involve a futures exchange "local" (floor trader).

A trader's identity would be known on the exchange floor, but not away from it. Sometimes even basic data fall in this category. Some analyses of foreign exchange dynamics include prices and quantities of recent trades. Yet there is no general trade reporting in this market, and the details of the trade are often known only to the buyer and seller.

In a decomposition of the random-walk variance, a nonpublic variable may well possess strong explanatory power. This should be kept in perspective. The variable's contribution to σ_w^2 may accurately reflect the economic value of the information to the few agents in possession. It almost certainly overstates, however, the contribution that would arise if the variable were made public. Forcing disclosure of the information would change the incentives for its production. Futhermore, if the disclosure relates to the trading process (e.g., the disclosure of order attributes or originator identification), then disclosure will probably change trading behavior.

Private information need not directly relate to security payoffs. Section 5.6, for example, demonstrates that knowing that previous traders were uninformed may be valuable. From a random-walk decomposition perspective, a price change that appears permanent conditional on the public information set may be transitory when the expectation is conditioned on private information.

This discussion ends on a note of caution. The techniques described in this chapter allow us to identify variance components in the efficient price that are attributed to trades. The logic of the sequential and strategic trade models broadly connect the trade-related variance components to asymmetric information. The variance measures, and other microstructure-based information asymmetry proxies, such as price impact coefficients and spreads, may readily be estimated in many important settings. It is then tempting to relate the cross-sectional and time-series variation in these proxies to changes or differences in regulation, reporting, disclosure, or any events that might plausibly be hypothesized to affect the information environment. Because stakes in these questions are high, we emphasize that there is little corroborating evidence that these microstructure based proxies are meaningfully connected to asymmetric information, at least as it pertains to securities' cash flows. Neal and Wheatley (1998) examine the spreads of closed-end mutual funds. The most meaningful valuation number for these securities is their net asset value. As this is publicly known, information asymmetries are presumably low. Despite this, they carry substantial spreads. Saar and Yu (2002) show that price-impact proxies for U.S. firms are not reliably correlated with other informational variables. The proxies furthermore exhibit time variation around index rebalancing periods, events which should be unrelated to the firm's cash flows.

9.7   Implementation Issues

9.7.1   Timing and Signing

Typically the basic data consist of a time-stamped record of bid and ask quotes and transactions. If the data originate in a limit order market, the sequencing of events, in particular the interleaving of quote changes and trades, is likely to be highly accurate. On the other hand, if the data arise in a hybrid market, if the data follow different dissemination paths, if the time stamps are not sufficiently precise, or if there are manual steps to the process, the sequencing is likely to be suspect.

Relative timing of quotes and trades is important because the prevailing quote midpoints are generally used to sign the trades (infer the direction of the order, q_t). If all executions occur at posted quotes, we set $q_t = +1$ for a trade priced at the prevailing ask and $q_t = -1$ for trades priced at the bid. This is generally successful, however, only in limit order markets (where the book can be accurately reconstructed), and then only when all executions occur against visible (as opposed to hidden or reserve) limit orders. More generally we might set $q_t = Sign(p_t - m_t)$, reasoning that a trade priced above the quote midpoint is more likely to be buyer initiated. Even this rule, however, leaves unclassified trades occurring exactly at the midpoint. In some samples, this is a frequent occurrence. When this rule fails, an alternative is to assign to the trade the sign of the most recent price change.[1]

9.7.2   Signed Order Variables

The example structural model uses only one trade variable—the direction, q_t. In most cases, the execution price and quantity of the trade are known. Because most economic considerations suggest that larger orders should have a higher information content, it makes sense to include signed volumes and/or signed monotone transformations of volume. Letting V_t denote the volume of the trade (in shares or value), the candidates would include $q_t V_t$, $q_t \sqrt{V_t}$, and so on. Hasbrouck (1991a) uses signed-squared volumes ($q_t V_t^2$). This transformation, however, is likely to amplify the effect of extreme dispersion of volumes (Gabaix et al. (2003)), leading to unstable estimates. In general, convex transformations should probably be avoided.

A VMA or VAR model applied to transformed data can capture certain nonlinear features while remaining computationally convenient. The capabilities and limitations are similar to those associated with linear regression on nonlinear functions of the explanatory variables. That is, transformations can locally rescale additive linear effects but cannot capture nonlinear interactions. For example, a specification like

$y_i = (x_{i,1})^{a_1}(x_{i,2})^{a_2} + \varepsilon_i$ can't be reworked as $y_i = \alpha_1 f_1(x_{i,1}) + \alpha_2 f_2(x_{i,2}) + \eta_i$ by artful choice of f_1 and f_2.

As a rough generalization, the estimated relation between order size and price impact is concave, becoming flat at large sizes (see, for example, Kempf and Korn 1999). Although it might seem obvious that signed order size should be included in the price change specification, it often contributes little incremental explanatory power above the signed trade direction variable (Jones, Kaul, and Lipson (1994)). A possible explanation for this draws on time variation in liquidity. If agents trade large amounts when price impact is low, and small amounts when price impact is high, the time-averaged price impact will appear relatively unaffected by order size (Coppejans, Domowitz, and Madhavan (2001) Mendelson and Tunca (2004). Barclay and Warner (1993) suggest that in U.S. equity markets most price changes are attributable to medium-size trades.

9.7.3   Event Time or Wall-Clock Time?

In the discussion, the subscript t is assumed to index trades. Thus, t is an event counter. Other possible event indexes are quote revisions or a mix of trade and quote revisions (i.e., t is incremented whenever a trade occurs or a quote is revised). Analyses can also be set in wall-clock time, with t indexing fixed intervals (e.g., minutes). With wall-clock time index, aggregation or transformation is often necessary to handle (possibly multiple) events occurring within the interval.

The choice depends on the goals of the analysis. If the analysis involves a single security and the data are precisely time stamped, an event index is probably the first choice. The guiding principle here is that the process is more likely to be covariance stationary in event time than in wall-clock time.

If the microstructure-based estimates are to be subsequently used in a cross-sectional analysis, though, comparability across securities may become the dominant consideration. This may militate in favor of wall-clock time. For example, volatility per minute is probably more comparable across firms than volatility per trade. Breen, Hodrick, and Korajczyk (2002) estimate the impact coefficient with a simple linear specification using daily aggregate data.

9.7.4   Trade Prices or Quote Midpoints?

The specifications discussed to this point have generally assumed that the p_t are actual trade prices. If the analysis is aimed at characterizing execution-related phenomena, like the pricing error variance or trade execution costs, this is the usually the correct choice. If the point of the study is estimation of long-run price impact or the contribution of trades to the efficient price variance, then the bid-ask midpoint is a sensible alternative price variable. Analysis of the present chapter's structural model would be more straightforward if it were based on $[\Delta m_t \quad q_t]$ instead of $[\Delta p_t \quad q_t]$.

Quotes have certain advantages over trade prices. Although they may be revised sporadically, they are normally regarded as active between revisions. A bid made at 10:01 A.M., for example, and next revised at 10:05 A.M. would be considered current at 10:02, 10:03, and 10:04. The price of a trade executed at 10:01 A.M. might well be stale by 10:02, even if it were still the most recent transaction. This point is particularly important when a wall-clock time scale is used. The quote prevailing at the end of an interval can usually be precisely determined. Quotes can furthermore be revised in the absence of trades. Because a quote setter's bid and ask can be picked off in response to new public information, there is a strong motivation to keep them up to date. For this reason, they may be presumed to reflect current public information more reliably that last-sale prices. Finally, trade prices are subject to bid-ask bounce, a source of transitory volatility. Although quote midpoints are not immune from transitory components, their short-run volatility is lower than that of trades. (The long-run volatilities are, of course, equal.) In this sense, quote midpoints are more precise price estimates.

9.8   Other Structural Models

The structural model described in section 9.2 was chosen for illustration and exposition. The literature contains a number of other structural models. The following are representative.

9.8.1   Glosten and Harris (1988)

Glosten and Harris (1988) (GH) estimate a model in which the efficient price is driven by the trade size (as well as the direction):

$$
\begin{aligned}
m_t &= m_{t-1} + w_t \\
w_t &= u_t + q_t(\lambda_0 + \lambda_1 V_t) \\
p_t &= m_t + q_t(c_0 + c_1 V_t).
\end{aligned}
\tag{9.26}
$$

where V_t is the (unsigned) volume of the trade. The information content of the trade is linear in size, as discussed earlier. The cost term is also linear in size. The exercise that follows is based this representation of the model.

GH actually estimate a version of this model that is distinctive in two key respects. First, the model has a methodical treatment of price discreteness. The p_t given in equations (9.26) is latent. The observed price is p_t rounded to the nearest tick (in GH's data, one-eighth of a dollar). Second, the GH data do not contain bid and ask quotes, so the q_t are latent variables as well. GH base inference on rounded prices and V_t and estimate the model using an innovative nonlinear filtering procedure. With so much of the model's content unobserved, estimation requires stronger distributional assumptions. GH treat V_t and q_t as exogenous and assume normality for the public information innovation u_t.

> *Exercise 9.1* (VMA analysis of GH) In the model given by equations (9.26), assume that the signed volume is $Q_t \sim N(0, \sigma_Q^2)$. Let $q_t = \text{sgn}(Q_t)$ and $V_t = |Q_t|$. p_t and q_t are observed (but m_t is not).
>
> a. Specify a VMA model $y_t = \theta(L)\varepsilon_t$ for $y_t = [\Delta p_t \quad q_t \quad Q_t]'$ and $\theta(L) = \theta_0 + \theta_1 L$. If $x \sim N(0, \sigma^2)$ then $E|x| = \sqrt{2\sigma^2/\pi}$. Using this result to compute $\text{Cov}(q_t, Q_t)$, specify $\Omega = \text{Var}(\varepsilon_t)$.
> b. Compute σ_w^2 directly from the expression for w_t in equations (9.26). Verify that equation (9.22) gives the same answer.
> c. Using alternative Cholesky decompositions, show that the amount of σ_w^2 that is explained by the direction variable q_t is $(\pi - 2)\lambda_0^2/\pi$ (when the ordering is Q_t, q_t, u_t) and $(\lambda_0 + \lambda_1\sigma_Q\sqrt{2/\pi})^2$. (when the ordering is q_t, Q_t, u_t). *Hint:* Although the covariance matrix is 3×3, the only off-diagonal elements are in the block containing q_t and Q_t. Under either permutation this block is 2×2, so the Cholesky decomposition may be computed using equation (9.17).

9.8.2 Madhavan, Richardson, and Roomans

Madhavan, Richardson, and Roomans (1997) (MRR) posit a model similar to the structural model in section 9.2, except that the signed trades are generated by an autoregressive process. Specifically, $q_t = \rho q_{t-1} + v_t$. This generates more persistent dependence than the moving average form.

> *Exercise 9.2* Suppose that the structural model is given by $m_t = m_{t-1} + w_t$, $w_t = u_t + \lambda v_t$, $q_t = \rho q_{t-1} + v_t$ (where $|\rho| < 1$), and $p_t = m_t + c q_t$. Show that the resulting system for $y_t = [\Delta p_t \quad q_t]$ can be written as a mixed vector autoregressive and moving average (VARMA) model $y_t = \varphi_1 y_{t-1} + \varphi_2 y_{t-2} + \theta_0 \varepsilon_t + \theta_1 \varepsilon_{t-1}$ where $\varepsilon_t = [u_t \quad v_t]'$ and $\Omega = \begin{bmatrix} \sigma_u^2 & 0 \\ 0 & \sigma_v^2 \end{bmatrix}$. For a VARMA model of the form $\phi(L)y_t = \theta(L)\varepsilon_t$, $\sigma_w^2 = A\Omega A'$ where A is the first row of $[\phi(1)]^{-1}\theta(1)$. Verify that this gives the structurally correct expression for σ_w^2.

9.9 Estimating Price Impact from Returns and Volume

The specifications discussed in this chapter regress returns against order flow that has been signed as to buyer- or seller-initiated. The sign is usually inferred by comparing high-frequency trade and quote prices. Many samples, particularly long-term historical databases, however, only include returns and (unsigned) volume aggregated over daily or longer intervals. These data can also be used to estimate price impact measures, but the estimates are necessarily best viewed as proxies.

If the true price impact model is $\Delta p_t = \lambda x_t + u_t$ where x_t is the series signed trades, then inference about λ based on $|\Delta p_t|$ and $|x_t|$ (the trade volume) is supported under certain distributional assumptions. In particular, if Δp_t and x_t are bivariate normal, then $|\Delta p_t|$ and $|x_t|$ are jointly bivariate half-normal. $E[|\Delta p_t|\,|\,|x_t|]$ is nonlinear, but of a known form, and estimation of λ could proceed (see Kotz, Balakrishnan, and Johnson (2000) also the correction at Mathstatica (2005)). Normality, however, is likely to be a poor assumption in most samples of returns and volumes. Furthermore, no simple analogous relation characterizes data that are time-aggregated.

There are a number of approaches to quantifying the contemporaneous return-volume relationship. The liquidity ratio is the time-series average $L = \overline{(|Vol_t|/|r_t|)}$ where t typically indexes days and the average is over all days in the month or quarter for which the return is nonzero. It is also sometimes called the Amivest liquidity ratio, after the now-defunct management firm that developed it. Amihud (2002) suggests the illiquidity ratio $I = \overline{(|r_t|/|Vol_t|)}$, where the average is over all days with nonzero volume. Both estimates are prone to extreme values, although the illiquidity ratio, due to the presence of volume in the denominator, is somewhat more stable. Hasbrouck (2005) finds that in the cross section, both measures are moderately positively correlated with λ coefficients estimated from high-frequency data, but that the illiquidity measure appears to be the better proxy. Besides Amihud (2002), illiquidity ratios have been used in asset pricing specifications by Acharya and Pedersen (2005).

10
Multiple Securities and Multiple Prices

Markets for different securities often interact. The standard theory of portfolio optimization is built on the assumption that securities share common-factor value determinants. The value of a derivative securities is generally linked to its underlying asset by arbitrage possibilities.

The trading process may reflect these long-term interactions and may exhibit other dependencies as well. Trades may be correlated for non-informational reasons. A trader buying into an index, for example, will place orders in many or all stocks of the index. A trade in stock A, for example, that conveys information about a factor that is also a value determinant of stock B may move the price of B. Arbitrage, too, usually requires trading.

The starting point for this chapter is models formed by simply stacking single-security specifications like those described in earlier chapters. These are useful, for example, in modeling the joint behavior of two stocks in the same industry or the joint dynamics of a stock and an index. The stacking approach fails, though, when we have multiple prices for the same security (like a bid and an ask, or the bid in two different trading venues) or when the securities being modeled are linking by arbitrage. To handle these cases, the chapter describes error correction models and the role of cointegration. Engle and Granger (1987) provide a formal analysis of cointegration; Hamilton (1994, Ch. 19) is a textbook presentation; Hasbrouck (1995) discusses microstructure applications.

10.1 Stacked Models of Multiple Prices

Consider a structural model of two stocks with Roll dynamics:

$$m_{it} = m_{i,t-1} + u_{it}$$
$$p_{it} = m_{it} + cq_{it} \quad \text{for } i = 1, 2. \tag{10.1}$$

We might allow for dependence between the u_{it} arising from common value components or between the q_{it} (reflecting commonality in purchases and sales). The observations are the price changes $\Delta p_t = [\Delta p_{1t} \quad \Delta p_{2t}]'$. Suppose that the $u_{i,t}$ values are uncorrelated white-noise processes: $Eu_{1t}u_{2t} = 0$ and $Eu_{it}^2 = \sigma_u^2 = 1$. The trade directions are correlated, however, with $Eq_{1t}q_{2t} = \rho$. The vector autocovariances are then

$$\Gamma_0 \equiv \text{Var}(\Delta p_t) = \begin{bmatrix} 2c^2 + \sigma_u^2 & 2\rho c^2 \\ 2\rho c^2 & 2c^2 + \sigma_u^2 \end{bmatrix};$$

$$\Gamma_1 \equiv \text{Cov}(\Delta p_t, \Delta p_{t-1}) = \begin{bmatrix} -c^2 & -\rho c^2 \\ -\rho c^2 & -c^2 \end{bmatrix},$$

(10.2)

with $\Gamma_k = 0$ for $|k| > 1$. These imply a VMA of the form $\Delta p_t = \theta(L)\varepsilon_t$ where $\theta(L) = I + \theta_1 L$.

The VMA parameters may be obtained by equating the autocovariances implied by the structural and MA representations (following the same logic as in the univariate case). The expressions for the VMA parameters in terms of the structural ones are complicated and not particularly intuitive. So we continue with specific numeric values $\sigma_u^2 = 1$, $c = 10$, and $\rho = 0.9$. With these parameters the VMA parameters are

$$\theta_1 = \begin{bmatrix} -0.830 & -0.100 \\ -0.100 & -0.830 \end{bmatrix} \quad \text{and}$$

$$\Omega = \text{Var}(\varepsilon_t) = \begin{bmatrix} 109.0 & 95.3 \\ 95.3 & 109.0 \end{bmatrix}. \tag{10.3}$$

The variance-covariance matrix of the random-walk components is $\theta(1)\Omega\theta(1)'$. Using (10.3), this is equal to 2×2 identity matrix. This is structurally correct: The efficient price innovations (the u_{it}) have unit variance, and they are uncorrelated.

We next seek to determine security 1's contribution to the efficient price variance of security 2. This question requires a bit of explanation. According to the structural model, this contribution is zero. But in an empirical situation we would be working from an estimate of the VMA representation. Because Ω is not diagonal, the variance decomposition requires a Cholesky factorization. With the given ordering (security 1 first), the Cholesky factorization is $\Omega = F'F$, where

$$F' = \begin{bmatrix} 10.44 & 0 \\ 9.13 & 5.07 \end{bmatrix}. \tag{10.4}$$

The first row of $\theta(1)F'$ is $[\theta(1)F']_1 = [0.862 \quad -0.507]$. The random-walk variance decomposition for the first stock is $(0.862)^2 + (0.507)^2 = 0.743 +$

$0.257 = 1$, implying that 74.3% of stock 1's random-walk variance $\text{Var}(u_{1t})$ is explained by its own innovations, and 25.7% is explained by the innovations in the other stock (and the reverse holds for stock 2).

These results are surprising. The statistical model seems to imply (incorrectly) that the efficient price for stock 1 is partially driven by stock 2. Although this conclusion is misleading, it has a sensible explanation. For stock 1, the filtered state estimate is:

$$f_{1t} = E^* \left[m_{1t} | p_t, p_{t-1}, \ldots \right]$$
$$= p_{1t} - cE^* \left[q_{1t} | p_t, p_{t-1}, \ldots \right].$$

The history of p_{2t} is useful in predicting m_{1t} because it helps predict q_{2t}, and by virtue of the correlated trade directions, q_{2t} is useful in predicting q_{1t}.

Does the model "get it right?" If the two securities are U.S. stocks, it would be likely that the m_{it} would be closely proxied by the publicly known quote midpoints. Market participants would see these midpoints evolving independently. The interdependence captured in the model does not, therefore, characterize agents' beliefs. It is an artifact of the econometrician's limited information set.

10.2   Cointegrated Prices

The stacked security model has interdependent price dynamics, but as the dependencies arise from correlated trade directions, they are inherently transient. The same VMA and VAR models would also be appropriate, though, if we had allow correlation in the efficient price changes. As long as $|\text{Corr}(u_{1t}, u_{2t})| < 1$, each price would evolve, at least in part, independently of the other. This means that in the long run, the prices of the two stocks would diverge, in principle without bound.

There are many situations, though, where the prices are so closely linked by economic factors that boundless divergence is an unattractive feature of the model. Bid and ask quotes on the same security, for example, reflect a single common value plus trade-related costs that may vary, but in a stationary fashion. Bids for the same security quoted in different market venues are like to vary considerably but not diverge relative to each other. Absence of divergence also characterizes bid, ask, and trade prices.

Other restrictions on long-run divergence arise from arbitrage. Forward/spot parity, for example, states that the forward price is equal to the spot price plus the cost of carry. Violations of this condition present arbitrage opportunities. If the arbitrage would incur trading costs, we would not expect the parity relationship to hold exactly and uniformly.

An increasing divergence between forward and spot prices would, however, run up against arbitrage. A similar principle applies to the prices of options and their underlying assets, as long as appropriate correction is made for nonlinearities in the valuation relationship.

When two or more variables individually follow random walk–like (formally, "integrated") processes, but there exists a linear combination of them that is stationary, the variables are said to be cointegrated. The bid and ask for a stock, for example, are both dominated by random walks. The difference between them, the spread, is approximately stationary. Engle and Granger (1987) provide a formal analysis of cointegration; Hamilton (1994, Ch. 19) is a textbook presentation; Hasbrouck (1995) discusses microstructure applications.

In the presence of cointegration, the statistical models we've used to this point must be modified. VARs especially exhibit specification problems. Fortunately, simple modifications usually clear up matters.

10.2.1 The Structural Model

The problems and remedies can be illustrated with a simple structural model.

$$m_t = m_{t-1} + u_t$$
$$p_{1t} = m_t + c\, q_t \qquad (10.5)$$
$$p_{2t} = m_{t-1}.$$

There is one efficient price m_t that is common to both prices. The first price is generated by the usual Roll mechanism. The second price has no bid-ask spread, but uses an efficient price that is one period stale. This model can be motivated as a description of trading in a primary market and a crossing market (discussed in section 2.6). The second price is the quote midpoint in the primary market, lagged to reflect transmission and processing delays.

10.2.2 The VMA Representation

Both prices are integrated (contain random-walk components), but $p_{1t} - p_{2t} = u_t + cq_t$ is stationary. Thus, the prices are cointegrated. By direct inspection, the vector time series Δp_t has a VMA(1) representation $\Delta p_t = \theta_0^* \varepsilon_t^* + \theta_1^* \varepsilon_{t-1}^*$, where

$$\theta_0^* = \begin{bmatrix} 1 & c \\ 0 & 0 \end{bmatrix}, \quad \theta_1^* = \begin{bmatrix} 0 & -c \\ 1 & 0 \end{bmatrix}, \quad \text{and } \varepsilon_t^* = \begin{bmatrix} u_t \\ q_t \end{bmatrix}. \qquad (10.6)$$

This form is not very useful, however. It is not invertible, that is, it cannot be transformed into a VAR. Nor can it be reworked into a standard VMA form, such as $\Delta p_t = \varepsilon_t + \theta_1 \varepsilon_{t-1}$. (The device used in section 9.2 does not work because θ_0^* is singular.)

There is an alternative VMA representation. The autocovariances of Δp_t are:

$$\Gamma_0 = \begin{bmatrix} 2c^2 + \sigma_u^2 & 0 \\ 0 & \sigma_u^2 \end{bmatrix}; \quad \Gamma_1 = \begin{bmatrix} -c^2 & 0 \\ \sigma_u^2 & 0 \end{bmatrix};$$

and $\Gamma_k = 0$ for $|k| > 1$. $\qquad\qquad$ (10.7)

The alternative VMA is obtained by equating the autocovariances implied by the general form $\Delta p_t = \varepsilon_t + \theta_1 \varepsilon_{t-1}$ and $\Omega = \mathrm{Var}(\varepsilon_t)$ to the autocovariances given in (10.7), and solving. We obtain:

$$\theta_1 = \left(c^2 + \sigma_u^2\right)^{-1} \begin{bmatrix} -c^2 & c^2 \\ \sigma_u^2 & -\sigma_u^2 \end{bmatrix}$$

$$\Omega = \mathrm{Var}(\varepsilon_t) = \begin{bmatrix} 2c^2 + \sigma_u^2 - \dfrac{c^4}{c^2 + \sigma_u^2} & \dfrac{c^2 \sigma_u^2}{c^2 + \sigma_u^2} \\ \dfrac{c^2 \sigma_u^2}{c^2 + \sigma_u^2} & \dfrac{c^2 \sigma_u^2}{c^2 + \sigma_u^2} \end{bmatrix}. \qquad (10.8)$$

As in the noncointegrated models, we consider the forecast:

$$f_t = \lim_{k \to \infty} E^*[p_{t+k}|p_t, P_{t-1}, \ldots] = p_t + E^*[\Delta p_{t+1}|\varepsilon_t, \varepsilon_{t-1}, \ldots]$$

$$= p_t + \theta_1 \varepsilon_t.$$

The forecast has the usual filtering interpretation $f_t = E^*[m_t|p_t, p_{t-1}, \ldots]$. The first difference is:

$$\Delta f_t = [I + \theta_1]\varepsilon_t = \left(c^2 + \sigma_u^2\right)^{-1} \begin{bmatrix} \sigma_u^2 & c^2 \\ \sigma_u^2 & c^2 \end{bmatrix} \varepsilon_t. \qquad (10.9)$$

Note that the rows of Δf_t are identical. This implies that the two projected efficient prices have identical dynamics, that is, that the same filtered efficient price underlies both securities. It is true that this is a feature of the structural model, but the important point is that this commonality is uncovered on the basis of the VMA representation.

Exercise 10.1 Suppose that $\sigma_u^2 = 1$ and $c = 2$ Using Cholesky factorizations with the two possible orderings, show that ε_{1t} (i.e., the innovation from the first price) explains between 20% and 55.9% of σ_u^2. (Both prices are informative about m_t. The first price is based on the current m_t but impounds the bid/ask bounce error. The second price has no bid/ask bounce noise, but is based on m_{t-1}. As c gets large, the information share of the first market declines; as c declines, the information share of the first market increases.)

10.2.3 Autoregressive Representations

For most of the VMA models considered up to this point, the VAR is an alternative representation that is particularly convenient for estimation. Here, though, if we attempt to determine the VAR coefficients, $\varphi(L)$ in $\varphi(L)\Delta p_t = \varepsilon_t$, by the usual method of series expansion of $(I + \theta_1 L)^{-1}$, we get an unpleasant surprise. The leading terms of the expansion are:

$$\varphi(L) = I + \left(c^2 + \sigma_u^2\right)^{-1} \left(\begin{bmatrix} c^2 & -c^2 \\ -\sigma_u^2 & \sigma_u^2 \end{bmatrix} L + \begin{bmatrix} c^2 & -c^2 \\ -\sigma_u^2 & \sigma_u^2 \end{bmatrix} L^2 \right.$$
$$\left. + \begin{bmatrix} c^2 & -c^2 \\ -\sigma_u^2 & \sigma_u^2 \end{bmatrix} L^3 + \cdots \right).$$

Apparently, the coefficients of the VAR representation do not converge. This difficulty is not specific to the present structural model. When variables are cointegrated, no convergent VAR representation exists for the first-differences.[1]

Fortunately, a modified version of the VAR does exist. This is the vector error correction model (VECM). The "error correction" attribute refers to a common early use of these specifications, the modeling of dynamic systems in disequilibrium. To build the VECM, note first that a VAR does in fact exist for the price levels. Because $\Delta p_t = (1 - L)p_t$, the VMA representation becomes $(1 - L)p_t = \theta(L)\varepsilon_t$. A VAR level representation, $\phi(L)p_t = \varepsilon_t$, would have the property that $\phi(L) = \theta(L)^{-1}(1 - L)$. Direct computation of this yields:

$$\phi(L) = I - \phi_1 L \quad \text{where } \phi_1 = \left(c^2 + \sigma_u^2\right)^{-1} \begin{bmatrix} \sigma_u^2 & c^2 \\ \sigma_u^2 & c^2 \end{bmatrix}. \tag{10.10}$$

We may work back to first differences as:

$$p_t = \phi_1 p_{t-1} + \varepsilon_t$$
$$\Delta p_t = p_t - p_{t-1} = (\phi_1 - I)p_{t-1} + \varepsilon_t$$
$$= \left(c^2 + \sigma_u^2\right)^{-1} \begin{bmatrix} -c^2 & c^2 \\ \sigma_u^2 & -\sigma_u^2 \end{bmatrix} p_{t-1} + \varepsilon_t \tag{10.11}$$
$$= \left(c^2 + \sigma_u^2\right)^{-1} \begin{bmatrix} -c^2 \\ \sigma_u^2 \end{bmatrix} \begin{bmatrix} 1 & -1 \end{bmatrix} p_{t-1} + \varepsilon_t.$$

Finally,

$$\Delta p_t = \beta z_t + \varepsilon_t$$
$$\text{where } \beta = \left(c^2 + \sigma_u^2\right)^{-1} \begin{bmatrix} -c^2 \\ \sigma_u^2 \end{bmatrix} \text{ and } z_t = p_{1t} - p_{2t}. \tag{10.12}$$

This is a VECM, and βz_t is the error correction term. z_t is the combination of two prices that is stationary. It is the error, not in the sense of any disequilibrium, but rather in the sense of discrepancy. β is the matrix of adjustment coefficients. If $z_t > 0$, the error correction term implies that p_{1t} will drop and p_{2t} will rise.

The present structural model is only illustrative, and as such exhibits some special features. The right-hand side of a VECM typically contains terms in lagged first differences $(\Delta p_{t-1}, \Delta p_{t-2}, \ldots)$. Given the absence of these terms, the error is eliminated in one step. The normalization of the error is natural but arbitrary. By appropriate scaling of β, we could have defined the error as $p_{2t} - p_{1t}$ or $(p_{2t} - p_{1t})/5$.

The relative magnitudes of the adjustment coefficients suggest something about price discovery and leadership. In a sense, the process is like a bargaining situation in which the two sides each concede something to reach agreement. The party that makes the smaller concession (changes position by the smallest amount) is the stronger. The party that moves the most is the weaker.

10.3   General VECM Specifications

10.3.1   Multiple Prices

We consider the case where there are n prices for a single security. In many applications, the prices arise from n different trading venues. The VECM has the general form

$$\Delta p_t = \phi_1 \Delta p_{t-1} + \phi_2 \Delta p_{t-2} + \cdots + \beta(z_{t-1} - b) + \varepsilon_t, \qquad (10.13)$$

where p_t is the $n \times 1$ vector of prices. A convenient expression for the error is:

$$\underset{(n-1)\times 1}{z_{t-1}} = \begin{bmatrix} p_{1,t-1} - p_{2,t-1} \\ p_{1,t-1} - p_{3,t-1} \\ \vdots \\ p_{1,t-1} - p_{n-1,t-1} \end{bmatrix} = A' p_{t-1}$$

$$\text{where } A' = \begin{bmatrix} 1 & -1 & 0 & \cdots & 0 \\ 1 & 0 & -1 & \cdots & 0 \\ & & & \ddots & \\ 1 & 0 & \cdots & & -1 \end{bmatrix}. \qquad (10.14)$$

Each component of z_{t-1} is a difference relative to the first price. It is convenient to order the prices so that the presumptively dominant one appears first. This facilitates interpretation of the β coefficients as speed-of-adjustment parameters toward the first price. From a statistical viewpoint, however, the ordering is arbitrary. The essential properties of the model are also unaffected if A is replaced by AP, where P is any non-singular square matrix of order $n-1$. Formally, A is considered a linear basis for the set of cointegrating vectors.

The b in the error correction term is an $(n-1)$ column vector of mean errors. From an economic perspective, the mean error is the target of the adjustment process. For example, if $p_t = [ask_t \; bid_t]'$, we'd expect the difference $z_t = ask_t - bid_t$ to tend toward the long-run average spread.

Equation (10.13) suggests a recursive procedure for forecasting. To construct impulse response functions, we set lagged price changes and disturbances to zero and work forward from an initial specified shock ε_t. By successively computing the impulse response functions for unit shocks in each variable, we may obtain the VMA representation for the price changes $\Delta p_t = \theta(L)\varepsilon_t$.

We may posit for the n prices a random-walk decomposition of the form

$$\underset{(n\times 1)}{p_t} = \underset{(n\times 1)}{m_t \times \iota} + \underset{(n\times 1)}{s_t} \quad \text{where } m_t = m_{t-1} + w_t, \tag{10.15}$$

where ι is a vector of ones. It is important to note that m_t is a scalar: The random-walk ("efficient price") component is the same for all prices in the model. The random-walk variance is: $\sigma_w^2 = [\theta(1)]_1 \Omega[\theta(1)]_1'$, where $[\cdot]_1$ denotes the first row of the matrix. One property developed earlier for the structural model, however, is general: The rows of $\theta(1)$ are identical. (In the computation of σ_w^2, the first row is as good as any.)

The random-walk variance decomposition was introduced in section 8.6. Letting $d = [\theta(1)]_1 F'$ where F is the Cholesky factor of $\Omega(=F'F)$, $\sigma_w^2 = \sum d_i^2$. In the context of section 8.6, the variance decomposition is used to make informational attributions about a diverse set of variables (such as prices and trades). Here, all variables are prices, but the principles are identical. The absolute contribution of the ith price's innovations to the common efficient price is d_i^2. We may also compute a relative contribution, d_i^2/σ_w^2. In the context of a model of multiple prices, the relative contribution is also known as price i's information share.

Cholesky factorization was used in section 9.4 to impose a causal ordering that was supported by economic logic (trades first). In multiple price analyses, however, one usually tries to preserve balance in the analysis by treating all prices symmetrically. In practice, this suggests calculating and reporting for each information share the minimum and maximum over all causal permutations.

Random-walk variance decompositions are probably more important here than in any other microstructure application. VECM models are often estimated for trade prices or quotes from different, competing trading venues. The venue with the largest information share is in some ways the most important. In a statistical sense, it is the price leader. Loosely speaking, the prices of other markets tend to follow its moves. It is the venue where most value-relevant information is first revealed. The social welfare importance of an informationally efficient price is appreciated by regulators. The dominant market can assert that it is the largest producer of an important social good and can make a case for regulatory preference based on something other than self-interest.

The VECM framework suggests other measures of market importance. One approach suggests measuring contributions by the elements of $\beta = \theta(1)_1/\iota'\theta(1)_1$, that is, the long-run VMA coefficients normalized to sum to unity. This vector has some interesting properties. In the permanent/transitory decomposition defined by $p_t = m_t^*\iota + s_t^*$ where $m_t^* = \beta'p_t$, it may be shown that s_t^* has no long-run effect on m_t^*. This permanent/transitory decomposition was originally suggested in a macroeconomic context by Gonzalo and Granger (1995)(GG). Chu, Hsieh, and Tse (1999) and Harris, McInish, and Wood (2002b) use the decomposition in microstructure analyses. The general properties and relative merits of information shares and GG factor components are discussed in a special issue of the *Journal of Financial Markets* containing Baillie et al. (2002), de Jong (2002), Harris, McInish, and Wood (2002a,b), Hasbrouck (2002), and Lehmann (2002).

10.3.2 Extensions

The basic price VECM easily accommodates several useful generalizations. We might expand the system to include other variables in addition to the cointegrated prices. These other variables might include orders associated with the cointegrated prices or prices of other securities (as long as they are not cointegrated with the original set of prices). An extended VECM of this sort would look like:

$$y_t = \phi_1 y_{t-1} + \phi_2 y_{t-2} + \cdots + \beta(b - z_{t-1})\varepsilon_t$$
$$\text{where } y_t = \begin{bmatrix} \Delta p_t \\ x_t \end{bmatrix} \text{ and } x_t = \begin{bmatrix} q_t \\ \Delta p_t^* \end{bmatrix}. \tag{10.16}$$

The q_t includes one or more order variables, and Δp_t^* contains the changes of the noncointegrated prices.

10.3.3 Testing and Estimating Cointegrating Vectors

The present discussion of cointegration has neglected several aspects of the topic that are usually accorded great attention in treatments motivated by macroeconomic applications. In macroeconomic analysis, testing for cointegration is important because the considerations that might cause it to arise are often not transparent. In microstructure analysis, however, cointegration or its absence tends to be an obvious structural feature.

The discussion has proceeded on the assumption that we know the cointegrating vectors, such as the price difference in the simple structural model (section 10.2) or the basis for the cointegrating vectors (A in equation (10.14)). In practice, this is almost always the case. The bids, asks, trade prices, and so on, even from multiple trading venues, for a single security cannot reasonably diverge without bound. In applications involving index arbitrage, the weights of the component prices are set by the definition of the index, and are known to practitioner and econometrician alike. (Of course, it might be easier, particularly in an exploratory analysis, to estimate the weights, rather than look them up.)

10.3.4   Pairs Trading

The previous remarks notwithstanding, there is one practical situation, in which the testing and estimation of cointegration vectors is important. Pairs trading is the strategy of identifying two securities or commodities with relative prices that are constant in the long run but exhibit considerable variation in the short run. When the relative prices diverge from the long-run value, one buys the (relatively) undervalued security/commodity and sells (or sells short) the overvalued (Gatev, Goetzmann and Rouwenhorst (2006)). The ratio of gold and silver prices, for example, arises in the analysis of commodities trading strategies.

Lest formal cointegration theory appear to put these strategies on a sound methodological footing, two potential problems should be noted. The first concerns data-snooping biases. The nominal size of a cointegration test (probability of incorrectly rejecting the null hypothesis of no cointegration) is likely to understate the true size if the price pair has been selected from a large number of candidates due to a history of "interesting" comovement. The second problem is that structural breaks can play havoc with the forecasts of cointegrated models. This is particularly true of breaks in the long-run means of the errors. What may look like extreme misvaluation on the basis of historical estimates may actually represent convergence to a new equilibrium point (Clements and Hendry (1999) Doornik and Hendry (1997)).

10.4   Time

The preceding chapter noted that in a single-security analysis, it is often useful to let t index events (e.g., trades). This is tenable because when the pace of trading accelerates, all events (trades, quote revisions, etc.) also occur more frequently. In a two-security model, though, if we let t index times when trades occur in both securities, we will end up throwing out trades that occur in one security only. If we let t index trades in either security, trades that occur sequentially in one security may wind up being separated by many intervals if there were intervening trades in the other security. In these models, then, event time is awkward. The common frame of reference provided by wall-clock time is more attractive.

If the specification is to be estimated in wall-clock time, what interval should be used? The precision of the time stamps (e.g., one second in TAQ data) sets a lower limit on the interval length. It is always possible to aggregate up to longer intervals, however, and analyses of this sort may use intervals of one minute or longer.

In most situations, aggregation reduces the information in a sample. In a VECM price discovery model, this loss is reflected in the disturbance covariance matrix Ω. Time aggregation may make events that are actually separated in time to appear contemporaneous. This leads to larger off-diagonal covariances in Ω. When Ω is diagonal, the information shares are precisely determined. As the off-diagonal elements increase in size, the information shares become more sensitive to the causal ordering imposed by the Cholesky factorizations. Over all causal permutations, the upper and lower bounds for the information shares will become wider. A shorter time interval is desirable, therefore, because it generally implies tighter bounds.

However, a short time interval has some apparent inconveniences. First, it is necessary to propagate prices past the time of their initial posting. For example, suppose that t indexes one-second intervals, a bid of 100 is posted at 10:00:15, and a bid of 101 is posted at 10:01:00. In the observation matrix, a price of 100 will entered at 10:00:15, 10:00:16, ..., 10:00:59. For bid and ask quotes, this is a sensible procedure because quotes in most markets are regarded as active and firm until withdrawn or revised. Suppose, however, that the prices are trade prices. A trade occurs at a particular time, and it cannot be suggested that the trade is repeated each second until a fresh transaction is recorded. Propagation of the trade price can still be justified, however, by interpreting the filled price series as a record of "last sales." The economic relevance of last sale prices is suggested by the fact that they are widely disseminated in market data streams and are in fact often displayed with no indication of the trade time. Last sale prices are also used for purposes of index computation.

Second, a side effect of propagating price levels is that the series of price changes may contain many zero observations. This should not suggest model misspecification. The VMA, VAR, and VECM specifications rest on the Wold theorem and covariance stationarity, neither of which preclude a data series dominated by zeros (or any other value).

Finally, a VECM specified for short intervals may have an excessively large number of parameters. For example, suppose that we wish to describe dynamics over one minute for a set of five prices with one-second resolution. Each coefficient matrix in the VECM will be 5×5, and there will be 60 such matrices, implying that the VECM will have at least 1,500 parameters. The parameter space can be greatly reduced, however, by the use of polynomial distributed lags.

When integrating data from multiple markets, one is often reliant on the time stamps provided by the markets. The quality of the time stamps depends on the accuracy of internal systems clocks, latencies in data processing and transmission, and the nominal reporting precision. Trading in some markets occurs are such a rapid pace that often multiple events are reported in the same second. When this happens, the sequencing of reporting is suspect.

Beyond a certain point, precise determination of when an event like a trade actually occurred is often a hopeless endeavor, involving considerations of when Smith transmitted a commitment or Jones received an acknowledgment. For many purposes, though, it suffices to determine when knowledge of an event entered the public awareness. This is, after all, the point when agents' information sets are updated. For this purpose, it is appropriate to use the timing and sequencing as reported in the real-time consolidated data feed. Most microstructure data sets are based on such sources and preserve the source timing.

11

Dealers and Their Inventories

Dealers, briefly discussed in section 2.3, are professional intermediaries. The descriptions of dealer behavior to this point have focused on their recovery of noninformational operating costs (via c in the Roll model) and their pricing under asymmetric information. This chapter examines other aspects of the dealer's role and behavior.

The discussion first considers the inventory control models. These analyses (which generally predate the asymmetric information models) essentially view the securities dealer as being similar in key respects to a dealer in any other commodity. Normally a vendor maintains an inventory to accommodate randomly arriving purchasers. A securities dealer, of course, must also accommodate randomly arriving sellers and in fact must replenish inventory by buying from these sellers. This complicates the inventory management problem. Control relies on order arrival rates that are sensitive to the prices posted by the dealer.

The inventory control models predict that the dealer will have a preferred inventory level. Such a preference, though, may also arise from risk aversion. The discussion develops this point, its implications for dealer quotes, and multisecurity extensions. The discussion then examines some of the evidence on dealer positions and statistical issues that arise in analyzing the dynamics of these positions.

In going through these analyses, it should be kept in mind that most of the analyses that focus on the behavior of dealers were developed in an era when the institutional distinctions between dealers and customers were sharper than they are at present. Fortunately, many of the analyses originally developed as models of dealers (in a narrowly defined sense) are also relevant for the more numerous agents whom we might describe as customers acting as dealers.

11.1   Inventory Control

11.1.1   Garman (1976)

Garman (1976) suggests that a dealer is needed because buyers and sellers do not arrive synchronously. In his model, buyers and sellers arrive randomly in continuous time, as Poisson/exponential arrival processes (section 6.1), and transact a single quantity. The arrival intensity for buyers is $\lambda^{Buy}(p)$, a function of the price they pay. The arrival intensity for sellers is $\lambda^{Sell}(p)$, a function of the price they receive. These functions are depicted in figure 11.1. They describe demand and supply, but not in the usual static sense. Market clearing in this context means that buyers and sellers arrive at the same average rate, that is, with the same intensity. If the dealer were to quote the same price to buyers and sellers, market clearing would occur where the intensity functions cross. This is defined by $\lambda^{Buy}(p^{Eq}) = \lambda^{Sell}(p^{Eq}) = \lambda^{Eq}$. As long as the intensities are the same, the dealer is on average buying and selling at the same rate.

If the dealer is buying and selling at the same price, of course, there is no profit. If the dealer quotes an ask price to the buyers and a bid quote to the sellers, he will make the spread on every unit turned over (the "turn"). The dealer's average profit (trading revenue) per unit time is:

$$\begin{aligned} \pi\left(Bid, Ask\right) &= \left(Ask - Bid\right)\lambda^{Buy}\left(Ask\right) \\ &= \left(Ask - Bid\right)\lambda^{Sell}\left(Bid\right), \end{aligned} \tag{11.1}$$

where we have maintained the condition that is $\lambda^{Buy}(Ask) = \lambda^{Sell}(Bid)$, that is, supply and demand balance (on average). Setting a wide spread increases the profit on each trade but depresses the rate of arrivals.

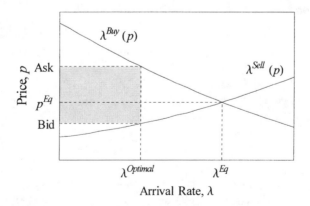

Figure 11.1. Arrival rates of buyers and sellers.

The profits are defined by the shaded rectangle in figure 11.1. The dealer sets the bid and ask to maximize this area.

Exercise 11.1 Suppose that the (inverse) intensity functions are given by $p(\lambda^{Buy}) = 3 - \lambda^{Buy} + 0.2(\lambda^{Buy})^2$ and $p(\lambda^{Sell}) = 2 + 0.2\lambda^{Sell} + 0.2(\lambda^{Sell})^2$, where the units of λ^{Buy} and λ^{Sell} are arrivals per minute. Determine the equilibrium price and arrival rate. Determine the dealer's optimal bid and ask and the average profit per minute.

To accommodate the asynchronous buying and selling, the dealer needs to maintain buffer stocks of the security and cash. The key constraint is that the dealer's inventories of the security and cash cannot drop below given levels, taken without loss of generality to be zero. If $\lambda^{Buy}(Ask) = \lambda^{Sell}(Bid)$, holdings of stock follow a zero-drift random walk. Cash holdings follow a positive-drift random walk (due to the turn). Garman points out that in this case, the dealer is eventually ruined with probability one. (A zero-drift random walk will eventually hit any finite barrier with probability one.) Furthermore, with realistic parameter values, the expected time to ruin is a matter of days.

The dealer in this variant of the Garman model sets the bid and ask prices once and for all. As he sees an inventory barrier approaching, he simply watches and hopes that the barrier isn't hit. Commenting on the short expected failure times implied by this strategy under realistic parameter values, Garman notes, "The order of magnitude makes it clear that the specialists [dealers] must pursue a policy of relating their prices to their inventories in order to avoid failure." This statement lays out the intuition behind the inventory control principle. The essential mechanism is that dealers change their bid and ask quotes to elicit an expected imbalance of buy and sell orders to push their inventories in the direction of their preferred long-run position.

Before discussing this mechanism further, we note that ruins do occur (market makers occasionally fail), but these are infrequent events. They generally arise because security inventories are levered (partially financed with debt). A sudden price movement triggers a default in the dealer's borrowing arrangements. In a sense, ruin is caused not by moving inventory hitting a fixed barrier but by a moving barrier hitting the existing level of inventory. The relationship between credit and liquidity is modeled by Brunnermeier and Pedersen (2005).

11.1.2 Amihud and Mendelson (1980)

The Amihud and Mendelson (1980) model has much in common with the Garman framework. There is a monopolistic dealer. Buyers and sellers come to the market asynchronously, as Poisson arrivals where the arrival intensities depend on the posted quotes. The market maker's inventory of the security is constrained to lie between given upper and lower bounds, which may be thought of as arising from credit constraints. The market maker maximizes expected profits per unit time.

The model has a number of important predictions. First, the dealer has a preferred inventory level lying between the two extremes. This arises from the opportunity cost of being at an extreme point. As the dealer's position nears the upper boundary, for example, he must set the bid quote to lessen (and at the boundary, force to zero) the expected arrival rate for customer sell orders. Similar considerations come into play near the lower boundary. When the arrival rate is low on either side of the market, the rate at which the dealer earns the bid-ask spread is also low.

Figure 11.2 depicts the relation between the inventory position and bid/ask prices. It is clear that:

- Bid and ask are monotone decreasing functions of the inventory level.
- There is a positive spread.
- The spread is increasing in distance from preferred position.
- The quotes are not set symmetrically about the "true" value.

Implicit in the figure is another important prediction. Because bids and asks are depend only on the inventory level, and the inventory level is mean reverting toward the preferred position, the price effects of inventory imbalances are transient.

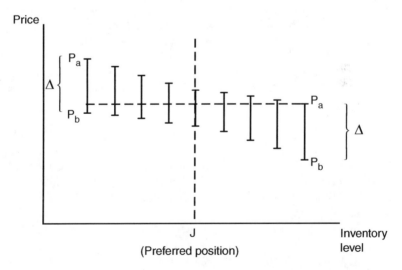

Figure 11.2. The dependence of bid and ask prices on inventory position.

11.2   Risk Aversion and Dealer Behavior

In the Amihud and Mendelson model, an extreme inventory position depresses the expected profits of a risk-neutral dealer. Aversion to extreme positions may also arise, however, due to simple risk aversion on the part of the dealer. That is, a dealer can be viewed much as any other risk-averse expected utility maximizer who forms a portfolio. The distinction is that in disseminating a bid or offer quote, the dealer is allowing for the possibility of a shock to his portfolio. If the dealer is initially at his portfolio optimum, he will set the bid and offer prices to impound compensation for being pulled off his optimum, if the bid or offer is hit. To illustrate, we consider a version of a model originally due to Stoll (1978).

The framework assumes a risky asset with a normally distributed payoff and an agent (the dealer) with an exponential utility function. This setup is often used in economic modeling, and because exponential utility exhibits constant absolute risk aversion (CARA), it is often called the "CARA-normal" framework. The agent's preferences over final wealth W are given by $U(W) = -e^{-\alpha W}$. He chooses a strategy to maximize expected utility $EU(W)$. Under normality, that is, if $W \sim N(\mu_W, \sigma_W^2)$, then expected utility simplifies to $EU(W) = -e^{-\alpha \mu_W + \alpha^2 \sigma_W^2/2}$.[1] To optimize this, it suffices to maximize $\alpha \mu_W - \alpha^2 \sigma_W^2/2$, or equivalently to maximize the certainty equivalent $CE(\mu_W, \sigma_W^2) = \mu_W - \alpha \sigma_W^2/2$.

Returning to the dealer's problem, we assume that the security has random payoff $X \sim N(\mu_X, \sigma_X^2)$ and that all borrowing and lending is at a zero rate of interest. Prior to bidding or offering the dealer holds n units (shares) of the security (not necessarily an optimum), with $n < 0$ corresponding to a short position. Now suppose that he posts a bid B for one share. If the bid is not hit, his terminal wealth is $W = nX$. If the bid is hit, he acquires one more share for which he pays B, and $W = (n+1)X - B$. For the dealer to be indifferent to an execution, his certainty equivalent must be the same whether or not his bid is hit: $CE(n\mu_X, n^2\sigma_X^2) = CE((n+1)\mu_X - B, (n+1)^2\sigma_X^2)$. This equivalence implies

$$B = \mu_X - (2n+1)\alpha\sigma_X^2/2. \qquad (11.2)$$

The bid is equal to the expected payoff plus or minus a differential. If the dealer starts out with $n > -1/2$ (allowing for fractional holdings) the bid depends inversely on σ_X^2 and α. If the initial position is $n < -1/2$, however, the dealer bids above the expected payoff, and the excess depends positively on σ_X^2 and α.

Setting the bid to maintain the expected utility whether or not the bid is hit is optimal, however, only if the dealer already holds an optimal number of shares. Suppose that prior to bidding, the dealer can buy or sell the security at a notional price P. (Stoll suggests that P be viewed as the dealer's subjective valuation.) The dealer's terminal wealth, then (assuming zero initial endowments of shares and cash), is $W = n(X - P)$.

Maximizing the certainty equivalent of this over n gives the optimal holdings as $n^* = (\mu_X - P)/(\alpha\sigma_X^2)$. Substituting this for n in equation (11.2) gives $B = P - \alpha\sigma_X^2/2$. This value of B leaves the dealer indifferent between execution and remaining at his optimum.

An advantage of incorporating risk aversion into the analysis is that it highlights the role of correlation in market making across multiple securities. To illustrate this, suppose that there are two risky securities with payoffs $X \sim N(\mu, \Omega)$, where X and μ are column vectors and Ω is the payoff covariance matrix. If the holdings are $n = [n_1 \quad n_2]'$, then the terminal wealth is $W = n'X$, so $\mu_W = n'\mu$ and $\sigma_W^2 = n'\Omega n$. The dealer makes a bid B_1 for the first security. If the bid is hit, his terminal wealth is $W_{Hit} = [n_1 + 1 \quad n_2]X - B_1$. Equating the certainty equivalents of being hit and not being hit gives:

$$B_1 = \mu_1 - \frac{\alpha\sigma_1}{2}\left[(1 + 2n_1)\sigma_1 + 2\rho n_2 \sigma_2\right], \qquad (11.3)$$

where $\rho = \mathrm{Corr}(X_1, X_2)$. Thus, the dealer will bid less aggressively if the securities are positively correlated. This conforms to the usual intuition that positive correlation aggravates total portfolio risk.

On the other hand, if we assume (as before) that the dealer is starting at his optimum, then $B_1 = P_1 - \alpha\sigma_1^2/2$. Surprisingly, this is the same result as in the one-security case. In particular, the correlation coefficient drops out. This is a consequence of offsetting effects. The optimal n_1 and n_2 in equation (11.3) depends negatively on ρ, leaving the bracketed term invariant to changes in ρ. (Although this offset is a general feature of the problem, the complete disappearance of ρ in the final expression for the bid is a consequence of CARA utility.)

11.3 Empirical Analysis of Dealer Inventories

11.3.1 A First Look at the Data

Changes in the dealer's position reveal the dealer's trades, which may disclose strategy and profitability. Position records for dealers (in fact, for all traders) are therefore difficult to obtain. There are no public data sets. Most published research is based on data collected for regulatory purposes and/or made available to the researcher under the condition of no further redistribution.

NYSE specialist inventories are analyzed by Madhavan and Smidt (1991, 1993), Hasbrouck and Sofianos (1993), and Madhavan and Sofianos (1998). The graphs of typical daily closing positions reported by Hasbrouck and Sofianos are a good place to start. Figure 11.3 depicts the positions for stock A. The salient features are:

- Inventory are sometimes negative (short positions).
- There is no obvious drift or divergence.

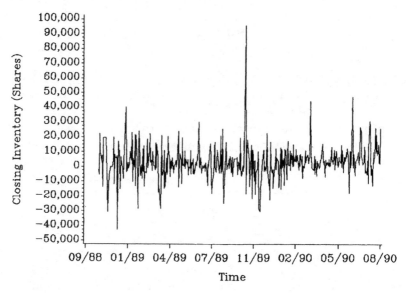

Figure 11.3.   Inventory for stock A.

- The mean inventory is near zero. Although not obvious from the figure, overnight positions are small: Dealers tend to "go home flat."

This inventory path is consistent with the economic logic presented to this point. Other specialist inventories, however, are not as well behaved. The specialist position for Hasbrouck and Sofianos's stock C depicted in figure 11.4 also appears to be mean-reverting but has protracted departures (on the order of several months) from the mean. The variation in holdings seems to be better characterized by long-term components, operating at horizons normally associated with investment decisions. The specialist may in fact be pursing short-term inventory control, but toward preferred positions that are slowly time-varying. The graph demonstrates that even traders who are officially designated dealers are not necessarily well characterized by the standard inventory perspective. (The plot for stock B, not reproduced here, exhibits swings of even longer duration and size.)

The next section discusses statistical issues related to the univariate characterization of inventory series and studies that incorporate inventories into dynamic price/trade models.

11.3.2   Inventories and Trades: Levels and Differences

If the dealer is counterparty to all trades and all trades are for one unit, then the trade direction variable used earlier is $q_t = -\Delta I_t$, where I_t is the

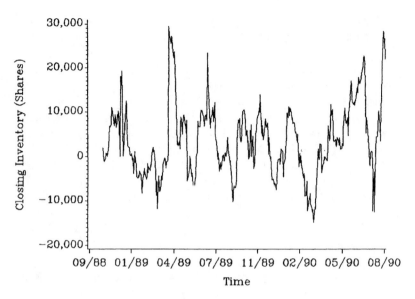

Figure 11.4. Inventory for stock C.

dealer's inventory. (If we wanted to allow for various quantities, we'd just use the signed order volume in lieu of q_t.) If the q_t values are uncorrelated, as in the basic Roll model, then I_t will follow a random walk, diverging over time (as noted by Garman). But suppose we start by assuming that I_t is well behaved. In particular, if I_t is covariance stationary, what does that imply about q_t?

11.3.3 Stationarity

In the first place, how do we decide whether a time series is a random walk or covariance stationary? The question is actually ill-phrased. In the Roll model, for example, the price is neither a random walk nor stationary. It's a mixture of both sorts of components. A somewhat better question is, how do we know if a time series contains a random-walk component? From a statistical viewpoint, however, even this is too vague. For reasons that will shortly become clear, it's more precise to ask, "Does the process contain a unit root?" Formally, the material in this section applies to processes that might have a unit root and are covariance stationary after first differencing. Statistical issues related to unit roots are discussed in Hamilton (1994, pp. 475–543) and Fuller (1996, pp. 546–663).

   The term *unit root* arises in connection with the autoregressive representation for a time series. Consider the autoregressive form of a time series x_t in terms of the lag polynomial: $\phi(L)x_t = \varepsilon_t$ where $\phi(L) = 1 + \phi_1 L + \phi_2 L^2 + \cdots + \phi_K L^K$. The stationarity of x_t depends on the form of $\phi(L)$ and in particular on the solutions to the polynomial equation $\phi(z) = 0$.

The criterion for stationarity is that all of the solutions to $\phi(z) = 0$ must lie outside of the unit circle. Consider the simplest case, an autoregression of order one. If $x_t = \phi_1 x_{t-1} + \varepsilon_t$, then $\phi(z) = 1 - \phi_1 z = 0$ implies $z = \phi_1^{-1}$, and the requirement that $|z| > 1$ is equivalent to $|\phi_1| < 1$. Alternatively, if we factor the polynomial as $\phi(z) = (1 - a_1 z)(1 - a_2 z) \ldots (1 - a_K z)$, the roots correspond to the a_i^{-1}. If the ith root is equal to one, then $a_i^{-1} = 0$, and the lag polynomial will be of the form $\phi(L) = (1 - L)\ldots$. In this case, we say that "x_t has a unit root." If one root lies on the unit circle and the others lie outside, then x_t is stationary after first differencing.

The Roll model also provides a nice illustration. The structural model has the MA representation $(1 - L)p_t = \theta(L)\varepsilon_t$ where $\theta(L) = 1 + \theta_1 L$. The autoregressive representation for the price *level* is $\phi(L)p_t = \varepsilon_t$ where $\phi(L) = \theta(L)^{-1}(1 - L)$. We can identify at least one root here, and its value is unity. This is not surprising because we built a random walk into the structural model.

If we did not have a structural model, though, we'd have to make an inference based on a sample of data. There are various statistical unit root tests available. It is quite possible in microstructure situations, though, to hypothesize situations in which the tests would be misleading. In the Roll model, for example, a large trading cost coupled with a small random-walk volatility can generate a sample in which the dominant feature is bid-ask bounce and the sample path is apparently stationary.

11.3.4 Invertibility

The economic models unambiguously assert that the inventory series I_t is mean-reverting. If it is also covariance stationary, then by the Wold theorem it possesses a moving average representation: $I_t = \theta(L)\varepsilon_t$. The first difference is stationary as well and possesses the MA representation $\Delta I_t = (1 - L)\theta(L)\varepsilon_t$.

When we encountered in the analysis of the Roll model a series (like p_t) that was (or contained) a random-walk component, we constructed a stationary process by differencing. Suppose that we aren't sure whether I_t possesses a unit root or not. To be on the safe side, shouldn't we take the first difference anyway? If the series is stationary to begin with, the first difference is still stationary, so by this criterion there is no harm done.

"Overdifferencing" does create one difficulty, however. It ruins the recursion that underlies the autoregressive representation for the series. To see this, consider the simple case where $I_t = \varepsilon_t$. The recursion then becomes $\Delta I_t = \varepsilon_t - \varepsilon_{t-1} = \varepsilon_t - (\Delta I_{t-1} + \varepsilon_{t-2}) = \cdots = \varepsilon_t - \Delta I_{t-1} - \Delta I_{t-2} - \cdots$, from which it is clear that the coefficients on the lagged ΔI_t never converge. Few statistical software routines will alert the user to noninvertibility. It is always possible to compute least squares estimates for autoregressive models in finite samples. Often these estimated models will appear quite reasonable, with apparently well-behaved residuals, and respectable goodness-of-fit tests.

Sometimes, in lieu of dealer inventories, the data set identifies dealer trades: "100 shares purchased from the dealer, 200 shares sold by the dealer, etc." The trade series is (minus) the first difference of the inventory series. So if inventories are stationary, the trade series is noninvertible. A noninvertible moving average model cannot be estimated by inverting an estimated VAR. It can, however, be estimated directly by Kalman filter maximum likelihood methods (Hamilton (1994, p. 387)).

11.4   The Dynamics of Prices, Trades, and Inventories

It is obvious that dealers (at least those who survive) monitor their inventories and keep them from diverging to arbitrarily large long or short positions. No such clarity, however, characterizes our view of the control mechanisms.

The mechanism described in section 11.1 is quote-based. Some early empirical studies found evidence for this mechanism in that inventory changes had a negative effect on quote changes. As predicted, when a customer purchased from a dealer (depleting her inventory) the dealer bid and ask would rise, presumably as the dealer sought to encourage an offsetting sell order and discourage another incoming buy order. The problem is that the same short-term relation is predicted by the asymmetric information models. (Is the dealer raising the quotes on account of the possibility that the purchaser is informed?) To differentiate the two effects empirically, it is necessary to consider the long-run behavior. Information effects of trades are permanent, while inventory effects are temporary (Hasbrouck (1988)). That is, when offsetting trades restore the inventory to the desired position, the inventory control component of the quotes should vanish. Madhavan and Smidt (1991) describe a theoretical model of dealer behavior that incorporates both inventory and asymmetric information effects (also see Madhavan and Smidt (1993)).

For NYSE data, Hasbrouck and Sofianos (1993) estimate VARs that include price changes, signed orders, and specialist inventory positions. In a market where all trade is against the dealer, $q_t = -\Delta I_t$, so an analysis that includes current and lagged q_t and I_t would suffer from multicollinearity (excessive dependence in the explanatory variables). The problem does not arise in the NYSE data because the specialist does not participate in all trades. Hasbrouck and Sofianos find that most of the quote dynamics are attributable to trades, with inventories contributing little explanatory power. Positions are not apparently managed by adjustment of publicly quoted bids and offers.

This should not be too surprising. A dealer using public quotes would be signaling to the world at large his desire to buy or sell, putting him at a competitive disadvantage. Other liquidity suppliers face a similar sort of dilemma. A customer bidding with a limit order runs the risk that his bid will be matched by others in the market (quote matching) and that his order will be executed after those other bids or (in the worst case) not at all.

If inventory management is not effected with publicly posted bid and offer quotes, though, how is it accomplished? There are a number of alternative mechanisms. They may be grouped in three categories: selective, nonpublic quoting; interdealer markets; and market-specific rules that allow dealers to participate in trades without public quoting.

The first of these mechanisms typically arises from the practice (common in dealer markets) of making firm bids and offers only in response to an inquiry by a customer and visible and accessible only by that customer. Yao (1997) analyzes the U.S. dollar/Deutschmark deals of a major foreign exchange dealer, and finds that the terms of trade are partially determined by the inventory position of the dealer in the direction predicted by the inventory control hypothesis. The disadvantage of broad public dissemination is avoided, but the mechanism relies on a sustained flow of customers. Dealers may also trade directly with each other in an interdealer market (described in section 2.3.1).

In consideration of their market-making obligations, designated dealers on regulated exchanges often have methods of trading that are not available (or as readily available) to other participants. These typically involve discretion concerning participation in a trade. Madhavan and Sofianos (1998) document that NYSE specialist inventory positions are partial determinants of specialist participation. For example, a specialist with a neutral inventory position would be inclined to let an incoming customer buy order transact against sell orders in the limit order book. With an undesired long position he might sell to the incoming customer himself. (To do this, he would have to sell at a price below that of any public limit sell order.) This last-mover advantage is further explored in section 13.5.

11.5 Concluding Remarks

Garman's view of dealers as smoothers of buy/sell order imbalances continues to be useful. His model focuses on asynchronous arrivals of individual traders, but the perspective also applies when temporary order imbalances arise in the aggregate. Dealers are agents who (for a price) accommodate these imbalances (see Grossman and Miller (1987); Campbell, Grossman, and Wang (1993); Saar (1998); Llorente et al. (2002). At the same time, the lines between dealers and customers in many markets have blurred. Professional intermediaries are no longer invariably seen as necessary to any well-functioning market. The effects modeled in these studies certainly remain pertinent, but the dealers are best considered as a broad set, not limited to those agents officially designated as such.

The notion that dealers are characterized by inventory control seems less relevant in today's markets. Nor does the logic of achieving inventory control by positioning of the posted quotes seem as compelling as it once did. On the other hand, if inventory control is more broadly interpreted as position management, the issues are as pertinent as ever. The underlying concerns of risk and credit exposure, formerly viewed as important mostly (or solely) for dealers, are in fact pertinent for a large number of agents that may, in the course of their trading decisions, act as liquidity suppliers.

Finally, although trade has become disintermediated in many markets (such as actively traded equities), dealers remain important in many other markets (bonds, foreign exchange, swaps, etc.). The role they play and how they should be regulated are ongoing concerns of practical interest.

12

Limit Order Markets

The worldwide proliferation of limit order markets (LOMs) clearly establishes a need for economic and statistical models of these mechanisms.
This chapter discusses some approaches, but it should be admitted at the
outset that no comprehensive and realistic models (either statistical or
economic) exist.

One might start with the view that a limit order, being a bid or offer,
is simply a dealer quote by another name. The implication is that a limit
order is exposed to asymmetric information risk and also must recover
noninformational costs of trade. This view supports the application of
the economic and statistical models described earlier to LOM, hybrid,
and other nondealer markets.

This perspective features a sharp division between liquidity suppliers
and demanders. This dichotomy is a useful modeling simplification, and
it will be used again in later chapters. The essence of a LOM, however, is
that these roles are blurred. Agents dynamically decide whether to supply
liquidity with limit orders or consume it with market orders. Their decisions may depend quite generally on the state of the market. Liquidity, it
is sometimes said, is supplied by the customers.

Accordingly, this chapter concentrates mostly on models that prominently feature order choice. It is easy to see why this might alter our view of
the quotes. In most of the models considered earlier, dealer optimization
and competition lead to a zero expected profit condition: The dealer can't,
on average, lose money on trades. To a customer intent on accomplishing
a trade, however, a limit order might simply be an alternative superior to
a market order. The customer's bid need not satisfy a zero expected profit
condition. It might lose money and still be preferable to a market order.

The first section considers a simple one-period model of order choice. (A dynamic multiperiod model is described in a later chapter.)

It will become apparent from this analysis that a key determinant of order choice is the probability that a particular limit order will be executed. The model initially considered here features an exogenous execution mechanism: The probability that a limit order is executed depends on its price and nothing more. This greatly simplifies the individual's decision problem. In reality, of course, execution probabilities are determined by the order choice decisions of other agents. The ask price is another's sell limit order; the latent reservation values may trigger market orders. There is, therefore, a strong dependence between an agent's own order choice problem and the order choices made by others in the past and in the future. Ideally, the solution to the order choice problem should be consistent with the assumed price and execution processes. That is, the latter should arise when a set of other traders follows the strategy given by the former. This consistency is necessary for the market to be in dynamic equilibrium.

The close dependence between execution probability and order choice motivates the value of equilibrium analysis. The chapter considers two equilibrium models, due to Parlour (1998) and Foucault (1999), and some of the empirical analyses these models have motivated. The final section summarizes other models, and current directions.

12.1   The Choice between a Limit and Market Order

Most of our models of dealer quoting are characterized by indifference to execution. The zero expected profit condition underlying the Roll and asymmetric information models is conditional on a trade, in which event the dealer simply recovers his costs. The exceptions are the inventory control models where the dealer generally prefers to trade in one direction or the other. In this section we investigate a customer's order choice when there is a preference for trade. The conceptual framework is based on Cohen, Maier, Schwartz, and Whitcomb (1981) (CMSW). Related papers include Angel (1994) and Harris (1998).

We can set up a simple order choice situation by building on the model considered in section 11.2. In one version of that model, a dealer already at his portfolio optimum set his bid to include compensation for being pulled away from that optimum. The bid is defined by the condition that the expected utility is the same whether or not a customer actually executes against the bid. The present model uses the same approach to describe a customer who enters the market with a portfolio imbalance and can enter a market order, place a limit order, or do nothing.

The model is set in the CARA-normal framework. As in section 11.2 an agent (the customer) has exponential utility $U(W) = -e^{-\alpha W}$. If wealth is normally distributed, $W \sim N(\mu_W, \sigma_W^2)$, then $EU(W) = -e^{-\alpha\mu_W + \alpha^2\sigma_W^2/2}$. There is a single security with payoff $X \sim N(\mu_X, \sigma_X^2)$, and borrowing or lending is at a zero rate of interest. If the customer currently holds n shares, her expected utility is $EU_{Base} \equiv EU(W)$ where $\mu_W = n\mu_X$ and $\sigma_W^2 = n^2\sigma_X^2$. If she places a limit order to buy at price L and the limit order is hit (executed), then her expected utility is $EU_{Hit}(L) \equiv EU(W)$, computed using $\mu_W = (n+1)\mu_X - L$ and $\sigma_W^2 = (n+1)^2\sigma_X^2$. The expected utility of the limit order strategy is then $EU_{Limit}(L) = \Pr_{Hit}(L)EU_{Hit}(L) + [1 - \Pr_{Hit}(L)]EU_{Base}$ where $\Pr_{Hit}(L)$ is the probability of execution.

The limit order's execution probability is an important and difficult-to-model aspect of the problem. If the order is displayed (and in a modern electronic market, it usually will be), it changes the information and strategic incentives of other market participants. Execution probability is therefore properly modeled as an equilibrium phenomenon. Although some equilibrium models will be discussed in subsequent sections, these analyses are stylized and do not claim to achieve full and realistic characterizations of execution probabilities.

What are the underlying determinants of execution uncertainty? One way to look at things is to suppose that potential sellers arrive randomly over time, for example, as in the Poisson process assumed by Easley et al. (2002). There is then some chance that in any finite interval, no sellers will arrive.

Alternatively (or additionally), there may be uncertainty about the reservation prices of potential sellers. The dynamics of double auction start-ups often involve a progressive narrowing of the spread as buyers and sellers compete to outbid and outoffer each other. It is natural to suppose that the agents with the strongest demands for trade take the lead in this process. Yet one strategy involves letting others narrow the spread and hitting the bid or offer when this convergence is judged to be substantially complete. A newly arriving agent's visible limit order may trigger such an action.[1]

Suppose that the ith potential seller in the market is characterized by an unexpressed reservation price denoted c_i. The seller monitors the market, and if she sees a buy limit order priced at c_i or higher, she immediately enters a market order to sell. Let C denote the minimum unexpressed reservation price across all sellers in the market. A limit buy order priced at L will execute if $C \leq L$. Suppose that C is exponentially distributed with density $f(C) = \lambda \exp[-\lambda(C - \theta)]$. In this context the exponential parameter λ may be interpreted as a measure of seller aggressiveness. The lower bound of the distribution is θ (no seller reservation prices are below θ). The execution probability is simply the distribution function corresponding to this density, $\Pr_{Hit}(L) = 1 - \exp[-\lambda(L - \theta)]$ for $L \geq 0$.

With the exponential execution probability, the expected utility of a limit order strategy may be computed. For purposes of illustration, we'll assume parameter values $\alpha = 1, \mu_X = 1, \sigma_X^2 = 1, \lambda = 1$, and $\theta = 0$.

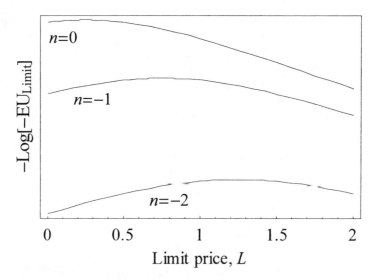

Figure 12.1. Limit order placement strategies.

Figure 12.1 depicts expected utility as a function of buy limit price for initial holdings $n=0, -1$, and -2. The concavity reflects the trade-off between paying a low price with an unaggressive limit order that rarely executes and paying a high price with an aggressive limit that is highly likely to execute.

A customer who is short one unit $(n=-1)$ can be viewed as an agent with a hedging demand. With the given numerical parameter values, her optimal limit order is priced at $L=0.75$ (and has a 53% probability of execution). This is obviously preferable to submitting no order.

Now suppose that the current ask quote in the market is A, representing a dealer or a limit order seller. With a market buy order, the customer can purchase with certainty, paying A, and achieving expected utility $EU_{Market}(A) \equiv EU(W)$, computed using $\mu_W = (n+1)\mu_X - A$ and $\sigma_W^2 = (n+1)^2\sigma_X^2$. A market order can be preferable to doing nothing. The customer is indifferent between these two strategies when $EU_{Market}(A) = EU_{Base}$. With $n=-1$ and the other assumed values, $A=1.5$. If $A < 1.5$, the customer will strictly prefer a market buy order to doing nothing.

We now turn to a comparison of market and limit order strategies. A limit order priced at $L=0.75$ is obviously preferable to a market order when $A=1.5$, because the expected utility of the latter strategy is identical to that of doing nothing. Suppose now that A moves downward from 1.5. At what point will the customer switch from a limit to a market order? The value of A such that $EU_{Limit}(L=0.75) = EU_{Market}(A)$ is $A=1.17$.

It is noteworthy that the switch point is well above the optimal limit price. CMSW compare this to gravitational pull. (When the market ask price, approaching from above, hits 1.17, the limit order buyer is pulled to the ask—switches to a market buy order.) CMSW show that the principal necessary condition for gravitational pull is that $\lim_{L \to A} \Pr_{Hit}(L)$ is bounded away from unity, that is, that there is a discontinuity in the execution probability at the ask price. Even as L approaches A in the limit, some execution uncertainty remains. They suggest that the gravitational pull effect can explain the existence of a finite bid ask spread, even when prices are continuous.

12.2   Equilibrium

The order choice model relies on an exogenous (and ad hoc) execution mechanism. In reality, execution probabilities are fundamentally endogenous. An agent's own choice depends on the execution probability, which in turn depends on her conjectures about the choices faced by other agents who arrive after her. This linkage will tend to mitigate the direct effect of a change in the market environment. Something that makes an immediate market order more expensive (e.g., an access fee) will make a limit order more attractive. But customers arriving later will also prefer limit orders, driving down the execution probability, thereby making an immediate limit order *less* attractive. The outcome of these opposing forces is best characterized by an analysis of the equilibrium (as noted, for example, by CMSW).

Equilibrium analyses of limit order markets have been suggested by Kumar and Seppi (1994), Chakravarty and Holden (1995), Parlour (1998), Foucault (1999), Foucault, Kadan, and Kandel (2001), and Goettler, Parlour, and Rajan (2005). The following sections describe two representative models.

12.2.1   The Parlour (1998) Equilibrium Model

In the Parlour model, executions arise from market orders submitted by other traders facing their own order choice problems. The model abstracts from many familiar features of a security market. There is no uncertainty about the asset's cash flows, nor is there price determination (at least in the usual sense). Despite these limitations, however, it elegantly illustrates the key equilibrium interaction that connects an agent's order choice and her beliefs about similar choices made by others in the future.

There is one security. It is traded in day 1 and pays off a certain amount V on day 2. On day 1, at each of the times $t = 1, \ldots, T$, a randomly drawn customer (agent t) arrives at the market. Agents are first characterized as potential buyers or sellers. With probability one-half, the arriving agent is a potential buyer: She has an endowment of cash that she can use to purchase one share. Otherwise the agent is a potential seller: She holds one share, which can be sold for cash. Agent t's preferences are given by a utility function $U(C_1, C_2) = C_1 + \beta_t C_2$, where β_t is a time preference parameter. Across agents, the β_t are randomly distributed over an interval $(\underline{\beta}, \bar{\beta})$. The form of the distribution, and in particular the likelihood of outcomes near the endpoints, will affect agents' eagerness to trade. Several alternative distributions will be considered. A potential seller with a low value of β_t will be eager to sell; a potential buyer with a low β_t will be disinclined to purchase. Despite strong preference for current consumption, he cannot sell short. Nor can a potential seller with a high β_t buy on margin. An agent, on arriving at the market, may decide to submit no orders and keep his existing positions.

We now turn to the details of the trading mechanism. The bid and ask prices B and A are fixed, with $B < V < A$. The limit order book is described by the number of shares on the bid and ask sides, n_t^B and n_t^A, immediately prior to the arrival of agent t. If agent t enters a limit buy order, then $n_{t+1}^B = n_t^B + 1$ (and similarly for limit sell orders). If $n_t^A \geq 1$ and agent t enters a buy market order, then $n_{t+1}^A = n_t^A - 1$, that is, the order executes against the book. Limit orders in the book are executed in first-in, first-out time priority. If agent t enters a buy market order when the book is empty, the order will execute (at price A) against a dealer. Dealers stand ready to buy any amount at B or sell any amount at A. They must yield to customers, in that any customer limit order must be filled before a dealer can buy or sell. Dealers do not behave strategically or actively.

Agent's beliefs and optimal strategies are determined by recursively working backward from time T. This recursion can be described as follows. For agent T, a limit order is pointless, because there are no remaining opportunities for a market order to arrive. If she is a potential seller, she will compare the utility of doing nothing ($\beta_T V$) with the utility of selling at the bid (B). If $\beta_T V < B \Leftrightarrow \beta_T < B/V$, then she'll enter a market sell order. Given a particular distribution for β_T, we can compute the probability that agent T will enter a market sell order. A similar computation gives the probability of a market buy order.

Now consider agent $T - 1$. If he's a buyer and $n_{T-1}^B = 0$, he can enter a buy limit order. This will be executed if agent T enters a market sell order, the probability of which we just computed. If $n_{T-1}^B \geq 1$, agent $T - 1$'s limit buy will not be first in the execution queue, and therefore cannot be executed in the one remaining period. Given agent $T - 1$'s direction (potential buyer or seller), n_{T-1}^B, n_{T-1}^A, and the limit order execution probabilities, his optimal strategy depends on β_{T-1}. Parlour demonstrates that there are cutoffs $\underline{\beta}_{Limit}^{Buy}$ and $\bar{\beta}_{Limit}^{Buy}$ (functions of time, the state of the book, and the execution probabilities) such that if $\beta_{T-1} < \underline{\beta}_{Limit}^{Buy}$, agent $T - 1$ does nothing; if $\underline{\beta}_{Limit}^{Buy} < \beta_{T-1} < \bar{\beta}_{Limit}^{Buy}$, he enters a limit buy order; and if $\bar{\beta}_{Limit}^{Buy} < \beta_{T-1}$, a market buy order. Given the distribution of β_{T-1} we can compute the probabilities of these events. These define the limit

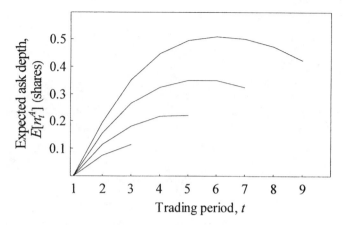

Figure 12.2. Depth of the book over time.

order execution probabilities for time $T - 2$ limit orders, which define agent $T - 2$'s optimal strategies, and so on.

For many of the models discussed in this book, exposition is simplified by focusing exclusively on one side of the market (e.g., buy market orders hitting the ask side of the book). It is noteworthy that we can't do this for the Parlour model, for example, by restricting the backward recursions to computations involving limit sell execution probabilities. The reason is that a limit sell order can only be executed by market buy orders occurring in the future. The relative attractiveness of these buy market orders will depend on the execution probabilities of limit *buy* orders. Thus, execution probabilities for buy and sell limit orders are jointly determined over time.

The equilibrium features can be illustrated by numerical example. We set $V = 5.5$, $B = 5$, and $A = 6$. Initially, we assume that the β_t are uniformly distributed over the interval $(0, 2)$. Figure 12.2 depicts the expected depth of the limit order book over time for trading days of $T = 3$, 5, 7, and 9 periods. Starting from an empty book at $t = 1$, the depth increases as the book tends to fill. The books fill more rapidly for the markets with larger Ts: with longer trading days, a limit order is more attractive because there are more opportunities for it to be executed. Near the end of the trading day, however, the depth drops.

Next, consider the model with $T = 5$. Figure 12.3 depicts the probabilities of various events at each trading opportunity. Limit order usage declines over time, while market order usage increases.

Next we consider alternative hypotheses about the agents' preferences. Figure 12.4 depicts three candidate distributions for the β_t. Panel A is the uniform distribution used in the previous examples. The distribution in panel B is triangular. It is concentrated around unity, and exhibits a relatively low likelihood of extreme realizations (few eager traders).

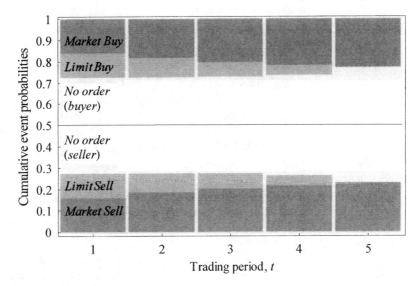

Figure 12.3. Event probabilities.

Panel C depicts an inverted triangular distribution in which the probabilities are elevated at the ends (many eager traders).

Intuition suggests that the expected depths of the book across the distributions should be inversely related to the likelihood of extreme values. (More eager traders imply more market orders and fewer limit orders.) This is indeed the case. For a market with a total of $T=7$ trading

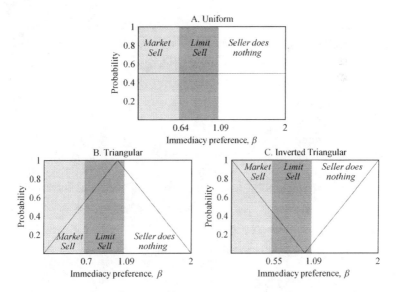

Figure 12.4. Distribution of betas.

periods, expected depth prior to the third arriving agent is $E\left[n^A_{T=3}\right]$ is 0.19 when the β_t are inverted triangular, 0.27 for the uniform, and 0.37 for the triangular distributions.

What may initially seem less intuitive is the behavior of the strategy cutoff points. Figure 12.4 also depicts for each distribution the β regions where a potential seller who arrives at time $t = 3$ and encounters an empty book will use a market order, use a limit order, or do nothing. For the uniform distribution, the cutoff between a market and limit order is $\underline{\beta}^{Limit}_{Sell} = 0.64$. A potential seller with $\beta_3 = 0.65$ would prefer a limit order. The corresponding cutoff for the triangular distribution is $\underline{\beta}^{Limit}_{Sell} = 0.70$, implying that a seller with $\beta_3 = 0.65$ would prefer a market order. That is, holding β_3 fixed, switching from a uniform to triangular distributions shifts the agent from a limit to a market order. Yet we have argued that the triangular distribution implies less urgency and therefore fewer market orders in equilibrium.

The resolution of this apparent inconsistency lies in the fact that agent 3's decisions are driven by the expected future actions of others. With the triangular distribution, extreme realizations for β_4, β_5, β_6, and β_7 are less likely. It is less probable that a limit order entered by agent 3 will be executed, so for this agent a market order becomes more desirable. The value of equilibrium models lies in their ability to illuminate interactions of this sort.

The Parlour model has a number of empirical implications for the dynamics of prices and orders. The predictions most commonly invoked in empirical modeling, however, concern the relation between limit order usage and the state of the book. These may be stated as follows:

i. An increase in book depth on the bid side decreases the probability that a buyer will submit a limit order.
ii. An increase in book depth on the offer side increases the probability that a buyer will submit a limit order.

Predictions for sell limit orders are symmetric. Prediction (i) is a consequence of limit order queuing: An order added to a book when there is already large depth has more orders standing in front of it, and a lower probability of execution. This same logic will be used by future sellers conditioning on the offer side of the book. High offer-side depth decreases the attractiveness of limit orders for them, making it more likely that they will use a market sell order. This gives prediction (ii).

12.2.2   The Foucault (1999) Equilibrium Model

The Foucault model also exhibits a dynamic consistency that links execution probabilities with order choice. Whereas the implications of the

Parlour model primarily involve dynamic order choice, Foucault's results are cross-sectional. As in the Parlour model, at each time $t = 1, \ldots, T$ an agent arrives in the market. Here, though, T is a random stopping time: At each t, the probability that trading will terminate is $(1 - \rho)$. If trading terminates, the security pays off $V_T = v_0 + \sum_{t=1}^{T} \varepsilon_t$ where the ε_t are independently distributed value innovations, $\varepsilon_t = \pm\sigma$, with each realization having a probability of one-half.

At each time t (assuming that the game is not over), a trader arrives. The trader is characterized by the reservation price, $R_t = v_t + y_t$, where $y_t = \pm L$, with each realization having a probability of one-half. y_t is independent of v_t at all leads and lags, and hence is not informative about the value. Instead, it arises from portfolio or liquidity considerations that are not explicitly modeled. y_t drives the direction of the agent's desired trade (buy or sell).

If a trade is executed at price P, a buyer will have utility $U(y_t) = V_T + y_t - P$. A seller will have utility $U(y_t) = P - (V_T + y_t)$. The state of the book at the arrival of agent t is $s_t = \{A_t, B_t\}$, the best ask and bid in the book. If there is nothing on the bid side, $B_t = -\infty$; if there is nothing on the ask side, $A_t = +\infty$. Agent t knows s_t, v_t, and y_t and can take one of the following actions. If the book is not empty, he can hit either the bid or the ask with a market order. Alternatively, he can place both a limit buy and a limit sell order. If the book is empty, this latter strategy is the only one available (apart from the suboptimal strategy of doing nothing).

A trader gets one shot at the market. He doesn't have the opportunity to return and revise the order. Furthermore, limit orders are valid only for one period. This implies that the book is either empty or full. The probability of execution for a limit order depends on the limit price in the usual way. Here, though, the execution probability is not an ad hoc functional form but instead arises endogenously. Specifically, agent t knows the distribution of v_{t+1}, and the distribution of the characteristics for the agent $t + 1$. This enables him to derive the execution probability for any given limit price.

Despite the simplicity of the model, the strategic considerations regarding order choice are quite rich. First consider execution risk of a limit order when there is no possibility of change in the underlying asset value ($\sigma = 0$). Part of the execution risk arises from the random characteristics of the next trader. If $y_t = +L$ (a natural buyer) and $y_{t+1} = +L$ as well, a trade is unlikely. So a limit order can fail to execute because the two parties wish to trade in the same direction. A limit order submitted at time t might also fail to execute, however, because $t + 1 = T$, that is, the market closes.

If we now allow for nonzero value innovations ($\sigma > 0$), a buy limit order submitted at time t (for example) also faces the risk that $\varepsilon_{t+1} = -\sigma$. This corresponds to the real-world situation of a limit order that can't be canceled promptly in response to a public news announcement. This is a form of the winner's curse. It increases the chance that an agent's limit order will execute but decreases the agent's gain from the trade (and perhaps drives it negative). The limit order is said to be picked off subsequent to a public information event.

A move in the other direction ($\varepsilon_{t+1} = +\sigma$) decreases the chance of execution (but increases the agent's gains from an execution). This situation occurs in actual trading situations when the market "moves away" from a limit order, often leaving the trader (a) wishing he'd originally used a market order, and (b) chasing the market with more aggressively priced limit or market orders. (This strategy is considered in chapter 15 but is not available to agents in the Foucault model.)

The predictions of the model are sensible. As in the analyses of individual order choice, when the opposite side quote is distant, a trader is more likely to use a limit order. The fundamental risk of a security, σ, is a key variable. If σ increases (higher fundamental risk) then a given limit order faces a higher pick-off risk. This causes limit order traders to fade their prices (make them less aggressive) and the spread widens. Market orders become more expensive, leading traders to favor limit orders. The order mix shifts in favor of limit orders, but fewer of them execute. This is a comparative statics result and thus best viewed as a cross-sectional prediction (across firms) rather than dynamic one (what happens when the volatility changes over time).

12.3 Empirical Event Models

Initial studies of limit order markets focused on the Tokyo Stock Exchange (Lehmann and Modest (1994) and Hamao and Hasbrouck (1995)) and the Paris Bourse (Biais, Hillion and Spatt (1995)). The latter noted that for many purposes the evolution of a market can be described by a sequence of well-defined events. A minimal set of events for a LOM, for example, consists of order submissions (buy or sell, market or limit) and cancellations. We might refine this classification by treating limit orders at different prices as different events and similarly for cancellations. The content of the equilibrium models lies in their predictions about the relative probabilities of these events.

A natural statistical framework for modeling the event occurrences is the multinomial logit model. (Greene (2002) provides an excellent discussion.) Let the possible events (outcomes) be indexed by $j = 0, \ldots N$, and let Y_t denote the outcome at time t. Outcome probabilities are then given by the system of equations:

$$\frac{\Pr(Y_t = i)}{\Pr(Y_t = 0)} = \exp[\alpha_i + Z_t \beta_i] \quad \text{for } i = 1, \ldots, N. \tag{12.1}$$

Z_t is a vector of conditioning variables (which must be known prior to outcome determination). The model parameters are the intercepts α_i and the coefficients β_i. Note that although there are $N+1$ outcomes, there are only N equations. This is a consequence of the requirement that the probabilities sum to one. Outcome zero is the reference event. The conditioning information Z_t will presumably include summary statistics on the depth in the book, recent volume and volatility, and (in a cross-sectional application) security-specific information, such as return variance, market capitalization, and so on. One can push the definition of *predetermined* to include order size. Even though this is not public information prior to the outcome determination, it is presumably known to the agent making the decision.

In modeling discrete choices, it is sometimes possible to order the outcomes. For example, observations of daily weather that are coded as cold, mild, and hot are logically modeled as ordered transformations of an underlying continuous variable (the temperature) that is unobserved (at least within the context of the model). If a car buyer's color preferences are observed to be red, blue, or green, however, there is no obvious natural ordering.

Ordered outcomes often result in a more parsimonious model. An ordered multinomial logit model, for example, has the form:

$$\text{logit}(\Pr(Y_t \leq i)) = \alpha_i + Z_t\beta \quad \text{for } i = 0, \ldots, N, \tag{12.2}$$

where the logit transformation is $\text{logit}(x) = x/(1-x)$. One key difference between equations (12.1) and (12.2) is that the β coefficients in the ordered logit model are common to all outcomes. This may simplify estimation, presentation, and interpretation of the results, particularly if Z_t is large.

Does the set of limit order market events have a natural ordering? Within a single direction (buy or sell), limit orders are clearly ordered by price. Market orders can be placed on the same ordering by imputing to them a limit price equal to the bid or offer which they hit. (Many systems in fact require all orders to be priced.) The Parlour model suggests such an ordering, with β_t as the latent continuous variable. It may also seem natural to place buys and sells in the same ordering, implicitly viewing sales as resulting from negative demand. However, this is not generally compatible with the Parlour model, as the β ranges associated with optimal strategies overlap for buyers and sellers. It is also difficult to place cancellations on this scale.

Representative analyses using unordered logit specifications include Smith (2000), Ellul et al. (2002) Hasbrouck and Saar (2003); Griffiths et al. (2000) and Renaldo (2004) employ ordered specifications. The studies differ in their particulars and often in their conclusions. In describing dynamic variation in order choice, the most consistent finding concerns the bid-ask spread: When the spread is wide, order choice tilts in favor of a limit order. The Parlour prediction that same-side depth favors a market order is supported by Renaldo, Ellul et al., and Hasbrouck and Saar.

Support for the hypothesis that an increase in opposite-side depth favors limit orders, however, is less clear. The effects of volatility in the cross-section (across firms) are also mixed (Hasbrouck and Saar (2003), Smith (2000)).

The sequential event analyses discussed herein are motivated the economic analyses considered earlier in the chapter and are best viewed as attempts to test these analyses and guide their refinement. LOMs are sufficiently complex, however, that a case can be made in some situations for atheoretic statistical modeling (Farmer, Patelli, and Zovko (2005)).

13

Depth

In addition to best bid and offers, most modern financial markets present their customers with full price/quantity schedules, essentially supply and demand curves for instantaneous trade. This chapter explores the determinants of these schedules and what might be learned from their analysis.

The stylized empirical fact is that the supply and demand schedules appear to be too steep. As an illustration, recall that in the basic sequential trade model, the price at which an order is executed is equal to the expectation of the security value (conditional on the trade). Because trade prices are equal to expectations, trade price changes mirror the revisions in expectations. In a sequence of three buy orders, for example, the price at which the last order is executed is the expected security value conditional on all three orders. Now suppose that in a limit order market, the purchases are combined into one order for three units. The order executes against the ask side of the book, at progressively higher prices as quantities at lower prices were exhausted. It would seem reasonable to suppose that the price at which the last part of the order is executed will be the new expected security value, around which the book would reform shortly after the trade.

Sandas (2001) examines a sample of OMX data. Figure 13.1 (figure 1 in the original) depicts three summary price schedules for two stocks. The steepest lines (dashed) in each graph are the mean book price schedules. The quantities on the horizontal axis are signed as the demand of the incoming market order (a negative demand is a sale that executes against the bid side of the book). The next steepest lines (dash/dotted) are the median book price schedules. The differences between mean and

131

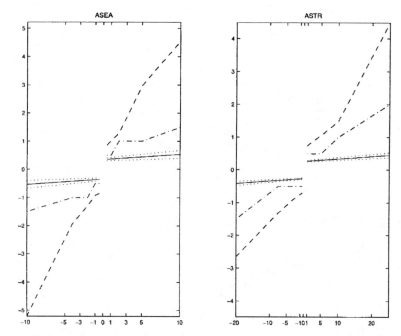

Figure 13.1. Estimated limit order book and price revision schedules for two representative OMX stocks.

median are suggestive of outliers, times when depth is extraordinarily low. The shallowest lines (solid with dotted confidence intervals) are the price revisions estimated from dynamic regression specifications similar to those discussed in chapter 8.

The differences between the price schedules in the book and the price revision functions are striking. They suggest that following a large order (one that walks deeply through the book), depth reappears at prices that are better than the marginal execution price of the order (sometimes called backfilling). The finding also suggests that agents with large quantities to buy or sell could trade more cheaply on average by splitting the orders into smaller quantities and sending them to the market over time.

This chapter discusses the connections between the price schedules posted by liquidity suppliers and the information possessed by liquidity demanders. The foundation of the chapter is a family of models originally presented by Glosten (1989, 1994). The analysis considers three canonical types of liquidity suppliers and the market environments: competitive dealer, limit order, and monopolistic dealer markets. We then turn to the liquidity demanders (customers), modeling their informational and noninformational motives for trade, and considering equilibrium in each of the three market settings. The equilibrium price schedules embody consistent beliefs and optimizing behavior across liquidity suppliers and their customers. The chapter then returns to the empirical evidence, and extensions.

13.1 Market Structures and Liquidity Suppliers

Glosten's market structures are representative of settings commonly encountered in securities trading.

13.1.1 The Competitive Dealer Market

The liquidity suppliers in this market are dealers. Each dealer quotes a price schedule that specifies a unit price for the entire amount the customer wishes to trade. A customer discloses the full size of his trade. This rules out the possibility of order splitting. A customer with 100,000 shares to buy, for example, cannot approach two dealers and buy 50,000 shares from each at the price corresponding to a full order size of 50,000 shares (which is what each dealer sees). The customer can in principle buy 50,000 shares with each dealer, as long as each dealer knows that the full amount is 100,000 shares. The customer gains nothing from this, however, as each dealer sets the unit price based on the full amount.

In this situation the customer has an obvious incentive to lie. Normally, he would be tempted to disclose an amount smaller than the true quantity, although if he wished to momentarily establish a fictive price he might exaggerate the total quantity. Though there is no foolproof way for the dealer to detect such cheating, unusual volume or price movements may be suggestive. Dealers may punish suspected infractions by subsequently offering poor terms of trade or completely refusing to deal with the customer.

The dealer's pricing criterion is the one familiar from the sequential and strategic trading models: The price must be equal to the expected value of the security conditional on the trade. If the price is higher than this expectation, competitors will find it profitable to offer more aggressive terms; if the price is lower, the dealer will lose money. Equilibrium is not inevitable. If the informational advantage of the customers is sufficiently high, no feasible pricing schedule may exist, and the market fails.

13.1.2 The Limit Order Book

The price schedule in a limit order book is the aggregation of unexecuted orders, typically small orders submitted by numerous and diverse traders. For pricing, however, the distinctive feature of the book is that the agent who places a limit order does not know the total size of the incoming order that will cause his own order to execute. Unlike the dealer in the last section, the limit order trader does not get the opportunity to set the terms of order based on knowledge of the total incoming order. A large marketable order will "walk through the book," with the first portion executing at the most favorable price and subsequent portions on less favorable terms. For this reason, executions against the book are discriminating, in the same sense that a discriminating monopolist picks customers off the demand curve based on their willingness to pay.

Discrimination changes the incentives to provide liquidity. To see this, suppose that the best ask in the market is $20.10, and that the total quantity offered at this and higher prices is 100,000 shares. A trader is contemplating a limit sell order for 100 shares at $20. In the standard sequential trade model, his offer price of $20 would be the expectation of the security value, conditional on an incoming customer order to purchase 100 shares. But in the book his order will also be executed (at $20) if the incoming order is a purchase of 100,100 shares. This larger quantity obviously conveys a stronger positive signal about the security value. There is ample opportunity for ex post regret, because the trader might sell at $20 while (nearly simultaneously) sellers deeper in the book are selling at higher prices. The limit order seller cannot prevent this from happening, but he can set his price to reflect the possibility. In a discriminating book, therefore, a limit order is priced at the "tail expectation," that is, the expected value of the security conditional on an incoming order of a size just sufficient to trigger execution or anything larger.

13.1.3 A Monopolistic Dealer

Most security markets are well approximated by the competitive dealer or limit order paradigms just described. But in a market for a thinly traded security or one in which there are regulatory or institutional barriers to entry, a dealer may possess market power. In the third setting we consider a monopolistic dealer.

One feature of this situation is the standard result. The monopolist enjoys rents, abnormal profits that are not competed away. A more surprising result is that a monopolistic market may benefit customers (relative to the competitive dealer market). In a competitive dealer market (or in the limit order market, for that matter) each point on the price schedule is a competitive equilibrium, in the sense that it is open to entry by new liquidity suppliers. If one point in the price schedule is profitable, a new entrant can supply liquidity at that point only. This rules out price schedules dependent on cross-subsidization, for example, with profits on numerous small trades subsidizing losses on infrequent large trades. A monopolistic dealer, however, is not so restricted. He seeks to maximize expected profits over the entire price schedule. Profitable points on his price schedule are not contested and so may offset losses at other points. Cross-subsidization may enable the market to stay open when a competitive dealer market might fail.

13.2   The Customers

To most effectively compare and contrast the three market regimes, we will analyze them holding constant the remaining features of the economy. This characterization is stylized, in keeping with the demands of model tractability. The notation is similar to Glosten's.

The model is set in the CARA-normal framework described in section 11.2. There is one risky security with random payoff $X \sim N(\mu_X, \sigma_X^2)$. An incoming customer initially has n units of the security and may purchase q additional units. The initial endowment may be negative, reflecting a previously established short position or a hedging demand not explicitly modeled. Likewise, a negative q corresponds to a sale of the security. The customer has no initial endowment of cash. To finance purchases, he may borrow at zero interest. Proceeds of sales are invested at zero interest.

A purchase of q requires an expenditure of $R(q)$, which is interpreted as the total revenue received by the liquidity supplier(s). In the dealer models, the customer trades the entire quantity at a single quoted price, and $R(q) = P(q) \times q$ where $P(q)$ is the dealers' pricing schedule. In the limit order market, though, $R(q)$ arises from walking through a continuum of prices. Subsequent to trading, the risky payoff is known. At this point the customer's terminal wealth is $W = (n + q)X - R(q)$. The customer chooses q to maximize an expected utility function of the form $EU(W) = E[-e^{-\rho W}]$. The first-order condition for maximization of the certainty equivalent is

$$\mu_X - (q + n)\rho\sigma_X^2 - R'(q) = 0. \qquad (13.1)$$

Prior to trade the customer receives a signal (noisy indication) of the security value $S = X + \varepsilon$ where $\varepsilon \sim N(0, \sigma_\varepsilon^2)$ independent of n. Using the bivariate normal projection results introduced in section 7.1, conditional on S, $X \sim N(\mu_{X|S}, \sigma_{X|S}^2)$ where $\mu_{X|S} = (\sigma_\varepsilon^2 \mu_X + \sigma_X^2 S)/(\sigma_\varepsilon^2 + \sigma_X^2)$, and $\sigma_{X|S}^2 = \sigma_\varepsilon^2 \sigma_X^2/(\sigma_\varepsilon^2 + \sigma_X^2)$.

We now turn our attention to what the liquidity suppliers can infer given the customer's trade. If the liquidity suppliers knew n, then given q (and, of course, their revenue function) they could deduce the customer's signal. Both parties would then have the same information, and there would be no informational motive for trade. A richer and more realistic interaction results when the liquidity suppliers do not know the endowment n. More precisely, we assume that across the population of potential customers, endowments are normally distrubted, $n \sim N(0, \sigma_n^2)$, independent of X and ε. The customer's trade now arises, in the liquidity suppliers' view, from a mix of informational and noninformational motives.

The customer's first-order condition plays a crucial role in the liquidity suppliers' inference. Noting that $\rho > 0$, equation 13.1 may be rearranged as

$$M + q\rho\sigma_{X|S}^2 = \mu_{X|S} - \rho\sigma_{X|S}^2 n, \tag{13.2}$$

where $M \equiv R'(q)$ is the suppliers' marginal revenue, or equivalently (at the optimum) the customer's marginal valuation. Conditional on the trade, the suppliers know M and q, and therefore the left-hand quantity in equation (13.2). Knowing the total does not suffice to resolve the two terms on the right-hand side, the informational ($\mu_{X|S}$) and hedging ($\rho\sigma_{X|S}^2 n$) components. It does, nevertheless serve as a useful signal. Denoting this quantity as ω,

$$\omega = \mu_{X|S} - \rho\sigma_{X|S}^2 n = \frac{\sigma_\varepsilon^2 \mu_X + \sigma_X^2 \left(X + \varepsilon - \sigma_\varepsilon^2 \rho n\right)}{\sigma_\varepsilon^2 + \sigma_X^2}. \tag{13.3}$$

To the liquidity suppliers, therefore, ω is a noisy signal of X. ω and X are jointly bivariate normal with means $\mu_\omega = \mu_X$. Using the normal projection results, $\mu_{X|\omega} \equiv E[X|\omega] = \mu_X + (\omega - \mu_X)\sigma_{\omega X}/\sigma_\omega^2$, where $\sigma_\omega^2 = \sigma_X^4 \left(\sigma_X^2 + \sigma_\varepsilon^2 + \rho^2\sigma_n^2\sigma_\varepsilon^4\right)/\left(\sigma_X^2 + \sigma_\varepsilon^2\right)^2$ and $\sigma_{\omega X} = \sigma_X^4/\left(\sigma_X^2 + \sigma_\varepsilon^2\right)$.

13.3   Equilibrium in the Three Regimes

13.3.1   The Competitive Dealer Market

We conjecture a linear price schedule: $P(q) = k_0 + k_1 q$, where k_0 and k_1 are yet-to-be-determined constants. Then $M = R'(q) = \partial/\partial q[q(k_0 + k_1 q)] = k_0 + 2k_1 q$. Thus $\omega = (k_0 + 2k_1 q) + q\rho\sigma_{X|S}^2$. The equilibrium condition is $P(q) = \mu_{X|\omega}$, which then becomes

$$k_0 + k_1 q = \mu_X + \left[\left((k_0 + 2k_1 q) + q\rho\sigma_{X|S}^2\right) - \mu_X\right]\sigma_{\omega X}/\sigma_\omega^2. \tag{13.4}$$

This must hold for all q, giving:

$$k_0 = \mu_X \quad \text{and} \quad k_1 = \frac{\rho\sigma_X^2\sigma_\varepsilon^2}{\rho^2\sigma_n^2\sigma_\varepsilon^4 - \sigma_X^2 - \sigma_\varepsilon^2}. \tag{13.5}$$

For the price schedule to be upward-sloping (and therefore a valid equilibrium), it is necessary that $\sigma_\varepsilon^2 \left(\rho^2\sigma_n^2\sigma_\varepsilon^2 - 1\right) - \sigma_X^2 > 0$. Furthermore,

$$\frac{\partial k_1}{\partial\sigma_X^2} > 0, \quad \frac{\partial k_1}{\partial\sigma_\varepsilon^2} < 0, \quad \frac{\partial k_1}{\partial\sigma_n^2} < 0, \quad \text{and} \quad \frac{\partial k_1}{\partial\rho} < 0.$$

The intuition for these results lies in the fact that the essential danger for the liquidity suppliers is loss associated with buying at $P(q) > X$ or selling at $P(q) < X$. Higher σ_X^2 increases this likelihood. Higher σ_ε^2 however, decreases the customer's certainty in his signal, and so lessens the motive for informational trade. Higher σ_n^2 or ρ increases the likelihood that the customer is trading mostly for liquidity reasons.

It is worth emphasizing that the $\sigma_\varepsilon^2 \left(\rho^2 \sigma_n^2 \sigma_\varepsilon^2 - 1 \right) - \sigma_X^2 > 0$ condition can be violated by reasonable parameter values. In these cases, no equilibrium price schedule exists, and the market fails. When this happens, customers forgo the hedging benefits from trading (risk sharing). If they could credibly disclose their signals, they would willingly do so, forgoing any informational advantage from their trades but benefiting from better hedging.

13.3.2 The Limit Order Market

We will consider limit orders on the offer side of the market. A customer purchase of q shares executes by walking through the book. The price schedule $P(q)$ gives the price of the last limit order executed.

Let m denote the random marginal valuation of incoming customer, and let $\underline{m}(q)$ denote the value of m for which the limit order priced at $P(q)$ is the last limit order executed. Obviously $P(q) \geq E[X|m = \underline{m}(q)]$. That is, the liquidity supplier won't regret the trade if his is the last order executed. His order, however, will also be executed with the arrival of any larger quantities. Taking into account this possibility, his price must be at least as large as $E[X|m \geq \underline{m}(q)]$. That is, any customer with $m > \underline{m}(q)$ will purchase more than q units. The competitive equilibrium condition is therefore $P(q) = E[X|m \geq \underline{m}(q)]$. The right-hand-side quantity is sometimes described as the upper-tail (conditional) expectation. It should be noted that although this condition prevents ex post regret in expectation across all order sizes, certain trade sizes may still be unprofitable.

The computation of the upper-tail expectation uses the properties of truncated normal variables (see Greene (2002)). Truncation refers to the restriction of a random variable to a region above (or below) a given cutoff point. If $X \sim N(\mu, \sigma^2)$ then the truncated expectation is

$$E[X|X \geq \underline{X}] = \mu + \sigma \left[\phi \left(\frac{X - \mu}{\sigma} \right) \bigg/ \left(1 - \Phi \left(\frac{X - \mu}{\sigma} \right) \right) \right], \qquad (13.6)$$

where ϕ and Φ are the standard normal density and distribution functions. Next consider the linear projection when Z and Y are bivariate normal: $X - a_0 + a_1 Z + e$. Under bivariate normality Z and e are independent, so $E[X|Z \geq \underline{Z}] = a_0 + a_1 E[Z|Z \geq \underline{Z}]$.

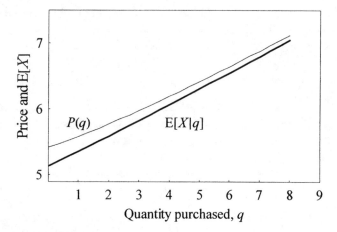

Figure 13.2. Price and expectations revision schedules in a limit order book.

Although the equilibrium condition differs from that of the competitive dealer model, the customer's first-order condition and the joint normality of ω, X and m. Using (13.2) and (13.3),

$$E[X|m \geq \underline{m}] = \mu_X + \frac{\sigma_{\omega X}\left(q\rho\sigma_{X|S}^2 - \mu_X + E[m|m \geq \underline{m}]\right)}{\sigma_\omega^2}. \qquad (13.7)$$

At any given quantity q, a customer will trade if his marginal valuation $m \geq P(q)$. In equilibrium, $P(q) = E[X|m \geq \underline{m}]$. This must be solved numerically, and doing so for the continuum of quantities yields the price schedule.

Figure 13.2 depicts $P(q)$ for the indicated parameter values. As noted, this is the upper-tail expectation. The second line in the figure is the point expectation given the total size of the order. There are several features of interest. Both functions are nonlinear (due in part to the nonlinearity of the upper-tail expectation). Also note that some limit orders will be unprofitable ex post. Consider the marginal limit order priced to sell at $q = 2$. If the size of the incoming order is in fact $q = 2$, the limit order is profitable: $P(q=2) > E[X|q=2]$. The limit order will also execute, however, if $q = 8$, in which case $P(q=2) < E[X|q=8]$, the limit order incurs a loss. Finally, $\lim_{q \to 0^+} P(q) > \mu_X = 5$, that is, even a infinitesimal purchase will incur a transaction cost. Another way of putting this is that the bid-ask spread is positive even for arbitrarily small quantities. (In the competitive dealer model, in contrast, $\lim_{q \to 0^+} P(q) = \lim_{q \to 0^-} P(q) = \mu_X$.) The pricing schedule is sufficiently discriminatory that a ω considerably greater than μ_X is necessary before the customer will consider an even an infinitesimal purchase.

The relationship between the supply schedule and expectation revision functions is broadly similar to the empirical finding depicted in figure 13.1, with the latter lying below the former. Price discrimination in the book can therefore potentially account for the empirical evidence. We will subsequently return to this point.

13.3.3 The Monopolistic Dealer

The monopolistic dealer sets a price schedule to maximize $E[P(q) - E[X|q]]$, where the outer expectation is over all incoming customers (or equivalently, quantities). As the customer demands depend on $P(q)$, $P(q)$ implicitly enters into $E[X|q]$. We will not present the general solution here, but will instead discuss the solution associated with the parameter values used to illustrate the limit order book. Using the same parameter values as in the previous cases, the monopolistic dealer market has prices and expectations depicted in figure 13.3.

As in the limit order case, some quantities are unprofitable. The reason for this, however, is quite different here. The dealer knows the full q (as in the competitive dealer case) and is not exposed to an upper-tail expectation. Instead, the region of losses is necessary to ensure the separation that makes trades at smaller quantities profitable. If the dealer would, for example, refuse to sell at $q > 6$, customers who sought large amounts would submit the largest feasible order, pooling at $q = 6$. This would lead to losses at $q = 6$ larger than the figure indicates.

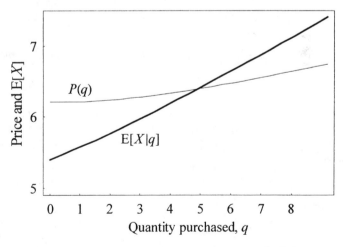

Figure 13.3. Price and expectations revision schedules for a monopolistic dealer.

13.4   Additional Empirical Evidence on Limit Order Book Price Schedules

Sandas (2001) estimates for his OMX data a modified version of the Glosten model. Sandas's model is dynamic in the sense of allowing for successive order arrivals. It is assumed that the book is in a static equilibrium prior to each order arrival. The specification also assumes an exogenous order process. Finally, although the earlier exposition was simplified by allowing prices to be continuous, Glosten (1994) actually uses discrete prices. Sandas's model uses discrete prices as well.

The security value (conditional on public information) is X_t, with dynamics: $X_t = X_{t-1} + d_t$. The increment d_t reflects the information content of orders that have arrived through time t and additional public nontrade information. As before, we'll analyze only the sell side of the book and arriving buy orders. Treatment of the bid side is symmetric. The ask (sell) side of the book is described by a price vector $(p_1 \ p_2 \ \cdots \ p_k)$ ordered so that p_1 is the lowest (most aggressive). The associated vector of quantities is $(Q_1 \ Q_2 \ \cdots \ Q_k)$.

The incoming order is a purchase of b shares, where the distribution of b is assumed exponential with parameter λ: $f(b) = e^{-b\lambda}/\lambda$. The revision in beliefs subsequent to the order is given by: $E[X_{t+1}|X_t, b] = X_t + \alpha b$, where $\alpha > 0$. The order processing cost is γ. If a limit order priced at p_1 is executed, the profit (per unit traded) is $p_1 - \gamma - E[X_{t+1}|X_t, b] = p_1 - X_t - \gamma - \alpha b$.

Suppose that the sell limit orders at the price p_1 are ordered in time priority, the trader wish to sell an infinitesimal amount at p_1, and the cumulative quantity (her order plus everyone who is ahead of her) is q. Her order will execute if the incoming quantity is at least as high as q. Her expected profit conditional on execution is

$$E\pi_1 = E[p_1 - X_t - \gamma - \alpha b | b \geq q] = \int_q^\infty (p_1 - X_t - \gamma - \alpha b) f(b) db$$
$$= -e^{-q/\lambda}(X_t + \gamma + \alpha(q + \lambda) - p_1).$$

She will be indifferent to adding her order to the queue at this price when $q = Q_1$ where $Q_1 = (-X_t - \gamma - \alpha\lambda - p_1)/\alpha$. This might be negative for X_t just below p_1, in which case $Q_1 = 0$. At p_2 the expected profit for executed orders is:

$$E\pi_2 = E[p_2 - X_t - \gamma - \alpha b | b \geq Q_1 + q] = \int_{Q_1+q}^\infty (p_1 - X_t - \gamma - \alpha b) f(b) db$$
$$= -e^{-(q+Q_1)/\lambda}(X_t + \gamma + \alpha(q + \lambda) - p_2 + \alpha Q_1).$$

The point of indifference is given by $Q_2 = (-X_t - \gamma - \alpha\lambda + p_2 - \alpha Q_1)/\alpha$. Quantities $Q_3, Q_4, \ldots$ are computed in similar fashion. Figure 13.4 depicts

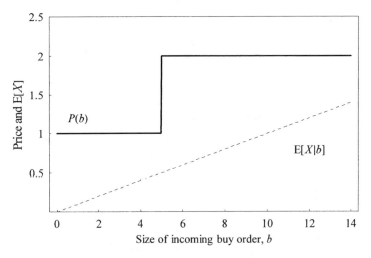

Figure 13.4. Price and expectations revision schedules in a
limit order book with discrete price levels.

the ask side of the book for parameter values $X_t = 0$, $\alpha = 0.1$, $\gamma = 0$, and
$\lambda = 5$. As in the continuous case, the expectation revision function lies
entirely below the price schedule.

In Sandas's framework, there are two sorts of conditions that can be
used to estimate the expectation revision coefficient α. One estimate is
based on the subsequent dynamic revision in prices, similar to that discussed in connection with figure 13.1. The other is based on the break-even
conditions already derived for the quantities on the book. The estimates
differ substantially. The break-even-based schedules are generally closer
to the observed schedules, the dynamic revision-based schedules are still
relatively shallow. Tests for overidentifying restrictions strongly reject
the joint use of break-even and dynamic conditions, however. The price
schedules on the book are still too steep relative to the price revisions.

With a view toward future research directions, Sandas examines a
number of model assumptions that could potentially lead to misspecification. The results suggest allowing for a more flexible distribution of
incoming order sizes, time variation in parameters, endogenous order
sizes, and effects related to intertrade times.

13.5 Hybrid Markets and Depth Improvement

In the competitive dealer market, dealers can condition on the total size
of the incoming order. Limit order traders do not have this opportunity.
Seppi (1997) models a hybrid market in which a public limit order book is
augmented by a dealer. The dealer must yield to public orders: He cannot

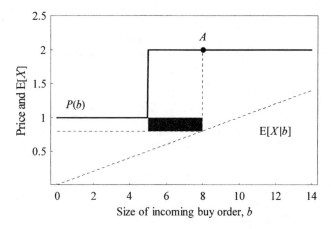

Figure 13.5. Depth improvement.

sell at a price while public customer offers at that price are left unexecuted. On the other hand, he can condition on the total order size in deciding how much to sell.

The situation can be depicted in the context of the Sandas version of the Glosten model (figure 13.5). An incoming purchase order for eight units would normally execute by walking through the book, buying five units at a price of one and three additional units at a price of two. But the revised expectation conditional on this purchase is only 0.8. The dealer would like to displace the sellers at $P = 2$, but cannot, due to public priority. He can, however, sell three units at $P = 1$. This is permissible because all public sellers at that price are satisfied. The dealer's expected profit from doing this is the shaded area.

The phenomenon is sometimes called depth improvement (see Bacidore (2002)). The buyer purchases at a lower average price than the he would have expected given the state of the book. From his viewpoint, more was available at $P = 1$ than the book was showing. The public limit order traders, on the other hand, are disadvantaged. In equilibrium, they will be less willing to provide liquidity and will post smaller quantities. The practice whereby a dealer outbids public interest was widely termed eighthing (when the tick size in U.S. equity markets was $0.125) and is sometimes now described as pennying. The depth improvement mechanism arises from a last-mover advantage enjoyed by the dealer. Rock (1990) discusses the general features of this phenomenon. He notes that it can also lead to "price improvement," because the dealer may buy or sell at prices that are better than the best published bid and offer.

14

Trading Costs: Retrospective and Comparative

T his chapter and the next address trading costs and their relation to strategy and institutional features. Economic logic suggests a definite ordering for these topics. Most economic data are the outcomes of strategies that are, at least from agents' ex ante perspectives, optimal. Thus arises the ideal paradigm of first defining agents' objectives, then enumerating the feasible strategies, mapping these strategies to costs, determining optimal (cost minimizing) strategies, and finally performing econometric analysis of observed outcomes taking into account their dependence on all prior stages of the process. The exposition will follow this sequence but is heavily shaped by the limitations of the data. The present chapter describes the microstructure literature that aims primarily at comparisons of alternative trading venues. The objectives and trading strategies considered in this context are mostly simple ones. The next chapter describes more realistic trading problems, but in a framework that is more normative and less relevant for analysis of actual data samples.

In most of the economic models considered to this point, trading problems have been posed as investment or portfolio problems, albeit ones with short horizons. Neither the identification of a trading strategy distinct from the investment decision nor the imputation of a trading cost as such has been useful or necessary. In practice, however, although investment and trading decisions should be made jointly, they are usually analyzed and implemented separately. This separation is most clearly visible in managed portfolios, where allocation decisions are made by an investment manager (stock picker) and the actual buying and selling is conducted by trading desk. The framing perspectives of the decisions can be characterized plainly as long-term versus short-term, but there are usually fundamental and far-reaching differences in the skills and information sets of the two groups.

The portfolio manager's communication of an order to the trading desk ("desk release") is only the first step in a chain of delegation. The desk may assign the order to be worked by particular broker. The broker will send the order to a particular trading venue. At each step involving discretion there is an agency relationship, which must be monitored and managed according to some observable (and ideally, quantifiable) criterion. The trading costs considered in this chapter are imputations that serve this purpose.

14.1 Overview

Some components of trading cost are direct and obvious. In this category fall commissions, transfer taxes, order submissions fees, and various account service fees. These arc usually itemized on the customer's invoice or account statement, and so are easily identified. I will generally ignore these costs, noting that in practice they can be added back in at the final stage. I suppress them not because they are trivial but because their inclusion clutters the analysis and obfuscates more subtle effects.

Trading involves many indirect costs. The most important (and usually the most easily identifiable) is the price concession associated with an execution. This is usually measured by the difference between the actual transaction price and some benchmark price that represents a "fair" market value. There are many possible choices for a benchmark, but the most common is the quote midpoint prevailing prior to the trade. This is generally called the effective cost, and corresponds to c in the basic Roll model.

Finally, because many trading strategies do not culminate in an execution, we need to impute a cost for failures. This often the most difficult determination because the consequences of failure must be assessed relative to some original intention that is rarely fully articulated.

14.2 The Implementation Shortfall

The implementation shortfall, initially suggested by Perold (1988), is a construct that both provides intuition into the aforementioned effects and contains as special cases most commonly used measures of trading cost. It is based on the divergence between actual and idealized investment cash flows. More precisely, it is the difference between the cash flows for an actual portfolio and those of a hypothetical paper portfolio for which purchases and sales occur at benchmark prices.

The mechanics can be illustrated with a simple two-date model. Suppose that there are $i = 1, \ldots, N$ securities, with the first being cash (the numeraire). Let n_0 be the vector of actual initial portfolio holdings (in shares, or, for $i = 1$, dollars), and let π_0 denote the vector of initial benchmark prices. The paper portfolio is described by a vector of holdings, v. This is a "desired" portfolio and reflects a hypothetical reallocation by the portfolio manager assuming that purchases and sales could be accomplished at the benchmark prices. Thus, the initial values of the actual and paper portfolios are equal: $n_0' \pi_0 = v' \pi_0$. The reallocation in the actual portfolio is accomplished by purchases and sales at actual trade prices p, and the final share holdings in the actual portfolio are n_1. The actual and desired holdings will diverge due to, among other things, failed trading attempts. Because a cash account is included among the assets, the reallocation is accomplished with no net cashflow in or out of the portfolio: $(n_1 - n_0)' p = 0$.

The implementation shortfall is the difference in terminal values between the paper and actual portfolios, with both valued at end of period benchmark prices π_1, and may be written as:

$$\begin{aligned} \text{Implementation Shortfall} &= (v - n_1)' \pi_1 \\ &= \underbrace{(n_1 - n_0)'(p - \pi_0)}_{\text{Execution cost}} + \underbrace{(v - n_1)'(\pi_1 - \pi_0)}_{\text{Opportunity cost}}. \end{aligned} \quad (14.1)$$

An element $n_{1,i} - n_{0,i}$ for $i > 1$ represents the number of shares of security i bought (if positive) or sold (if negative); the first element $n_{1,1} - n_{0,1}$ is the change in the cash account (noting that $\pi_{0,1} = \pi_{1,1} = p_1 = 1$). The first term on the right-hand side of equation (14.1) thus represents the cost of actual executions accomplished at actual trade prices rather than benchmark prices. The second term is driven by the divergence between actual and desired holdings and the change in benchmark prices. The implementation shortfall thus impounds the cost of establishing a particular position and the cost of divergence between that position and the one judged (by some other criteria) to be optimal. In other contexts, the second (opportunity) cost is known as the tracking error.

When the order is executed at one time but at multiple prices, p is interpreted as the share-weighted average execution price. This is also appropriate when the order is executed over time, as long as the agent being measured (trader, broker, etc.) in fact had discretion over the timing. In this case, the benchmark π_0 should be taken prior to the first execution.

Ex post either or both components of the realized implementation shortfall may be negative. An execution cost may be negative, for example, if the stock is purchased below the benchmark. An opportunity cost may be negative if an intended purchase was not completed for a stock that subsequently declined in value.

The separation of investment and trading decisions is implicit in the assumed constancy of the desired portfolio. In practice, a portfolio manager would certainly take expected trading costs into account when determining v. It is furthermore likely that v would be revised dynamically, conditional on price movements and the outcomes of previous order strategies. Thus, $(v - n_1)(\pi_1 - \pi_0)$ establishes (approximately) the worst possible case. Consider a buy order that has failed because the price has moved out of range, $\pi_1 \gg \pi_0$. The opportunity cost term is approximately the cost of buying the shares at the new, higher price. But at the new price, quite possibly the portfolio manager might seek fewer shares. This suggests that the real opportunity cost may actually be lower than the formula suggests.

Subject to this qualification, the distribution of the implementation shortfall, perhaps as summarized by its mean and variance, is a plausible basis for evaluating a trading strategy. Bearing this in mind, it is useful to consider the distributions that common strategies might imply.

First, most strategies will generally face a trade-off between expected execution and opportunity costs. Suppose we take the quote midpoint as the benchmark, and we wish to purchase a stock. A market order will achieve execution with certainty, but at a price generally above the midpoint. This will give a positive execution cost, but zero opportunity cost. Alternatively, we might submit a limit order priced below the midpoint. If the limit order is hit, the execution cost component will be negative. If the limit order is not hit, however, it is most likely to be that the price has increased, leading to a positive opportunity cost.

Second, assuming typical price dynamics, execution costs are likely to have low variance. Most limit orders are submitted near the quote midpoint. If there is no fill, the execution cost is zero. Otherwise, it is the distance between the limit price and the quote midpoint. For the unfilled portion of the order, however, opportunity costs are likely to be highly volatile, as $\pi_1 - \pi_0$ is the price change over a possibly long horizon. There is also likely to be a trade-off between the expectation and volatility of the trading cost. A market order will usually have high expected trading cost, but with little variation. (A purchase order, for example, will execute at or very close to the ask.) A limit order priced far away from the market will have a low expected shortfall but high volatility. This trade-off drives some of the more formal trading models considered in the next chapter.

It is also noteworthy that the implementation shortfall is defined at the level of the portfolio rather than the individual security. The total volatility will then reflect correlation across securities in the outcomes of limit order strategies.

Over both sides of the trade, and of course in the aggregate, execution costs are a zero-sum game as long as everyone uses the same benchmark π_0.

Opportunity costs, on the other hand, are measured relative to desired positions. There is no mechanism to ensure that unconsummated demand equals unconsummated supply.

Infeasibility of aggregate desired positions can easily lead to misleading estimates of aggregate implementation shortfalls. For example, suppose that a dealer bids $99 for one unit of the security, and offers one unit at $101, and that the rules of the market require that these quotes be firm (available for immediate execution). There are 100 traders following the security. They all receive the same information, a positive signal that causes the security value to increase to $110. At this point, they all "simultaneously" attempt to lift the dealer's offer by submitting marketable limit orders for one unit, priced at $101. Subject to the vagaries of transmission delays, the first buy order to arrive will succeed, at an execution cost of $1(=$101 − $100, the quote midpoint). At this point, the dealer revises her quotes to $109 bid, offered at $111 (thus bracketing the new value). Each of the other 99 customers will perceive an opportunity cost of $10 (=$110 − $100) and may well attribute this to sloth on the part of their brokers or their systems. Thus, the aggregate opportunity cost is $990, for an aggregate implementation shortfall of $991. It is nonsensical, of course, to suggest that aggregate welfare could be enhanced by this amount if market frictions or broker ineptitude were eliminated.

The problem is that the benchmark price of $\pi_0 = \$100$ does not come close, given the new information, to clearing the market. The profits realized by the lucky first trader are akin to lottery winnings. Individual traders might attempt to gain advantage by increasing the speed of their order submission linkages, but because only one trader can arrive first, the situation is fundamentally a tournament (in the economic sense).

14.2.1   The Implementation Cost for Liquidity Suppliers

Is implementation cost a useful criterion for liquidity suppliers? The question is important because although institutional trading desks have traditionally been liquidity demanders, the modern variant may also seek profits by opportunistically supplying liquidity. Furthermore, empirical analysis may require imputation of implementation costs when the trading motive underlying the order is unknown.

If $v = n_0$, implying that the agent already holds his desired position, the implementation shortfall reduces to $-(n_1 - n_0)(\pi_1 - p)$, the minimization of which is equivalent to maximization of the ex post profit on shares bought or sold (assuming that the final position is marked to the final benchmark price). The implementation shortfall can thus be interpreted as plausible objective function for a liquidity supplier. The decomposition into execution and opportunity costs, however, is somewhat strained. For one thing, given that $v = n_0$, the opportunity cost actually applies to filled orders. The risk-neutral liquidity suppliers (such as the dealers in the sequential trade models or the limit order traders in Glosten 1994) are indifferent to whether their bids or offers are executed. Conditional on execution, of course, their orders are priced to satisfy a zero expected profit condition. But in the absence of execution, they incur no loss.

14.2.2 Benchmark Prices

The execution cost based on the pretrade bid-ask midpoint (BAM) is also known as the effective cost. Since 2001, the U.S. SEC has required U.S. equity markets to compute effective costs and make summary statistics available on the Web (U.S. Securities and Exchange Commission 1996). The rule (605, formerly numbered 11ac1-5 and commonly referred to as "dash five") also requires computation of the realized cost. The realized cost is the execution cost computed using as a benchmark the BAM prevailing five minutes subsequent to the time the market received the order. Letting p_t denote the trade price and m_t the prevailing quote midpoint, the relationship between the effective and realized costs for a buy order is:

$$\underbrace{p_t - m_t}_{\text{Effective cost}} = \underbrace{p_t - m_{t+5}}_{\text{Realized Cost}} + m_{t+5} - m_t. \qquad (14.2)$$

The difference between effective and realized costs, $m_{t+5} - m_t$, is sometimes used as an estimate of the price impact of the trade. The realized cost can also be interpreted as the revenue of the dealer who sold to the customer (at p_t) and then covered his position at the subsequent BAM.

When a timely BAM is not available, practitioners resort to alternatives. One common benchmark used by institutional fund managers is the value-weighted average price (VWAP) of all trades over a particular interval, typically one day. VWAP is easier to compute than the effective or realized cost because it does not require matching by time. It is in a sense the answer to the question, "How well did we do relative to the representative buyer or seller?" It is commonly used to evaluate brokers. In this connection, we might raise several objections. The first is that orders vary in their degree of difficulty. A broker who is sent difficult orders will fare poorly in a VWAP evaluation. Second, if we account for a large proportion of a day's volume, our weighted average execution price will approximate VWAP (they're almost the same thing) irrespective of how the orders were handled. Third, VWAP benchmarks can be gamed (see Harris (2003)).

Other benchmarks include the previous day's close or the same day's close. Among all benchmark choices, these are likely to lead to the most variable cost estimates. This is because they will tend to be further removed in time from the actual trade and so will impound price movements over a longer period. The previous day's close, however, is of some special interest as a benchmark price due to the large number of studies based on daily data that assume feasibility of trade at that price in formulating trading strategies.

14.3 Applications of the Implementation Shortfall

14.3.1 Institutional-Level Order Data

Within the professional investment community, monitoring trading costs is regarded as good professional practice (see, for example, CFA Institute 2002). Subject to qualifications already discussed, a portfolio manager can measure the cost of the fund's trades using the implementation shortfall approach. The measurements are more useful, however, if there is some basis for comparison. Raw trading data can be reverse-engineered to construct holdings and discern strategies, so managers will generally avoid disclosure. Thus, a small industry has arisen to provide anonymity and expertise. Portfolio managers turn their order data over to a firm, which then computes trading cost estimates. Finally the firm shares summary statistics computed across all its clients.

The institutional process starts when the portfolio manager sends an order to its trading desk (desk release). The order at this stage is a general indication of quantity, price limits, urgency, and so on. The order (or a component of it) is then sent to a broker ("broker release"). At this stage, the instructions are usually more explicit. The broker will then attempt to execute the order (possibly breaking it into smaller pieces) on one or more trading venues.

The timing of the benchmark BAM depends on which stages of the process are being evaluated. If the intent is to measure the cost of the entire trading process, then the BAM should taken as of the desk release time. The BAM at the broker release time would be used to evaluate brokers.

The opportunity cost depends on π_1. Assuming that for consistency with π_0 we use the BAM, how far into the future should we go, subsequent to commencement of the order strategy? In principle, the consequences of an unfilled order may persist indefinitely. Portfolio managers generally revise the target portfolio (v), however, in reaction to large price changes. This revision effectively terminates the original trading instructions and so should limit the accumulation of opportunity costs. In practice, however, this termination is rarely explicitly documented. Opportunity cost calculations instead often invoke a fixed horizon that is long enough to encompass most trading strategies but short relative to portfolio turnover. The Plexus Group, for example, computes the opportunity cost of unexecuted orders over a 30-day window.

A number of firms in the trading cost industry have shared order data with academic researchers (having taken steps to maintain customer anonymity). Studies of Plexus data include Keim and Madhavan (1995, 1996, 1997), Conrad, Johnson, and Wahal (2001, 2002, 2003), and Irvine, Lipson, and Puckett (2006). Analyses of SEI data include Chan and Lakonishok (1993, 1995, 1997). The aims of these studies vary. Some seek to characterize the general features of institutional order strategies and their determinants. Among these results, it is particularly noteworthy that the fill (execution) rates on these orders are quite high. Keim and Madhavan (1995) find average completion rates of about 95%. This is important because it suggests that opportunity costs for unfilled orders (which are difficult to measure) are apt to be smaller than execution costs.

14.3.2   Market-Level Order Data

Real-time and historical data on the basic market and limit orders entering a venue are becoming increasingly available. Relative to the institutional data considered before, the main limitation of these data is that it is generally impossible to link sequences of orders to reconstruct full order strategies. Also in contrast to the institutional-level data, execution rates are low. This is easily explained by noting that a desk order that eventually achieves 99% execution may have been worked using a strategy where limit orders were used and frequently revised. In the market-level order data, the revisions will appear as disconnected cancellations and submissions.

The low completion rate of the individual orders makes the opportunity cost imputation important. Analyzing a sample of NYSE limit orders, Harris and Hasbrouck (1996) assign a cost for canceled orders by assuming a hypothetical fill at the opposing quote prevailing at the time of cancellation. Expired orders are treated in a similar fashion.

The execution of retail customer market orders in U.S. equity markets became an important issue in the early 1990s. Concern initially arose due to increased fragmentation, internalization, and payment for order flow. This established the context for numerous studies of comparative execution costs across venues. The earliest studies analyzed execution costs inferred from trade and quote data (as described in the next subsection). A small number of later publications report costs computed from order data (see Bacidore, Ross, and Sofianos (2003); Werner (2003)). Bessembinder, Maxwell, and Venkataraman (2005) analyze effective costs in the U.S. bond market.

Since 2001, summary statistics on execution costs have been computed and made available by the various market centers (under SEC rule 605, formerly 11ac1-5). The methodology is not completely straightforward, however: The U.S. Securities and Exchange Commission (2001) describes the various interpretations, qualifications, and exclusions.

Furthermore, the raw data are generally not available, nor are the summary statistics independently audited or verified.

14.3.3   Market-Level Trade and Quote Data

In the absence of order data, execution cost imputations are often based on reported trades and quotes, where it is assumed that an execution price above the BAM originates from a market buy order, and below, from a sell order. Mathematically this implies that the execution cost is $|p - BAM|$. To distinguish this from a computation based on order data, we will describe it as *trade-based*.

Trade-based effective cost estimates have been widely used in studies of comparative market quality and to assess the effects of industry practices and regulations. Representative studies include Lee (1993), Huang (1996), Battalio (1997a, 1997b, 1998, 2003), Bessembinder and Kaufman (1997), Bessembinder (1999, 2003a), Venkataraman (2001), Peterson (2003), Bacidore (1997), Degryse (1999), de Jong, Nijman, and Roell (1995), and Renaldo (2002).

Issues that generally arise in the computation of trade-based effective cost estimates include the accuracy of the quote and trade time stamps and the validity of the buy/sell direction inference. Time stamps are of concern because reporting conventions differ for trades and quotes. Because stale bids and asks will tend to be hit when it is to the advantage of the incoming order, quotes will usually be updated promptly. Trade reports, on the other hand, simply make public information known to those involved in the trade. If trades are reported with a lag, the quote used to compute the execution cost may actually have been posted subsequent to the trade. Because the quotes will tend to move in the direction of the trade, a small delay will tend to reduce the estimated effective cost. A large delay may lead to error in the buy-sell inference (e.g., if a buyer-initiated transaction report is delayed to a time when the quote midpoint lies above the reported trade price). The time stamps in automated markets are generally more accurate. Even here, though, we would do well to remember that quote and trade streams are often consolidated from several venues. The delays inherent in consolidation may not be uniform, leading to trades and quotes that are improperly ordered across venues. The same trade-quote synchronization problems addressed earlier in connection with the signing of trades arise here (see chapter 9, note 1).

The trade direction inference is affected by the existence of hidden orders and other latent liquidity mechanisms. For example, a buy market order may execute at a price at or below the BAM computed on the basis of the prevailing visible quote if there is an aggressively priced hidden sell limit order. This may also occur if a market maker, possibly conditioning on the size or other attribute of the order, betters the prevailing visible offer.

14.3.4 Selection Effects

The obvious way to analyze execution cost estimates is to compute summary statistics over the full sample and subsamples of interest (e.g., by trading venue). Additionally, execution costs might be regressed against characteristics of the stock, market conditions, and/or the order. The results might then be used to guide customers in directing their orders and other aspects of trading strategy. One might, for example, use regression estimates to project the execution cost of a contemplated order strategy. Although these sorts of analyses are sensible first steps, they are based on samples that are generated with a selection bias. The source of this bias lies in the decisions of the traders who submitted the orders. Corrections to deal with this bias have been implemented by Madhavan and Cheng (1997) and Bessembinder (2004).

15

Prospective Trading Costs and Execution Strategies

In this chapter we discuss minimization of expected implementation cost in two stylized dynamic trading problems. Both analyses are set in discrete time, and in each instance a trader must achieve a purchase by a deadline. The first problem concerns long-term order splitting and timing. A large quantity is to be purchased over a horizon that spans multiple days. Strategic choice involves quantities to be sent to the market at each time, but order choice is not modeled. The second problem involves purchase of a single unit over a shorter horizon, typically several hours. Strategic choice involves order type (market or limit), and (if a limit order is chosen) price.

15.1 Models of Order Splitting (Slicing) and Timing

15.1.1 The Basic Problem

The present analysis follows Bertsimas and Lo (1998), a classic and readable treatment of the problem. Related work includes Almgren and Chriss (2000) and Almgren (2003). Over $t = 1, \ldots, T$ periods, we seek to minimize the expected cost of purchasing $\bar{s}$ units of the security. The timed purchases are $s_t, t = 1, \ldots, T$, and completion requires $\bar{s} = \sum s_t$. At the beginning of period t, the number of shares remaining in the order is $w_t = w_{t-1} - s_{t-1}$.

The price dynamics are partially stochastic and partially driven by our trades. The latter effects certainly include transitory components (such as noninformational components of the bid-ask spread). It is also common in strategy analyses to allow trades to have permanent price effects.

To facilitate the reader's access to this literature, this presentation will also allow for permanent effects. It should be emphasized, however, that trading strategies are formulated from the perspective of a particular agent who is presumed to know both who he is and what he knows. Unless the buyer expects to alter the real characteristics of the firm, his trades will have no permanent effect on cash flows or the security market price (see section 5.6).[1]

Nevertheless allowing for a permanent impact, the quote midpoint at the end of period t is m_t:

$$m_t = m_{t-1} + \mu + \lambda s_t + \varepsilon_t, \qquad (15.1)$$

where μ is the drift, λs_t term is the permanent price impact, and ε_t is a random innovation uncorrelated with our trades. The interpretation of drift in this situation is unusual. Generally in microstructure models, drift is associated with an unconditional expected return and is likely to be negligible in comparison with other terms (section 3.3.1). In this context, however, drift reflects the buyer's beliefs about short-term dynamics that may be large. For example, if the buyer believes that awareness of a recent news announcement is likely to diffuse over the next hour, she may believe that there will be a large price adjustment over the hour, that is, a drift over the trading horizon that is far from zero (and also unrelated to her trades).

Temporary impact is modeled as a discrepancy between the quote midpoint and the trade price, p_t:

$$p_t = m_t + \gamma s_t. \qquad (15.2)$$

γs_t is a transient impact because it does not persist over time or cumulate over multiple trades.

The general approach to solving this kind of problem is dynamic programming via backward optimization. This will be used in subsequent analyses, but it is not actually necessary here. The reason is that no new information develops over time that might cause us to modify our initial plans. If the security price goes up unexpectedly (a large positive ε_t), for example, we will regret not having purchased more stock earlier. We have learned nothing new, however, that will help us predict the future price change. We can therefore set up the problem as a static optimization. From this perspective, subject to the constraint $\bar{s} = \sum s_t$, the problem is:

$$\min_{s_1, \ldots, s_T} E_t \left[\sum_{t=1}^{T} p_t s_t \right] = \min_{s_1, \ldots, s_T} \sum_{t=1}^{T} s_t \left(t\mu + \lambda \sum_{j=1}^{t} s_j + \gamma s_t \right). \qquad (15.3)$$

With $T = 3$, for example, the objective function is:

$$\mu(s_1 + 2s_2 + 3s_3) + \gamma\left(s_1^2 + s_2^2 + s_3^2\right) + \lambda\left(s_1^2 + s_2^2 + s_3^2 + s_1 s_2 + s_1 s_3 + s_2 s_3\right).$$

If $\mu = 0$, the objective function is symmetric in its arguments, and the optimal trading strategy is level: $s_t^* = \bar{s}/T$. With $\mu \neq 0$,

$$s_t^* = \bar{s}\left(\frac{1}{T} + \frac{(T+1) - 2t}{2(2\gamma + \lambda)}\mu\right). \tag{15.4}$$

The order size changes linearly over time. With positive drift, we will accelerate a buy order. The amount of the acceleration depends positively on μ, of course, but it also depends inversely on γ and λ. As these increase, departures from the level strategy become more expensive.

In some respects the order slicing strategy resembles that of the informed trader in the Kyle model (section 7.2). Although in both cases trading is distributed over time, there are some important differences. Kyle's informed trader conditions on price and trades so as to leave no traces in the form of autocorrelations that might signal his information. The trading strategy here, however, is consistent with positive autocorrelation in the order flow.

15.1.2 Slowly Decaying Nonstochastic Temporary Effects

The temporary effects of our trades in this specification affect only the current trade price. This might be a tenable approximation if our trades account for only a small portion of overall activity. As the relative scale of the purchase increases, however, it is more likely that transient effects will spill over into subsequent periods. As a first approximation, it is reasonable to allow the initial impact to decay gradually over time. This can be incorporated into the analysis by the addition of a second state variable,

$$A_t = \sum_{i=0}^{t-1} \theta^i s_{t-i} + \theta^t A_0, \tag{15.5}$$

where θ is the geometric weight $(0 \leq \theta < 1)$. The first term reflects our trades. The second term can be viewed as summarizing the delayed effect of others' trades prior to the start of our own. For $t > 1$, $A_t = s_t + \theta A_{t-1}$. The trade price is:

$$p_t = m_t + \gamma A_t + \varepsilon_t. \tag{15.6}$$

To isolate the effect of our own trades, assume for the moment that other trading was sufficiently distant in the past that $A_0 \approx 0$. In this case, the first of our trades will be cheaper than later trades because it will not incur any persistent cost components of any earlier trades. On the other hand, the first trade will raise the costs for all later trades.

Balancing these two effects leads to U-shaped trading strategies. Figure 15.1(A) depicts the execution strategies for various horizons. Panel B graphs the initial execution on the first trade for a three-period

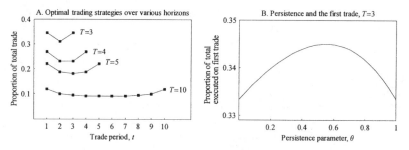

Figure 15.1. Characteristics of long-term trading strategies.

horizon, as a function of θ. With $\theta = 0$, the first trade share is 1/3 (as there is no persistence). This is also true, however, when $\theta = 1$: When persistence of the temporary impact is complete, the temporary impact is indistinguishable from the permanent impact.

We now indicate the effect of nonzero starting values A_0. It turns out that the first trade share is linearly declining in A_0. Thus, if previous trades have pushed up the temporary price component, we will tend to delay our own purchases, waiting until the initial cost component has decayed. If A_0 is sufficiently large, however, we will actually sell. In this case, the opportunity to take advantage of a temporarily inflated price by selling initially outweighs the gains from pursuing our overall purchase plan. Similarly, if A_0 is sufficiently low, it is optimal to buy shares in excess of $\bar{s}$, selling them at a profit when the price has risen.

15.1.3   Slowly Decaying Stochastic
Temporary Effects

It might be expected that the orders of others over our trading horizon would induce random variation in the evolution of A_t. This can be modeled by adding a disturbance:

$$A_t = s_t + \theta A_{t-1} + u_t. \tag{15.7}$$

Of course, if others' trades are correlated (as ours are), it might be desirable to allow for serial correlation in the u_t. Stochastic components to A_t complicate the solution process. Subsequent to time zero, we might seek to modify our trading plans in response to random changes in A_t. Static optimization is no longer appropriate, and the solution requires dynamic programming.

To implement this, we first define a value function, V_t, defined as the total expected expenditure on all purchases from time t onward, assuming that we make the best possible decisions at time t and subsequently. Because the program must be completed by time T, $V_{T+1} = 0$. At any time

$t \leq T$, V_t will depend on the most recently observed quote midpoint m_{t-1}, the number of units left to be purchased w_t, and the past-trade statistic A_{t-1}: $V_t = V_t(m_{t-1}, w_t, A_{t-1})$. At time T, the entire remainder must be purchased, so $s_T = w_T$. The expected cost is:

$$V_T(m_{T-1}, w_T, A_{T-1}) = E_T p_T s_T = E_T(m_{T-1} + \lambda w_T + \gamma A_T + \varepsilon_T) w_T$$
$$= (m_{T-1} + \theta \gamma A_{T-1} + (\lambda + \gamma) w_T) w_T. \qquad (15.8)$$

Looking ahead at time $T - 1$, we expect our remaining expenditures to be:

$$V_{T-1}(m_{T-2}, w_{T-1}, A_{T-2})$$
$$= \max_{s_{T-1}} E_{T-1} \left[V_T(m_{T-1}, w_T, A_{T-1}) + p_{T-1} s_{T-1} \right]. \qquad (15.9)$$

To find the optimal s_{T-1}, we substitute into the right-hand side using (15.8) and the dynamics for the state variables and maximize using differentiation. $V_{T-2}, \ldots, V_1$ are determined in a similar fashion.

The essential features of the solution, though, appear in

$$s_{T-1}^* = \frac{w_{T-1}}{2} - \frac{\gamma(1 - \theta)\theta}{2[\gamma(2 - \theta) + \lambda]} A_{T-2}. \qquad (15.10)$$

This is, in fact, identical to the solution one obtains for the deterministic A_t. In the deterministic case, though, we can compute A_{T-2} given what is known as of $t = 1$. In the stochastic case, we must wait until A_{T-2} is realized before making the trading decision. In both cases, however, the base solution (trading half the remaining amount) is augmented with a term that declines in A_{T-2}.

Exercise 15.1 (Predictable variation in the permanent impact parameter) Suppose that quote midpoint dynamics are given by $m_t = m_{t-1} + \lambda_t s_t + \varepsilon_t$, where the λ_t for $t = 1, 2, 3$ are known positive parameters. The trade price is simply $p_t = m_t$ (there is no transient price impact). Show that for $T = 3$ with $s_1 + s_2 + s_3 = 1$ the optimal order sizes are

$$s_1 = 1 + \frac{2\lambda_1 \lambda_3}{\lambda_2^2 - 4\lambda_2 \lambda_3}; \quad s_2 = \frac{\lambda_1(\lambda_2 - 2\lambda_3)}{\lambda_2(\lambda_2 - 4\lambda_3)}; \quad s_3 = -\frac{\lambda_1}{\lambda_2 - 4\lambda_3}.$$

Note that depending on how λ_t evolves, the optimal purchase may involve an initial sale (!). For example, when $\{\lambda_1 = 2, \lambda_2 = 1, \lambda_3 = 1/2\}$, $\{s_1 = -1, s_2 = 0, s_3 = 2\}$. The buyer is initially short selling (to drive the price down) and then purchasing to cover the short and establish the required position when price impact is low. Caution is warranted, however, because counterparties (and regulatory authorities) may view the intent of the initial sale as establishment of an "artificial" (i.e., "manipulative") price.

15.2   Models of Order Placement

The next analysis also deals with a purchase under a time constraint but with different emphasis. In the models of the previous section, trading costs are approximations that abstract from the details of order submission, and planned orders execute with certainty. This section considers dynamic order strategy. The strategic variable is order choice (limit or market, i.e., "make or take"), and execution is uncertain.

Though the present model examines the details of order submission, quantity is regarded as fixed (or determined in some prior optimization). The classic strategy for achieving execution involves initially placing a limit order, repricing it more aggressively over time, and ultimately (if necessary) using a market order. Angel (1994) and Harris (1998) analyze order choice strategies for various trading problems. The model discussed here is adapted from Harris.

15.2.1   The Basic Barrier Diffusion Model

The objective is to minimize the expected purchase price for a single unit of the security. The price follows a continuous time diffusion, but order decisions are only made at the discrete times $t = 1, \ldots, T$. The security must be purchased by the close of period T. At the beginning of each period, if the security has not yet been purchased, the agent may either submit a market order or a limit order. If the agent submits a limit order, he must decide on the limit price L_t (a continuous variable).

On the face of things, this problem seems very similar to the one-period order choice decisions considered in the single-agent and Parlour models discussed in chapter 12. In those settings, though, it is only necessary to model the execution mechanism. Price dynamics do not enter in any essential way. Multiperiod decisions are fundamentally different because when a limit order fails to execute, it is generally because the market price has moved away from the limit order. The trader is forced to chase the market, eventually achieving execution at an unfavorable price. This cost and its effect on strategy depend on the trader's beliefs about price movements.

The starting point is a simple model of price dynamics and limit order execution termed here the diffusion-barrier model. Various aspects of this approach are used in Handa and Schwartz (1996), Harris (1998), and Lo, MacKinlay, and Zhang (2002). Briefly, the market price follows a continuous time diffusion (Weiner) process, and a limit order executes when the market price hits the barrier corresponding to the limit price. More specifically, the price is p_t with dynamics:

$$dp_t = \mu dt + \sigma dz, \qquad (15.11)$$

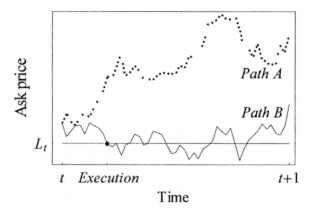

Figure 15.2. Limit order execution.

where μ is the instantaneous drift and σ is the standard deviation, both per unit time. In the context of a purchase problem, p_t is best thought of as the best (lowest) ask in the market. The buy limit price is denoted L_t. If at time t, $p_t \geq L_t$, then the agent has effectively submitted a marketable limit order, which achieves immediate execution. A limit order priced at $L_t < p_t$ will be executed during period t if $p_\tau \leq L_t$ for any time $t < \tau < t+1$. The situation is depicted in figure 15.2. A limit order priced at L_t executes if the stock price follows path B but not path A. This is a standard problem in stochastic processes, and many exact results are available.

The diffusion-barrier notion of execution is at best a first approximation. In many markets, a buy limit order might be executed by a market (or marketable) sell order while the best ask is still well above the limit price. We will subsequently generalize the execution mechanism to allow this. For the moment, though, it might be noted that the present situation is not without precedent. In the U.S. NASDAQ market, prior to the adoption of the Manning rules, a dealer holding a customer limit order was only required to fill the order when the opposing quote (the ask, in the case of a buy order) met the limit price (see appendix A, section A.3).

Like the long-term problem, the present one may be formulated as a dynamic programming exercise and solved via backward induction. The value function is denoted $V_t(p_t)$ and corresponds to the expected purchase price, that is, a cost to be minimized. If execution has not been achieved by the start of period T, then the trader must purchase using a market order. In this case, $V_T(p_T) = p_T$. The first substantive decisions occur if no execution has been achieved by the start of period $T - 1$. Should we use a market or limit order? If a limit order, at what price?

In period $T - 1$ if a limit order priced at L_{T-1} executes, the trader purchases at L_{T-1}; otherwise the problem continues into period T. Let $\Pr(L_t \ hit|p_t)$ denote the probability that a buy limit order priced at L_t

is hit in the coming period when the current ask is p_t. Obviously, $\Pr(L_t \text{ not hit}|p_t) = 1 - \Pr(L_t \text{ hit}|p_t)$. $E[p_{t+1}|p_t, L_t \text{ not hit}]$ is the expectation of p_{t+1} conditional on the initial ask and the limit order priced at L_t not being hit. Closed-form expressions for these functions are given in the chapter appendix. With this notation the value function at time $T-1$ is

$$
\begin{aligned}
V_{T-1}(p_{T-1}) = \min_{L_{T-1}} E[L_{T-1} \Pr(L_{T-1} \text{ hit}|p_{T-1}) \\
+ V_T(p_T) \Pr(L_{T-1} \text{ not hit}|p_{T-1})] \\
= \min_{L_{T-1}} \Big(L_{T-1} \Pr(L_{T-1} \text{ hit}|p_{T-1}) \\
+ E[p_T|p_{T-1}; L_{T-1} \text{ not hit}] \\
\times \Pr(L_{T-1} \text{ not hit}|p_{T-1}) \Big).
\end{aligned}
\tag{15.12}
$$

If $L_{T-1} = p_{T-1}$, the trader is essentially purchasing immediately with a market order. As L_{T-1} drops (becoming less aggressive), both terms on the right-hand side change as $\Pr(L_{T-1}\text{Hit}|p_{T-1})$ and $E[p_T|p_{T-1}; L_{T-1} \text{ not hit}]$ decline.[2]

An interesting result arises in the zero-drift case. If $\mu = 0$,

$$
\begin{aligned}
p_{T-1} = E[p_T|p_{T-1}] \\
= E[p_T|p_{T-1}, L_{T-1} \text{ hit}]\Pr(L_{T-1} \text{ hit}|p_{T-1}) \\
+ E[p_T|p_{T-1}; L_{T-1} \text{ not hit}] \Pr(L_{T-1} \text{ not hit}|p_{T-1}) \\
= L_{T-1} \Pr(L_{T-1} \text{ hit}|p_{T-1}) + E[p_T|p_{T-1}; L_{T-1} \text{ not hit}] \\
\times \Pr(L_{T-1} \text{ not hit}|p_{T-1}).
\end{aligned}
\tag{15.13}
$$

The first equality follows from the martingale property of a zero-drift Weiner process; the second, from the definition of conditional expectations; and the third, from the fact that once a driftless random walk hits a barrier, the expectation of its subsequent position is equal to the barrier level (using the reflection principle; see Karlin and Taylor (1975), pp. 345–52). By comparing (15.12) and (15.13), we see that the minimand of the value function is simply p_{T-1}. That is, there is no advantage to using a limit order, and the trader might as well buy immediately, paying p_{T-1} with a market order. The objective function here is the expected cost, but clearly using a limit order would result in a dispersion of outcomes. Thus an agent who was only slightly risk-averse would prefer a market order to a limit order. Perhaps not surprisingly, limit order usage in pre-Manning NASDAQ was reputedly low. If $\mu > 0$, then an immediate market order is strictly optimal. If $\mu < 0$, there is no interior optimum.

15.2.2   Random Execution

A more interesting and realistic model results from combining the diffusion-barrier model with an execution mechanism based on a random unexpressed reservation price, similar to the device used in the single-period order choice model (section 12.1). Specifically, suppose that at the beginning and throughout period t there is a group of potential sellers monitoring the market. Each seller has a unexpressed reservation price differential, a threshold such that when the distance between the visible ask and the buyer's limit bid price drops to the threshold, she immediately hits the limit bid. Let c_t denote the maximum reservation differential over the population of sellers over the interval. A limit buy priced at L executes during interval t if $p_\tau \leq L + c_t$ for some τ, $t \leq \tau < t+1$. Thus, execution can be viewed as the first passage to a random barrier. For tractability we assume that the c_t are independently and identically distributed, and that they are also independent of the price. (The independence assumptions ensure that c_t does not enter the problem as a state variable.)

The value function becomes

$$V_t(p_t) = \min_{L_t} E \begin{bmatrix} L_t \Pr\left(L_t + c_t \geq p_t | p_t\right) \\ + L_t \Pr\left(L_t + c_t \text{ hit}; \ L_t + c_t > p_t | p_t\right) \\ + V_{t+1}(p_{t+1}) \Pr\left(L_t + c_t \text{ not hit}; \right. \\ \left. L_t + c_t > p_t | p_t\right) \end{bmatrix}. \qquad (15.14)$$

The three terms in the brackets correspond to the possible outcomes of immediate execution, execution during the interval, and no execution. To develop the model further, it is useful to rework the problem so that the value function is expressed relative to the current ask price. Define the relative limit price as $\ell_t = L_t - p_t$ ($\ell_t < 0$ for a buy order). The cumulative price change over the interval is $\delta_\tau = p_\tau - p_t$ for $t \leq \tau < t+1$. Execution occurs if δ_τ hits (from above) a barrier located at $\ell_t + c_t$, and if $\ell_t + c_t \geq 0$, execution is immediate. Letting $\Pr(\alpha \text{ hit})$ denote the probability that δ_τ hits a barrier $\alpha < 0$, equation (15.14) may be written:

$$V_t(p_t) = p_t + \min_{\ell_t} E \begin{bmatrix} \ell_t \Pr\left(c_t \geq -\ell_t\right) \\ + \ell_t \Pr\left(\ell_t + c_t \text{ hit}; \ c_t < -\ell_t\right) \\ + (V_{t+1}(p_{t+1}) - p_t) \\ \times \Pr\left(\ell_t + c_t \text{ not hit}; \ c_t < -\ell_t\right) \end{bmatrix}, \qquad (15.15)$$

where the expectation is over price paths and c_t. A relative value function may be defined as $v_t = V_t(p_t) - p_t$. It does not depend on p_t, and so has the recursive structure:

$$v_t = \min_{\ell_t} \begin{bmatrix} \ell_t \Pr\left(c_t \geq -\ell_t\right) \\ + \ell_t \Pr\left(\ell_t + c_t \text{ hit}; \ c_t < -\ell_t\right) \\ + \{v_{t+1} + E[\delta_{t+1} | \ell_t + c_t \text{ not hit}; \ c_t < -\ell_t]\} \\ \times \Pr\left(\ell_t + c_t \text{ not hit}; \ c_t < -\ell_t\right) \end{bmatrix}. \qquad (15.16)$$

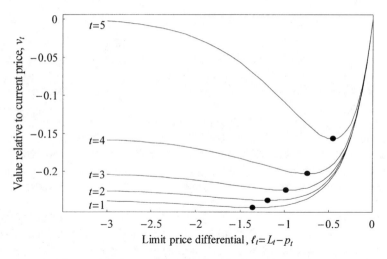

Figure 15.3. Value functions for six-period purchase problem.

Letting $f(c)$ denote the density function of c_t,

$$
v_t = \min_{\ell_t} \left[\begin{array}{l} \ell_t \int_{-\ell_t}^{\infty} f(c)dc + \ell_t \int_0^{-\ell_t} \Pr(\ell_t + c\ \text{hit})f(c)dc \\[2mm] + \int_0^{-\ell_t} \Pr(\ell_t + c_t\ \text{not hit}) \\[1mm] \times \{v_{t+1} + E[\delta_{t+1}|\ell_t + c_t\ \text{not hit};\ c_t < -\ell_t]\}f(c)dc \end{array} \right]. \tag{15.17}
$$

If c is an exponential random variable with density $f(c_t) = \lambda \exp(-\lambda c_t)$, most of the integrals have closed-form representations.

As a numerical illustration, we consider the problem fixing parameter values at $T = 6$, $\mu = 0$, $\sigma = 1$, and $\lambda = 5$. Figure 15.3 plots the value functions for the first five periods. (Recall that at $T = 6$, we have no choice but to hit the ask.) For the parameter values chosen, the value functions have global minima, which are marked with dots. The figure illustrates several features of interest. First, as we move earlier in the problem, the value function (expected purchase) declines for all choices of ℓ_t. This is reasonable, in that when the horizon is effectively longer, there is a greater chance that a limit order strategy will at some point succeed. Second, the limit order price increases as we move closer to the terminal time. Thus, within the framework of this model, we have demonstrated that it is an optimal strategy to initially submit limit orders far away from the market but making them more aggressive as the deadline approaches.

The next figure describes the effects of parameter changes on optimal limit order placement. Panel A of figure 15.4 illustrates the dependence on drift. With positive drift, the price is tending to move away from a buy

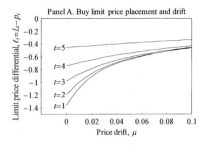
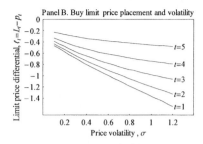

Figure 15.4. Dependence of limit order strategies on drift and volatility.

limit order. Thus, as drift increases, limit prices are more aggressive at all times. Panel B depicts volatility dependence. As volatility increases, the probability that a random walk will hit a given barrier increases. Volatility therefore increases the chance of execution, and limit orders are consequently priced less aggressively. The dependence of ℓ_t on the c distribution parameter λ is not depicted but is fairly intuitive. As λ increases, the distribution becomes more concentrated toward zero. There are likely to be fewer potential sellers with extreme values, and therefore the optimal limit orders must be priced more aggressively to succeed.[3]

15.2.3 Empirical Analysis of Limit Order Execution

The barrier-diffusion model and the extension with random reservation prices attempt to characterize the probability of execution over the decision interval. The length of the decision interval, though, is a property of the application (the strategic problem), not an essential characteristic of the limit order execution process. It is therefore more useful in practice to model a limit order's time to execution using duration analysis. Duration analysis seeks to characterize wall-clock times between events, in this case, between the submission of a limit order and its execution. The fundamentals of duration analysis are discussed in Lancaster (1997), Greene (2002), and Allison (1995). Lo, McKinlay, and Zhang (2002) apply these techniques to limit order executions.

The simplest duration specification is the Poisson/exponential model discussed in section 6.2. In the present context, it might arise as follows. Let τ denote the execution duration, the time between the submission and execution. In the case of a buy limit order, if it is alone at the best bid (i.e., it is the only order) and if market sell orders arrive with Poisson intensity λ, then τ is exponentially distributed with parameter λ.

The exponential model is the simplest duration specification, but there are many others. Among them is the diffusion-barrier model used here. Lancaster (1997) discusses its characteristics as basis for duration modeling. One distinctive feature is particularly relevant. If the diffusion price process has zero drift, then it will eventually (with probability one) hit any finite barrier. This implies that any limit order will eventually execute. This is also true of the exponential model (if $\lambda > 0$). In the diffusion model with nonzero drift, however, this is not the case. For example, in a limit buy situation with positive drift, there is a positive probability that the limit order will never execute.[4]

The barrier-diffusion model should be relatively easy to apply because the drift and volatility can be estimated directly from a sample of prices. In their sample, however, Lo et al. find that this model (which they call the first-passage time model) underestimates actual times to execution, that is, that the model is too optimistic, and that a generalized gamma alternative performs much better. Related work includes Challet and Stinchcombe (2003).

An important consideration affecting most duration models is censoring. This may involve observations at the start of the sample, for example, limit orders that were already on the book at the start of a sample and for which we have no record of the submission time. Censoring may also involve observations removed from the sample before the duration event occurred, for example, limit orders that are canceled. Econometrically, censoring is easily dealt with as long as the censoring process is independent of the duration being modeled. To illustrate the nature of the dependence, consider a medical study of mortality subsequent to diagnosis, where patients might drop out of the study because they move away and can no longer be followed by the investigator. The duration of a subject whose move results from a job transfer can reasonably be presumed to have been censored independently of the mortality process. This is not the case for a subject who moves to be closer to family because he is feeling poorly.

Censoring is important in limit order analysis because the vast preponderance of limit orders are canceled. In their sample, for example, Hasbrouck and Saar (2003) find that only roughly 13% of submitted limit orders are executed. The remainder are canceled, either explicitly or by expiration at the end of the day. Although tractability might dictate assuming otherwise, however, actual execution and cancellation processes are likely to be strongly dependent. One need look no further than the optimal strategies depicted in figure 15.3. Limit orders are canceled (and resubmitted with higher prices) when the price has moved away from the limit order, that is, because the likelihood of execution has fallen.

Appendix

Lancaster (1997) discusses the Weiner process barrier model in depth. The following are restatements of Lancaster's results in terms of the present problem. In what follows, the price is assumed to evolve as

$dp_t = \mu dt + \sigma dz$. A limit buy order is presumed to be priced at $L \leq p_t$. The time interval is assumed to be one unit.

For a limit buy order priced at L,

$$\Pr\left(Hit|p_t, L\right) = 1 - \Phi\left(\frac{p_t - L + \mu}{\sigma}\right) + \exp\left[\frac{2\mu(L - p_t)}{\sigma^2}\right]\phi\left(\frac{L - p_t + \mu}{\sigma}\right).$$

$$(15.18)$$

If the limit order is not hit, the density function for the end-of-period price is:

$f(p_{t+1}|p_t, L, No\ Hit)$

$$= \frac{-\exp\left[-\frac{2\mu(p_t - L)}{\sigma^2}\right]\phi\left[\frac{\mu + (L - p_t) + (L - p_{t+1})}{\sigma}\right] + \phi\left[\frac{\mu - (p_{t+1} - p_t)}{\sigma}\right]}{\sigma(1 - \Pr(Hit|p_t, L))}.$$

$$(15.19)$$

The corresponding expectation is:

$E[p_{t+1}|p_t, L, No\ Hit]$

$$= \mu + \frac{2(p_t - L)\exp\left[\frac{-2\mu(p_t - L)}{\sigma^2}\right]\Phi\left[\frac{\mu - (p_t - L)}{\sigma}\right]}{(1 - \Pr(Hit|p_t, L))}.$$

$$(15.20)$$

Additional results are developed in the *Mathematica* notebook associated with this chapter.

Appendix: U.S. Equity Markets

This appendix is an overview of the organization and recent history of U.S. equity trading. Many discussions of this material focus on the institutions: "listed" trading and the New York Stock Exchange (NYSE); and, "unlisted"/over-the-counter market (NASDAQ). These institutions are still important, but they are not as central as they once were, nor are they as well defined. Accordingly, it is better to start from a functional perspective that establishes the players and their relationships.

A.1 Functional Overview

The players in and components of U.S. equity markets may be summarized as follows:

- The customers are individuals and institutions (pension funds, mutual funds and other managed investment vehicles, collectively known as the buy side). The distinction between retail and institutional customers is mainly one of size, and should not be construed as naive versus sophisticated. Furthermore, customers often actively compete in the market-making process.
- Brokers act as agents for customer orders and often provide non-trading services as well (such as advice and research). Brokers and dealers are collectively known as the sell side.
- The market venues are simply places (real or virtual) where trades occur. The principal venues are:
  - The exchanges (also known as the listed market). Most important, the NYSE, but also including the American Stock

Exchange, Cincinnati and the regional stock exchanges (Philadelphia, Boston, Chicago, Pacific).
- NASDAQ (the "unlisted" market).
- Alternative trading systems (ATSs) include electronic communications networks (ECNs, e.g., Inet, Archipelago) and the crossing networks. Most ECNs are constituted as electronic limit order markets.

- The primary regulator of trading in U.S. equity markets is the Securities and Exchange Commission (SEC). In 1933, Congress created the SEC and delegated to it primary authority. The SEC has in turn delegated authority to industry entities known as "Self-Regulatory Organizations" (SROs). The NYSE and National Association of Securities Dealers (NASD) are the principal SROs. Congressional mandates on security markets generally take the form of broad directives that leave details up to the SEC, with the notable recent exception of decimalization (discussed later).
- Market data systems consolidate and disseminate trade reports, quotes, and so on.
- Intermarket linkage systems connect the trading venues and permit one trading venue to send an order to another for purposes of execution ("access"). As markets have become more fragmented, these systems have become very important, arguably transcending the importance of any single venue.

We now turn to a more detailed discussion of the components, beginning with the most important and complex: the market venues.

A.2   The NYSE

Historically, the NYSE dominated U.S. equity trading. An economist might describe it as a multiproduct firm, producing listing, regulatory, and trading services. The present analysis focuses mainly on the NYSE's trading activities.[1] NYSE trading protocols are complex because the exchange is a hybrid market that features an open outcry system, a dealer market, and an electronic limit order book. These mechanisms are not simply run in parallel isolation but are integrated in a fashion that attempts to balance their needs and features. The amalgam of these systems is now designated as the NYSE Hybrid Market (SM). It is perhaps easiest to approach these diverse mechanisms and their interaction by reviewing them in the order in which they arose historically.

A.2.1   The NYSE as an Open Outcry (Floor Market)

The NYSE was founded in 1792 and first functioned as an open outcry market (section 2.2). Floor trading procedures reflect the following principles.

- *Price priority.* As an illustration, someone who is bidding 101 should have priority over someone who's bidding 100. Here, it might be thought that self-interest of sellers would ensure price priority: Why would anyone sell at 100 when they could sell at 101? If the broker is acting as agent, he may care more about getting a customer order filled quickly than getting the best price, particularly if the customer can't easily monitor the market. The rule of price priority gives the other side (in this case, the bidder) the right to protest (and break) the trade. A trade at 100 when a buyer is bidding 101 is called a trade-through. The prevalence of trade-throughs has recently reemerged as an important regulatory concern (see section A.8).
- *Time priority.* First-come, first-served is a time-honored principle that rewards prompt action. In the present case, the first member to bid or offer at a price gets the first trade at that price. Beyond that, there is no time priority. In a crowd, it is relatively easy to keep track of who was first, but more difficult to remember who was second, third, and so on.
- *Trade reporting.* The practice of public last-sale reporting and dissemination of bids and offers date from the floor phase of the NYSE's history (and predates by many years the establishment of any external regulation).

A.2.2 The Dealer (Specialist)

The dealer part of the picture emerged in the 1870s. According to legend, a member broke his leg and while constrained by immobility decided to specialize in certain selected stocks. The practice was adopted by more ambulatory brokers, and the specialist system was born.

A specialist trades on his own account and is not an employ of the exchange. Specialists were originally small proprietorships, but recent consolidations have left only seven specialist units, some of which are subsidiaries of other financial firms. There is currently one specialist per stock. This has given rise to the expression *monopolistic specialist*. The specialist does enjoy some market power, but the qualifier greatly exaggerates its extent. The specialist participation rate (specialist purchases + specialist sales)/(2 × total volume) is about 15%.

The specialist's primary responsibility is to maintain a fair and orderly market. There a large number of rules that specify what the specialist should do (affirmative obligations) and what he should avoid (negative obligations). Among the specialist's affirmative obligations are duties to:

- Make a market, that is, bid and offer on his own account when necessary. The specialist has the sole authority and responsibility for the quotes.
- Act as agent for the limit order book and market orders. The specialist's role as agent for public orders became more prominent

with the prevalence of electronic delivery. The exchanges order delivery and routing systems (notably SuperDOT) send virtually all orders that don't require a broker's human attention to the specialist's workstation (DisplayBook).
- Maintain price continuity, that is, ensure that successive price variations are small.

Among the negative obligations, the specialist is:

- Prohibited from trading ahead of a public customer at the same price (e.g., buying at 100 when a customer is bidding 100).
- Discouraged from "trading in a destabilizing fashion" (buying on an uptick or selling on a downtick).

A.2.3   The Limit Order Book

The book is maintained by the specialist. In floor trading protocols, the specialist acting as agent for the book is essentially considered a single floor trader. One implication of this is that although price/time priority is strictly observed within the book, the book as a single entity might not have priority over floor traders who arrived considerably after the limit orders in the book were posted.

A.2.4   The Bid and Ask Quotes

The specialist sets the bid and ask quotes. In doing so, he might be representing his own interest, orders on the book, bids or offers that a floor broker might want displayed, or a combination of all of these. If there are orders on the book at the bid or ask, they must be represented (under the SEC's Quote Display Rule), but the display is not automatic. Historically, the specialist could exercise considerable discretion in the display of customer limit orders. Presently, limit orders that better the existing quote must be executed or displayed within 30 seconds.

A.2.5   Executions

The NYSE has historically aggressively adopted technology to transmit orders and information but has been disinclined to automate the execution of orders. This reluctance has been justified by the necessity of human (specialist) judgment in the maintenance of a fair and orderly market. In response to competitive pressure and a customer clientele that placed a premium on speed of execution, however, the NYSE began to offer automatic execution. The NYSE Direct+ system came online in 2000 and was quickly judged a success. It has since been refined, and is now an integral part of NYSE trading.

Non-Direct+ market orders are delivered to the specialist's post and do not execute automatically. Acting as agent for the order, the specialist effectively auctions it off. The order may execute against an order on the book, against an order represented by a floor broker. The specialist may also act as counterparty himself.

Large executions (block trades) have traditionally had a size threshold of 10,000 shares, but nowadays many orders of that size would simply be allowed to follow the electronic route of small orders, as described. The terms of large orders are usually negotiated by customers and their brokers. Often the process involves the broker guaranteeing the customer a price and then working the order (feeding it to the market) slowly over time to minimize price impact. The general process is the same whether the stock is listed on an exchange or NASDAQ. (See following discussion.) When a broker has located both a buyer and seller for a block, he may, under certain circumstances, "cross" the block, that is, execute the trade without other buyers and sellers stepping in to take part or all of one or both sides (the "clean-cross rule"). Many markets (including the Euronext markets) have similar arrangements.

A.2.6   Opening and Closing Procedures

The opening procedure is effectively a single-price call auction. Brokers submit customer orders. The specialist tries to find a single price at which supply equals demand. To maintain a fair and orderly market, and in accordance with various other rules, the specialist may buy or sell at the open. A common scenario is one in which the specialist buys or sells a relatively small amount to resolve a minor buy-sell imbalance and clear the book at the opening price.

The closing procedure is sometimes described as an auction. Like any double-sided clearing, it balances expressed supply and demand, but beyond this, it bears little resemblance to any other auction procedure. The specialist is not relieved of responsibility for price continuity, which implies that he must not only balance static supply and demand but also establish a transition path to the closing price. The rules regarding entry and cancellation of orders to be executed "at the close" are complex in their specifics, but are generally aimed at early detection of imbalances. By way of contrast, the closing auction procedure in the Euronext markets involves cessation of continuous trading, followed by a five-minute window to enter orders, and a single-price clearing that is essentially identical to the opening mechanism.

A.2.7   Governance and Alliance

In April 2003, it was disclosed that the NYSE was investigating five of its seven specialist firms for violations of its trading rules. The SEC also initiated an investigation. The SEC's investigation lasted into 2005 and resulted in penalties being assessed not only against the specialists but also against the exchange itself for failing to adequately police their activities.

At the same time the specialist investigations were unfolding, the NYSE suffered a governance crisis. The exchange was (and still is, at present) organized as a not-for-profit corporation, largely governed by its members. This simple statement, however, fails to convey the extent of the members' divergence of interests and the consequent factions, coalitions, and politicking that achieved the consensus necessary for operation. The exchange's trading practices were clearly subject to external review and oversight, but the internal governance was much more opaque (certainly in comparison with the practices it mandated for its listed companies). In late summer 2003, public revelation of its CEO's compensation arrangements triggered internal dissent and attracted unprecedented external criticism. The NYSE reorganized its governance procedures, and by the end of the year had installed as a new CEO John Thain, a strong proponent of automation.

In 2004 Thain proposed two connected initiatives. The first was demutualization of the exchange, conversion into a for-profit corporation with the members as the initial shareholders. Demutualization had been accomplished by other exchanges, had earlier been considered by the NYSE, and was not a surprising suggestion. The second initiative, however, was more unexpected. This was a proposed merger between the NYSE and Archipelago, which operated a successful ECN. Both goals were accomplished. A parent corporation (the NYSE Group) operates the NYSE and Archipelago (now known as NYSE Arca). NYSE Group is a publicly traded corporation (under the ticker symbol NYX). The NYSE Group has recently proposed merger with Euronext.

As profound as the NYSE's changes were (and continue to be), however, the forces of transformation hit earlier and more powerfully at the other major U.S. equity market, NASDAQ.

A.3   NASDAQ

Historically, NASDAQ was primarily a dealer market with geographically dispersed dealers linked by electronic systems that displayed bid and ask quotes and last sale prices (Smith, Selway, and McCormick 1998). As of 1990, NASDAQ was distinctly a dealer market (see section 2.3). It was transformed in the 1990s by economic, political, and regulatory pressures. The changes greatly enhanced customer protection and reduced the power and profitability of NASDAQ members (brokers and dealers). The changes also weakened the authority and reach of NASDAQ as a central market operator. They unfolded in the following steps.

A.3.1   The Manning Rules

NASDAQ (like most dealer markets) traditionally gave little protection to customer limit orders. For example, supposing that the best market quotes were 100 bid, offered at 102, a NASDAQ dealer who received a customer limit order to buy at 101 did not have to display the order as a new, more aggressive quote. The dealer could furthermore buy for his own account at prices below 101 (thus trading through the customer order). The customer was only entitled to an execution when the market offer price dropped to 101 (essentially making the customer order marketable). The Manning rules were adopted in 1994 and 1995 by NASD to prohibit brokers from trading ahead of or through their customer limit orders.

A.3.2   The Collusion Charges

In 1994, a Vanderbilt University academic study revealed an interesting regularity. Christie and Schultz (1994) found that despite the 1/8 ($0.125) tick size used at the time in U.S. equity markets, NASDAQ dealers tended to bid and offer on a 1/4-point grid. They suggested that this might be a coordination device to maintain spreads at 1/4. This would be profitable for dealers because most retail trades occurred at the bid or and the ask. Furthermore with weak limit order protection (pre-Manning), there was little opportunity for customers to use limit orders to compete with dealer quotes.

Christie, Harris, and Schultz (1994) describe the aftermath. They had sought comments from industry participants, and, after the findings were peer-reviewed and accepted for publication, Vanderbilt issued a press release on May 24, 1994. Also on May 24, a meeting of major NASDAQ dealers was convened at the offices of Bear Sterns in New York. At this meeting, a NASD official encouraged dealers to reduce their spreads. The stated reason for this exhortation was an earlier rule change (January 1994) to a NASDAQ automatic execution system (SOES), not the Christie-Schultz study. Whatever the motivation, on May 27, spreads began to drop dramatically.

NASDAQ authorized an external review of the matter (the Rudman Commission); the SEC and the Department of Justice (DOJ) opened investigations; and civil lawsuits were filed against the NASDAQ dealers (on behalf of customers). In the sequel:

- The Rudman Commission examined NASD's governance and recommended that market operation and market regulation be separated. The latter was spun off as NASD. The separation was (and is) structurally complex and is now enmeshed with NASDAQ's demutualization.
- The SEC and DOJ investigations were concluded and settled. The investigatory report (U.S. Securities and Exchange Commission 1996b) describes the commission's findings.

- The civil law suits were consolidated and eventually settled in May 1999 for slightly under $1 billion.

A.3.3   The SEC's Rule on Order Execution Obligations

The SEC and DOJ investigations served to support constructive reform going forward. The most striking examples of this are rules 11Ac1-1 and 11Ac1-4 (now designated rules 602 and 604) on Order Execution Obligations. The extent of these rules was not limited to NASDAQ; they applied to all markets. They are most clearly understood, however, in the context of NASDAQ regulation. There are two components, the Display Rule and the Quote Rule. As stated in the final rule release (U.S. Securities and Exchange Commission (1996)):

> [The Display Rule] require[s] the display of customer limit orders priced better than a specialist's or over-the-counter ("OTC") market maker's quote or that add to the size associated with such quote. ... [The Quote Rule] require[s] a market maker to publish quotations for any listed security ... and to make publicly available any superior prices that a market maker privately quotes through certain electronic communications networks ("ECNs"). (page 1)

The Display Rule strengthened NASDAQ customer limit orders beyond the protections afforded by Manning. When display is required, a customer limit order can become the best bid or offer in the market. The Quote Rule was designed to curb a practice whereby NASDAQ dealers would set wide quotes that were visible to the public, but narrow quotes in the interdealer and institutional markets that were not visible to the public. This practice remains common in many other dealer markets (including foreign exchange and bonds).

A.3.4   SuperMontage

NASDAQ is largely defined by its information systems. The modern NASDAQ essentially came into being with the 1971 initiation of the quote montage system, which allowed for screen display of dealer quotes. Subsequently added systems allowed for trade reporting and confirmation (ACT), interdealer communication of trading commitments (SelectNet), small retail order execution (SOES), and so on.

At present, most of the functionality in these disparate systems is now consolidated in one system, SuperMontage. Conceptually, SuperMontage comes closest to resembling an electronic limit order book for dealers. That is, the display and trading protocols are similar to what would be found in an electronic limit order book, except that customers are not permitted direct access to the system. The system was designed to facilitate established NASDAQ practices like preferencing, and as a result the actual trading protocols are quite complex.

A.3.5   *Governance and Alliances*

Like the NYSE, NASDAQ entered the 1990s as a not-for-profit corporation owned by its members. When NASDAQ (the market operation) was divorced from NASD (the regulatory arm), it also entered onto a path of demutualization (conversion into a stockholder-owned for-profit corporation), a process that is still in progress. En route, NASDAQ sold equity stakes to outside investment groups.

Although ultimately winding up in a similar stance, NASDAQ's alliances over the past 10 years have been more numerous and more varied than the NYSE's. In 1998 NASDAQ announced that it would purchase the American Stock Exchange (Amex). The proffered strategic rationale was that a combination would be able to provide a broad array of dealer and exchange markets in stocks and derivatives. The two units were never integrated, however, and in 2003, Amex was sold. NASDAQ also established a link with Optimark (an innovative electronic market), but for reasons unrelated to the connection Optimark was not successful. NASDAQ recently acquired the INET (formerly Island/Instinet) and Brut ECNs.

A.4   The New Trading Systems

With the advent of communications and Internet technology in the 1990s, there arose considerable interest in devising new electronic trading mechanisms.[2] The general structure of U.S. regulation, however, was not well suited to dealing with these developments. For regulatory purposes, the principal trading institution was the national securities exchange. As this term was defined in narrow terms, the new entrants did not obviously belong in that category (or any other). It was also widely recognized that classification as an exchange brought with it considerable regulatory overhead.

The SEC initially accommodated the many new systems with "No Action" letters that provisionally authorized operation. But it soon became clear that a more consistent and cohesive regulatory structure was called for. The SEC's rule on the Regulation of Exchanges and Alternative Trading Systems (Regulation ATS) established a new framework. As described in the executive summary to the final rules (U.S. Securities and Exchange Commission (1998)), the key provision was,

> To allow new markets to start, without disproportionate burdens, a system with less than five percent of the trading volume in all securities it trades is required only to: (1) file with the Commission a notice of operation and quarterly reports; (2) maintain records, including an audit trail of transactions; and (3) refrain from using the words "exchange," "stock market," or similar terms in its name. (Section II.c)

Although there is considerable overlap between the ECN and ATS categories, many ATSs do not display orders and are therefore not considered ECNs. Examples include most crossing markets (section 2.6). The rule successfully provided regulatory latitude during an unusually active time in trading system development.

A.5 Decimalization

By the 1990s, most of the world's financial exchanges used prices quoted in regular (decimal) form. U.S. equity trading, however, was still being conducted in eighths (of a dollar). Although this might have been viewed as an annoying anachronism, the NASDAQ collusion investigations gave prominence to the possibility that a market's tick size might have a large effect on trading costs. To take the simplistic view, if the bid and ask are set by insiders, and outside customers can trade only at these prices, insiders would seek to keep spreads wide. The tick size sets a floor on how narrow the spreads can become. It was conjectured that if the tick size were mandated to be smaller, spreads would fall to the cost of providing dealer services.

Positioned as a populist issue, the outcome of the debate was in little doubt. Congress passed the Common Cents (cf. "sense") Pricing Act of 1997. The NYSE switched to sixteenths and then, as required by the law, to pennies. Spreads for most stocks declined (Stoll and Schenzler (2002)). Thus, decimalization is clearly viewed as having been beneficial to retail customers. The effects on institutional trading costs and practices, however, have been less clear (Goldstein and Kavajecz (2000); Werner (2003)).

A.6 The Consolidation and Fragmentation Debate

Consolidation or centralization brings all trading interest together in one place, thereby lessening the need for intermediaries. As a regulatory principle, however, it favors the establishment and perpetuation of a single trading venue, which may discourage innovation. Allowing new entrants (like the ATSs) fosters competition among trading venues, but at any given time the trading interest in a security is likely to be dispersed (fragmented) among the venues, leading to increased intermediation and price discrepancies among markets. The growing role of ATSs, increasing competition among market venues, and the experience of the NASDAQ reforms brought these tensions to the fore.

A public debate was occasioned by the call for the repeal of the NYSE's Rule 390. This rule embodied the principle that NYSE members were prohibited from conducting trades off the floor of the exchange. At one time, the rule had great force and reach, but by the 1990s it had been weakened considerably. It nevertheless stood as strong symbol of the exchange's anti-competitive power. The relationship of the NYSE (as the self-regulatory organization) and the SEC (as the final authority on approval of rules) required the NYSE to propose the rule change to the SEC. The SEC then solicited comment on the proposal and finally took action (modification and approval, in this case).

In soliciting comment, the SEC took the occasion to raise broader issues. In the "Rule 390 Concept Release" (U.S. Securities and Exchange Commission (2000)), the SEC laid out terms of the debate and raised the relevant policy questions. At about the same time, the U.S. Senate Banking Committee conducted hearings in New York on the Competitive Market Supervision Act (on February 28, 2000) and on the Financial Marketplace of the Future (February 29, 2000). Referred to as the "World Trade Center hearings," these meetings are noteworthy because for a brief moment it appeared that there was an emerging consensus in favor of a consolidated limit order book (CLOB). For reasons possibly having to do with uncertainties over how such a system might affect institutions' competitive positions, however, the momentum suddenly abated. Not since then has a CLOB been seriously considered as the sole mechanism for U.S. equities trading.

A.7   Access and Intermarket Linkage Systems

Accessing a market generally refers to a constructive interaction with the market, particularly the transmission of a marketable (immediately executable) order to the venue. An access system is therefore more powerful than a market data system, which only offers a view of the trading activity. Broad access facilitates competition among venues, and can so promote virtual consolidation of a fragmented market.

For a broker to have direct access to a trading venue, it has usually been necessary for the broker to be a member (if the venue is an exchange) or a subscriber (if the venue is an ECN). A broker will usually be linked to most if not all trading venues, thereby providing maximum flexibility in routing a customer order.

Other links connect the trading venues directly. The most venerable of these is the Intermarket Trading System (ITS). ITS links the NYSE and the regional stock exchanges. It allows brokers at one exchange to send orders directly to another. NASDAQ's SuperSOES system also provides access (among other things). It can automatically generate executions between different market makers, between a broker and a market maker, or even between a broker and an ECN.

Intermarket access systems became flash points for intervenue disputes. A major point of difference arose from the relative speeds of electronic and floor-based venues. To avoid trade-throughs, the former may be forced to send orders to the latter at a penalty in response time that some traders felt is substantial. The problem has been largely addressed, however, with the order protection rule component of Regulation National Market System (NMS), to which we next turn.

A.8   Regulation NMS

After the rescission of NYSE Rule 390, the SEC next addressed the balance between consolidation and fragmentation in fall 2003. Following extensive internal discussion, on February 26, 2004, the SEC released for public comment a group of proposed rules collectively named "Regulation NMS" (U.S. Securities and Exchange Commission (2004a)).[3] The proposed rule was extensive in scope and attracted an exceedingly large number of comments. The SEC held public meetings, modified the rule, and reproposed it, allowing for another comment period. Following more heated debate, the final rule was adopted in June 2005 (U.S. Securities and Exchange Commission (2005)), but only over the strong dissent of two commissioners (Glassman and Atkins (2005)).

Regulation NMS has five parts:

1. The order protection rule: Market centers are responsible for taking steps to prevent the occurrence of trade-throughs. (This rule is sometimes described, incorrectly, as trade-through prohibition.)
2. The access rule: Markets must allow nonsubscribers (outsiders) to submit executable orders on the same terms as their subscribers. The rule also capped the fee that can be charged for this access.
3. The subpenny rule: Stocks trading above $1 cannot be quoted in increments smaller than 1 cent.
4. Revised market data rules that define how market data revenues are to be allocated to trading centers.
5. Reorganization of rules ("to promote greater clarity and understanding").

The first four of these are substantive. The fifth was a useful updating, and attracted no comments (U.S. Securities and Exchange Commission (2005), p. 283). The rules apply to diverse aspects of market operation but share a common purpose, namely, promoting the efficiency of a market that is fundamentally fragmented. The rules define, for the moment at least, the limits to which a single trading venue can wall off its operations from the rest of the market.

The order protection rule had the most interesting evolution and engendered the most heated discussion. Trade-throughs were generally acknowledged to be indicative of a poorly integrated market, but some doubted their frequency, magnitude, and economic significance, and therefore the need for regulation. One view was that the broker's agency duty already covered the matter, for example, that a broker who executed a customer market purchase order at 100 when there was an available offer at 99 was not giving his client "best execution." The Commission was also ultimately concerned, however, with the order traded through (in this example, the offer at 99). It was felt that trade-throughs would discourage the submission of visible limit orders and therefore that the competition to establish aggressive bids and offers would be impaired.

It was noted earlier that existing market linkage systems had difficulties with the differing degrees to which participants valued response speed. Trade-through avoidance may require a venue to send an order elsewhere. If the destination venue delays responding to the order, the market might grind to halt, with all participants being forced to wait for the slowest respondent. The Commission's solution was to make a venue's best bid and offer protected against trade through only if they were available for automatic execution. This effectively requires venues to establish rapid and reliable links.

The access rule prevents venues from establishing differential terms on which they handle subscriber and nonsubscriber orders. The cap on access fees avoids the distortion that might result if execution costs were net of access fees, but the quoted bids and offers did not include these fees. In setting a lower limit on the price increment, the SEC essentially decreed that markets should not compete on the tick-size dimension.[4]

The market data rule is complex in its particulars but is broadly intended to reward a venue for the informational value of the data it provides. In trade reporting, the formula is weighted to reward both trade frequency and trade volume. The part of the rule dealing with quotes, though, represents a more significant innovation. Under the rule, markets are rewarded for matching the best visible bids and offers and also for improving on these prices. The rule marked a step forward from pre-existing allocational practices that were unrelated to informational value at best and distortionary at worst.

Overall, Regulation NMS represents a significant evolutionary step in regulators' attempts to address market failures that might result in higher costs to traders or impairment of the informational value of prices in a hybrid market.

Notes

Notes to Chapter 2

1. Historically, limit order books were usually maintained on paper or chalk-board. The descriptor *electronic* differentiates the modern form of these books. It is increasingly being dropped because it has become superfluous: "Electronic limit order book" has gone the way of "electronic computer."

2. A similar situation recently occurred on the Tokyo Stock Exchange. "During the initial public offering of J-Com, . . . an employee at Mizuho, a subsidiary of the Mizuho Financial Group, mistakenly typed an order to sell 610,000 shares at 1 yen, or less than a penny each, instead of an order to sell one share at 610,000 yen ($5,057) as intended, the brokerage said" (Fackler (2005)). The chair of the Tokyo Stock Exchange resigned in the aftermath (Morse (2005)).

3. At one point there were over 100 U.S. regional stock exchanges (U.S. Securities and Exchange Commission (1963), p. 948). Arnold et al. (1999) state that by 1940, there were eighteen, and this number dropped to seven by 1980 (mainly through mergers). Recent closures of trading floors include the Vancouver Stock Exchange (1989), the Toronto Stock Exchange (1997), the Tokyo Stock Exchange (1999), and the equity floor of the Pacific Stock Exchange (2001). There have been few (if any) start-ups of floor-based exchanges.

4. For example, suppose that the lowest price in all the bilateral deals is $10. If there exists someone who wanted to buy (but didn't) at a price above $10, or sell (but didn't) at a price below $10, then the total trade surplus is not maximized.

5. In *Securities and Exchange Commission v. Moises Saba Masri, et al.*, the SEC alleged that the defendants entered large buy orders near the close in a stock on which they had written a large number of (uncovered) put options and that by artificially boosting the price of the stock they could prevent exercise of the options (U.S. Securities and Exchange Commission (2004b)). In *SEC v. Rhino Advisors, Inc. and Thomas Badian*, the SEC charged that the defendants had sold short a stock in attempt to depress the price, in an attempt to increase the number of shares they would obtain under the terms of a conversion (U.S. Securities and Exchange Commission (2003)).

6. An order surcharge that increased as time to the next scheduled clearing declined was used by Wunsch Auction Systems (subsequently the Arizona Stock Exchange, now defunct), an alternative trading system for U.S. equities.

7. Under regulatory pressure, in 1991 U.S. Treasury security dealers began to publish bids, offers, and trade prices in the interdealer market on the GovPX system. The success of the GovPX initiative was later used to support the implementation of the TRACE (Trade Reporting And Compliance Engine) for municipal and corporate debt securities (Levitt (1999)).

Note to Chapter 4

1. Cos(t) in this formulation is a *deterministic* component of the series. Such components can also arise from time trends (linear or otherwise). When the deterministic component is periodic (like Cos(t)), it is said to be *seasonal*. Although the term originated in descriptions of monthly and quarterly patterns, it is now used to describe recurrent patterns at any frequency. Financial market data, for example, are said to exhibit intraday seasonalities: Trading volumes and return volatilities tend to be elevated at the start and end of trading sessions.

Note to Chapter 5

1. These remarks presume that trading has no ultimate impact on the real cash flows of the security. One possible mechanism that might lead to an interaction (at least, in the case of equity) would result from a purchaser who intends to managerial control over the enterprise. Alternatively, a seller (or more likely, a short seller) who succeeds in temporarily driving the price down may thereby cause the firm to lose customers who take the stock price as a signal of the firm's long-term viability.

Note to Chapter 6

1. Specifically, because the basic model does not allow for nonevent days, $\alpha = 1$. Next note that μ functions differently in the two models. In the basic model, it is simply the probability that a trader is informed: μ(in the simple model) $= PIN$. In the present model, though, μ is an expected arrival rate (informed traders per unit time). To obtain PIN (a probability per trade), it must be normalized by the arrival rate of all trades (the denominator in PIN). Alternatively, if we scaled the time unit in the arrival rates so that the total arrival rate was unity, then μ (rescaled to this time unit) would equal PIN.

Note to Chapter 9

1. Lee and Ready (1991) assess the merits of quote comparison and tick test procedures. Among other things, they suggest that in working with NYSE data, trade prices be compared to midpoints prevailing five seconds previous (based on reported times). There have been many improvements in the reporting procedures however, and in more recent data signing based on reported times (with no lag) is likely to be more accurate (Bessembinder (2003a); Piwowar and Wei (2006)). Odders-White (2000) compares the trade signs imputed from quote data with the directions of the actual underlying orders.

Note to Chapter 10

1. The mere fact that no convergent representation exists does not preclude computation of sample estimates. Unlike, for example, the case of perfect collinearity in a set of regressors, there is no obvious computational problem.

Note to Chapter 11

1. The details are as follows. The characteristic function of a random variable X is defined as $\phi(t) = Ee^{iXt}$ where $i = \sqrt{-1}$. If $X \sim N(\mu, \sigma^2)$, then $\phi(t) = e^{i\mu t - \sigma^2 t^2/2}$. Letting $t = i\rho$ yields $Ee^{-\rho X} - e^{-\mu\rho + \sigma^2 \rho^2/2}$. The coefficient of absolute risk aversion is defined for a general utility function as $-U''/U'$. For the exponential utility function $-U''/U' = \rho$.

Note to Chapter 12

1. This strategy, called *lurking*, may be very effective. Rust, Miller, and Palmer (1993) describe a tournament of automated double-auction algorithms in which a lurking strategy was the winner.

Notes to Chapter 15

1. It might be claimed that the permanent/transitory distinction is essentially a semantic one, for example, that a transitory impact that remains for a month is effectively permanent from the perspective of a purchase program that will executed over one day. The relevant horizon, however, is not the trading period but the holding period. Suppose the purchase pushes up the security price by $1. If the increase is truly permanent, the dollar will be realized (in cash) when the security is subsequently sold. If the price reverts before the sale, however, the position incurs a $1 loss. Viewing long-term (but ultimately transient) impacts as permanent causes trading costs to appear smaller than they actually are.

2. In practice, a trader might price a limit order above the current ask ($L > p_t$) if she thought that that the ask might move before her order could be conveyed to the market and executed. Petersen and Sirri (2002) discuss such orders.

3. The model used in this section is cast in the framework of Harris (1998), with the following essential differences. Harris permits only discrete limit prices. (Prior to penny pricing in the U.S. equity markets, the tick size, generally $0.125, was large relative to short-term price volatility.) Harris also assumes a different execution mechanism, based on the beta distribution. Finally, Harris considers alternative trading objectives.

4. Most of the distributions commonly used in duration analysis imply eventual execution. The reader/trader is cautioned against relying on these models beyond the durations found in the estimation sample.

Notes to Appendix

1. Hasbrouck, Sofianos, and Sosebee (1993) and Teweles and Bradley (1998) give basic background on the NYSE, but neither source is current. The NYSE

Constitution and Rules (New York Stock Exchange (2005)) is authoritative and complete in the details, but it is difficult to distill from this document an overall picture of how the market really functions. The clearest description of NYSE procedures I have encountered is the exchange's *Floor Official Manual*. This manual is a complete and well-organized account, but is not circulated externally.

2. The question of which was the first electronic stock exchange has no clear answer. One strong contender, though, is Instinet. Instinet began operation in 1979 as an electronic limit order book for institutions (mutual funds, pension funds, etc.). Instinet's growth accelerated when it began to allow participation by NASDAQ market makers. The NASDAQ market makers used the system essentially as their interdealer market, and this clientele became a substantial, perhaps the dominant, group of Instinet participants. Significantly, Instinet did not open itself to retail traders. This proved to be a forgone opportunity, as newer entrants successfully cultivated the retail business.

3. In the 1975 Securities Act, Congress directed the SEC to foster a "national market system" (NMS). The phrase has probably occasioned more commentary than any other expression in U.S. market regulation. It has been interpreted at one extreme as suggesting a sort of loose communication among trading venues, and at the other extreme as a clear charge for a CLOB. The inclusion of the expression in the title of the proposed rule is significant, though, because it prominently asserts the rationale for the rules in a way that connects them to specific authorizing legislation.

4. Although not cited in the Commission's discussion, one example may illustrate the need for such a rule. ESpeed, an electronic trading system for U.S. Treasury bonds, had offered its users the ability (by paying a higher commission) to slightly improve on visible bids and offers, thereby gaining priority over them. The feature engendered some ill will, however, and ESpeed decided to abandon the feature in January 2005 (Lucchetti (2005)).

References

Acharya, Viral V., and Lasse Heje Pedersen, 2002, Asset pricing with liquidity risk (Stern School of Business).

Admati, Anat, 1985, A noisy rational expectations equilibrium for multi-asset securities markets, *Econometrica* 53, 629–57.

Admati, Anat, and Paul Pfleiderer, 1988, A theory of intraday trading patterns: Volume and price variability, *Review of Financial Studies* 1, 3–40.

Alexander, Carol, 2001, *Market Models: A Guide to Financial Data Analysis* (John Wiley West Sussex, UK).

Allison, Paul D., 1995, *Survival Analysis Using the SAS System: A Practical Guide* (SAS Institute, Cary, NC).

Almgren, Robert, 2003, Optimal execution with nonlinear impact functions and trading-enhanced risk, *Applied Mathematical Finance* 10, 1–18.

Almgren, Robert, and Neil Chriss, 2000, Optimal execution of portfolio transactions, *Risk* 3, 5–39.

Amihud, Yakov, 2002, Illiquidity and stock returns: cross-section and time-series effects, *Journal of Financial Markets* 5, 31–56.

Amihud, Yakov, and Haim Mendelson, 1980, Dealership markets: Market-making with inventory, *Journal of Financial Economics* 8, 31–53.

Amihud, Yakov, and Haim Mendelson, 1987, Trading mechanisms and stock returns: An empirical investigation, *Journal of Finance* 42, 533–53.

Amihud, Yakov, and Haim Mendelson, 1991. Market microstructure and price discovery on the Tokyo Stock Exchange, in William T. Ziemba, Warren Bailley, and Yasushi Hamao, eds., *Japanese Financial Market Research, Contributions to Economic Analysis*, no. 205 (North Holland, Amsterdam).

Amihud, Yakov, Haim Mendelson, and Maurizio Murgia, 1990, Stock market microstructure and return volatility: Evidence from Italy, *Journal of Banking and Finance* 14, 423–40.

Amihud, Yakov, Haim Mendelson, and Lasse Heje Pedersen, 2005, Market microstructure and asset pricing (Stern School, New York University).

Angel, James J., 1994, Limit versus market orders (School of Business Administration, Georgetown University).

Ansley, Craig F., W. Allen Spivey, and William J. Wrobleski, 1977, On the structure of moving average prices, *Journal of Econometrics* 6, 121–34.

Arnold, Tom, Philip Hersch, J. Harold Mulherin, and Jeffry Netter, 1999, Merging markets, *Journal of Finance* 54, 1083–107.

Bacidore, Jeffrey M., 1997, The impact of decimalization on market quality: An empirical investigation of the Toronto Stock Exchange, *Journal of Financial Intermediation* 6, 92–120.

Bacidore, Jeffrey M., 2002, Depth improvement and adjusted price improvement on the New York stock exchange, *Journal of Financial Markets* 5, 169–95.

Bacidore, Jeffrey, Katharine Ross, and George Sofianos, 2003, Quantifying market order execution quality at the New York Stock Exchange, *Journal of Financial Markets* 6, 281.

Back, Kerry, 1992, Insider trading in continuous time, *Review of Financial Studies* 5.

Back, Kerry, and Shmuel Baruch, 2004, Information in securities markets: Kyle meets Glosten and Milgrom, *Econometrica* 72, 433–65.

Back, Kerry, C. Henry Cao, and Gregory A. Willard, 2000, Imperfect competition among informed traders, *Journal of Finance* 55, 2117–55.

Baillie, Richard T., G. Geoffrey Booth, Yiuman Tse, and Tatyana Zabotina, 2002, Price discovery and common factor models, *Journal of Financial Markets* 5, 309–22.

Barclay, Michael J., and Jerold B. Warner, 1993, Stealth trading and volatility: Which trades move prices?, *Journal of Financial Economics* 34, 281–305.

Battalio, Robert H., 1997a, Do competing specialists and preferencing dealers affect market quality?, *Review of Financial Studies* 10, 969–93.

Battalio, Robert H., 1997b, Third market broker-dealers: Cost competitors or cream skimmers?, *Journal of Finance* 52, 341–52.

Battalio, Robert H., 1998, Order flow distribution, bid-ask spreads, and liquidity costs: Merrill Lynch's decision to cease routinely routing orders to regional stock exchanges, *Journal of Financial Intermediation* 7, 338–58.

Battalio, Robert H., 2003, All else equal?: A multidimensional analysis of retail, market order execution quality, *Journal of Financial Markets* 6, 143–62.

Bertsimas, Dimitris, and Andrew W. Lo, 1998, Optimal control of execution costs, *Journal of Financial Markets* 1, 1–50.

Bessembinder, H., 2004, Does an electronic stock exchange need an upstairs market?, *Journal of Financial Economics* 73, 3–36.

Bessembinder, Hendrik, 1999, Trade execution costs on NASDAQ and the NYSE: A post-reform comparison, *Journal of Financial and Quantitative Analysis* 34, 382–407.

Bessembinder, Hendrik, 2003a, Issues in assessing trade execution costs, *Journal of Financial Markets* 6, 233–57.

Bessembinder, Hendrik, 2003b, Quote-based competition and trade execution costs in NYSE-listed stocks, *Journal of Financial Economics* 70, 385–422.

Bessembinder, Hendrik, and Herbert Kaufman, 1997, A cross-exchange comparison of execution costs and information flow for NYSE-listed stocks, *Journal of Financial Economics* 46, 293–319.

Bessembinder, Hendrik, William F. Maxwell, and Kumar Venkataraman, 2005, Market transparency and institutional trading costs (Social Sciences Research Network).

Beveridge, Stephen, and Charles R. Nelson, 1981, A new approach to decomposition of economic time series into permanent and transitory components with particular attention to measurement of the "business cycle," *Journal of Monetary Economics* 7, 151–74.

Biais, Bruno, Lawrence R. Glosten and Chester Spatt, 2005, Market microstructure: A survey of microfoundations, empirical results, and policy implications. *Journal of Financial Markets* 8, 217–64.

Biais, Bruno, Pierre Hillion and Chester Spatt, 1995, An empirical analysis of the limit order book and the order flow in the Paris Bourse. *Journal of Finance* 50, 1655–89.

Breen, William J., Laurie S. Hodrick, and Robert A. Korajczyk, 2002, Predicting equity liquidity, *Management Science* 48, 470–83.

Brunnermeier, Markus K., 2001, *Asset Pricing under Asymmetric Information* (Oxford University Press, Oxford).

Brunnermeier, Markus K., and Lasse Heje Pedersen, 2005. Market liquidity and funding liquidity (Stern School, NYU).

Caballe, Jordi, and Murugappa Krishnan, 1994, Imperfect competition in a multi-security market with risk neutrality, *Econometrica* 62, 695–704.

Camerer, Colin, and Richard H. Thaler, 1995, Anomalies: Ultimatums, dictators and manners, *Journal of Economic Perspectives* 9, 209–19.

Campbell, John Y., Sanford J. Grossman, and Jiang Wang, 1993, Trading volume and serial correlation in stock returns, *Quarterly Journal of Economics* 108, 905–39.

CFA Institute, 2002, Trade Management Guidelines, CFA Institute (formerly the American Institute for Management Research), available online at http://www.cfainstitute.org/standards/pdf/trademgmt_ guidelines.pdf.

Chakravarty, Sugato, and Craig W. Holden, 1995, An integrated model of market and limit orders, *Journal of Financial Intermediation* 4, 213–41.

Challet, Damien, and Robin Stinchcombe, 2003, Non-constant rates and over-diffusive prices in a simple model of limit order markets, *Quantitative Finance* 3, 155–62.

Chan, Louis K. C., and Josef Lakonishok, 1993, Institutional trades and intraday stock-price behavior, *Journal of Financial Economics* 33, 173–99.

Chan, Louis K. C., and Josef Lakonishok, 1995, The behavior of stock prices around institutional trades, *Journal of Finance* 50, 1147–74.

Chan, Louis K. C., and Josef Lakonishok, 1997, Institutional equity trading costs: NYSE versus Nasdaq, *Journal of Finance* 52, 713–35.

Choi, J. Y., Dan Salandro, and Kuldeep Shastri, 1988, On the estimation of bid-ask spreads: Theory and evidence, *Journal of Financial and Quantitative Analysis* 23, 219–30.

Christie, William G., Jeffrey H. Harris, and Paul H. Schultz, 1994, Why did NASDAQ market makers stop avoiding odd-eighth quotes?, *Journal of Finance* 49, 1841–60.

Christie, William G., and Paul H. Schultz, 1994, Why do NASDAQ market makers avoid odd-eighth quotes?, *Journal of Finance* 49, 1813–40.

Chu, Quentin C., Wen-Liang Gordon Hsieh, and Yiuman Tse, 1999, Price discovery on the S&P 500 index markets: An analysis of spot index, index futures and SPDRs, *International Review of Financial Analysis* 8, 21–34.

Clements, M. P., and David F. Hendry, 1999, *Forecasting Non-stationary Economic Time Series* (MIT Press, Cambridge, MA).

Cochrane, John H., 2005, *Asset Pricing* (Princeton University Press, Princeton, NJ).

Codding, Jamey, 1999, Trading floors to shut in Sydney and London, *Futures* 28, December 1999, 16–17.

Cohen, Kalman J., Steven F. Maier, Robert A. Schwartz, and David K. Whitcomb, 1981, Transaction costs, order placement strategy, and existence of the bid-ask spread, *Journal of Political Economy* 89, 287–305.

Coles, Stuart, 2001, *An Introduction to the Statistical Modeling of Extreme Values* (Springer-Verlag, London).

Comerton-Forde, Carole, and James Rydge, 2004, A review of stock market microstructure (Securities Industry Research Centre of Asia-Pacific, Sydney).

Conrad, Jennifer S., Kevin M. Johnson, and Sunil Wahal, 2001, Institutional trading and soft dollars, *Journal of Finance* 56, 397–416.

Conrad, Jennifer S., Kevin M. Johnson, and Sunil Wahal, 2002, The trading of institutional investors: Theory and evidence, *Journal of Applied Finance* 12, 13.

Conrad, Jennifer S., Kevin M. Johnson, and Sunil Wahal, 2003, Institutional trading and alternative trading systems, *Journal of Financial Economics* 70, 99–134.

Copeland, Thomas, and Dan Galai, 1983, Information effects and the bid-ask spread, *Journal of Finance* 38, 1457–69.

Coppejans, Mark, Ian Domowitz, and Ananth Madhavan, 2001. Liquidity in an automated auction (Department of Economics, Duke University).

Dacorogna, Michel M., Ramazan Gencay, Ulrich A. Muller, Richard B. Olsen, and Olivier B. Pictet, 2001, *High-Frequency Finance* (Academic Press, New York).

de Jong, Frank, 2002, Measures of contributions to price discovery: A comparison, *Journal of Financial Markets* 5, 323–28.

de Jong, Frank, Theo Nijman, and Ailsa Roell, 1995, A comparison of the cost of trading French shares on the Paris bourse and on SEAQ international, *European Economic Review* 39, 1277–301.

Degryse, Hans, 1999, The total cost of trading Belgian shares: Brussels versus London, *Journal of Banking and Finance* 23, 1331–55.

Domowitz, Ian, and A. Mahmoud El-Gamal, 1999, Financial market liquidity and the distribution of prices (Social Sciences Research Network).

Doornik, Jurgen A., and David F. Hendry, 1997, The implications for econometric modelling of forecast failure, *Scottish Journal of Political Economy* 44, 437–61.

Duffie, Darrell, 2001, *Dynamic Asset Pricing Theory*, 3rd ed. (Princeton University Press, Princeton, NJ).

Easley, David, Soeren Hvidkjaer, and Maureen O'Hara, 2002, Is information risk a determinant of asset returns?, *Journal of Finance* 57, 2185–221.

Easley, David, Nicholas M. Kiefer, and Maureen O'Hara, 1997, One day in the life of a very common stock, *Review of Financial Studies* 10, 805–35.

Easley, David, and Maureen O'Hara, 1987, Price, trade size, and information in securities markets, *Journal of Financial Economics* 19, 69–90.

Easley, David, and Maureen O'Hara, 1991, Order form and information in securities markets, *Journal of Finance* 46, 905–27.

Easley, David, and Maureen O'Hara, 1992, Time and the process of security price adjustment, *Journal of Finance* 47, 576–605.

Eckbo, B. Espen and Jian Liu, 1993, Temporary components of stock prices: new univariate results. *Journal of Financial and Quantitative Analysis* 28, 161–76.

Ellul, Andrew, Craig W. Holden, Pankaj Jain, and Robert H. Jennings, 2002, Determinants of order choice on the New York Stock Exchange (Kelley School, University of Indiana).

Embrechts, Paul, Claudia Kluppelberg, and Thomas Mikosch, 1997, *Modelling Extremal Events for Insurance and Finance* (Springer-Verlag, London).

Engle, Robert F. and Clive W. J. Granger, 1987, Co-integration and error correction: representation, estimation and testing. *Econometrica* 55, 251–76.

Esser, Angelika, and Burkhart Mönch, 2005, The navigation of an iceberg: the optimal use of hidden orders (Social Sciences Research Network).

Euronext, 2003, Harmonized Market Rules I, Euronext, available online at http://www.euronext.com/editorial/documentation_rules/wide/0,5371,1732_4558617,00.html.

Fackler, Martin, 2005, Tokyo Exchange struggles with snarls in electronics, *New York Times*, December 13, 2005.

Farmer, J. Doyne, Paolo Patelli, and Ilija I. Zovko, 2005, The predictive power of zero intelligence in financial markets, *Proceedings of the National Academy of Sciences (Economic Sciences)* 102, 2254–59.

Foster, F. Douglas, and S. Viswanathan, 1990, A theory of the interday variations in volume, variance, and trading costs in securities markets, *Review of Financial Studies* 3, 593–624.

Foster, F. Douglas, and S. Viswanathan, 1996, Strategic trading when agents forecast the forecasts of others, *Journal of Finance* 51, 1437–78.

Foucault, Thierry, 1999, Order flow composition and trading costs in a dynamic limit order market, *Journal of Financial Markets* 2, 99–134.

Foucault, Thierry, Ohad Kadan, and Eugene Kandel, 2001, Limit order book as a market for liquidity (Social Sciences Research Network).

Friedman, Daniel, and John Rust, 1993, *The Double Auction Market: Institutions, Theories and Evidence* (Addison-Wesley, New York).

Fuller, Wayne A., 1996, *Introduction to Statistical Time Series,* 2nd ed. (John Wiley, New York).

Gabaix, Xavier, Parameswaran Gopikrishnan, Vasiliki Plerou, and H. Eugene Stanley, 2003, A theory of power law distributions in financial market fluctuations, *Nature* 423, 267–70.

Garman, Mark, 1976, Market microstructure, *Journal of Financial Economics* 3, 257–75.

Gatev, Evan, William N. Goetzmann and K. Geert Rouwenhorst, 2006, Pairs trading: Performance of a relative-value arbitrage rule. *Review of Financial Studies* 19, 797–827.

Glassman, Cynthia A., and Paul S. Atkins, 2005, Dissent of Commissioners Cynthia A. Glassman and Paul S. Atkins to the Adoption of Regulation NMS, available online at http://www.sec.gov/rules/final/34-51808-dissent.pdf.

Glosten, Lawrence R., 1989, Insider trading, liquidity, and the role of the monopolist specialist, *Journal of Business* 62, 211–35.

Glosten, Lawrence R., 1994, Is the electronic open limit order book inevitable?, *Journal of Finance* 49, 1127–61.

Glosten, Lawrence R., and Lawrence E. Harris, 1988, Estimating the components of the bid/ask spread, *Journal of Financial Economics* 21, 123–42.

Glosten, Lawrence R., and Paul R. Milgrom, 1985, Bid, ask, and transaction prices in a specialist market with heterogeneously informed traders, *Journal of Financial Economics* 14, 71–100.

Goettler, Ronald L., Christine A. Parlour, and Uday Rajan, 2003, Welfare in a dynamic limit order market (GSIA, Carnegie Mellon University).

Goettler, R. L., C. A. Parlour and U. Rajan, 2005, Equilibrium in a dynamic limit order market. *Journal of Finance* 60, 2149–92.

Goldstein, Michael A., and Kenneth A. Kavajecz, 2000, Eighths, sixteenths, and market depth: Changes in tick size and liquidity provision on the NYSE, *Journal of Financial Economics* 56, 125–49.

Gonzalo, Jesus, and Clive Granger, 1995, Estimation of common long-memory components in cointegrated systems, *Journal of Business and Economic Statistics* 13, 27–35.

Goodman, George (writing as Adam Smith), 1967, *The Money Game* (Random House, New York).

Gourieroux, Christian, and Joanna Jasiak, 2001, *Financial Econometrics* (Princeton University Press, Princeton, NJ).

Green, Richard C., Burton Hollifield, and Norman Schuerhoff, 2005, Financial intermediation and the costs of trading in an opaque market (David A. Tepper School of Business, Carnegie Mellon University).

Greene, William H., 2002, *Econometric Analysis* (Macmillan, New York).

Griffiths, Mark D., Brian F. Smith, D. Alasdair S. Turnbull, and Robert W. White, 2000, The costs and determinants of order aggressiveness, *Journal of Financial Economics* 56, 65–88.

Grossman, Sanford J., and Merton H. Miller, 1987, Liquidity and market structure, *Journal of Finance* 43, 617–33.

Hamao, Yasushi and Joel Hasbrouck, 1995, Securities trading in the absence of dealers: trades and quotes on the Tokyo Stock Exchange. *Review of Financial Studies* 8, 849–78.

Hamilton, James D., 1994, *Time Series Analysis* (Princeton University Press, Princeton, NJ).

Handa, Puneet, and Robert A. Schwartz, 1996, Limit order trading, *Journal of Finance* 51, 1835–61.

Harris, Frederick H. deB, Thomas H. McInish, and Robert A. Wood, 2002a, Common factor components vs. information shares: A reply, *Journal of Financial Markets* 5, 341–48.

Harris, Frederick H. deB, Thomas H. McInish, and Robert A. Wood, 2002b, Security price adjustment across exchanges: An investigation of common factor components for Dow stocks, *Journal of Financial Markets* 5, 277–308.

Harris, Lawrence E., 1990, Statistical properties of the Roll serial covariance bid/ask spread estimator, *Journal of Finance* 45, 579–90.

Harris, Lawrence E., 1998, Optimal dynamic order submission strategies in some stylized trading problems, *Financial Markets, Institutions and Instruments* 7, 1–76.

Harris, Lawrence E., 2003, *Trading and Exchanges* (Oxford University Press, New York).

Harris, Lawrence E., and Joel Hasbrouck, 1996, Market vs. limit orders: The SuperDOT evidence on order submission strategy, *Journal of Financial and Quantitative Analysis* 31, 213–31.

Hasbrouck, Joel, 1988, Trades, quotes, inventories, and information, *Journal of Financial Economics* 22, 229–52.

Hasbrouck, Joel, 1991a, Measuring the information content of stock trades. *Journal of Finance* 46, 179–207.

Hasbrouck, Joel, 1991b, The summary informativeness of stock trades: An econometric analysis. *Review of Financial* Studies 4, 571–95.

Hasbrouck, Joel, 1993, Assessing the quality of a security market: A new approach to transaction-cost measurement. *Review of Financial Studies* 6, 191–212.

Hasbrouck, Joel, 1995, One security, many markets: Determining the contributions to price discovery. *Journal of Finance* 50, 1175–99.

Hasbrouck, Joel, 1996a, Modeling microstructure time series, in G. S. Maddala, and C. R. Rao, eds., *Handbook of Statistics 14: Statistical Methods in Finance* (Elsevier North Holland, Amsterdam).

Hasbrouck, Joel, 1996b, Order characteristics and stock price evolution: An application to program trading, *Journal of Financial Economics* 41, 129–49.

Hasbrouck, Joel, 2002, Stalking the "efficient price" in market microstructure specifications: an overview, *Journal of Financial Markets* 5, 329–39.

Hasbrouck, Joel, 2005, Trading costs and returns for US equities: The evidence from daily data (Stern School of Business, New York University).

Hasbrouck, Joel, and Thomas S. Y. Ho, 1987, Order arrival, quote behavior, and the return-generating process, *Journal of Finance* 42, 1035–48.

Hasbrouck, Joel, and Gideon Saar, 2003, Technology and liquidity provision: the blurring of traditional definitions (Stern School, New York University).

Hasbrouck, Joel, and George Sofianos, 1993, The trades of market makers: An empirical examination of NYSE specialists, *Journal of Finance* 48, 1565–93.

Hasbrouck, Joel, George Sofianos, and Deborah Sosebee, 1993. New York Stock Exchange trading systems and procedures (New York Stock Exchange).

Holden, Craig W., and Avanidhar Subrahmanyam, 1992, Long-lived private information and imperfect competition, *Journal of Finance* 47, 247–70.

Holden, Craig W., and Avanidhar Subrahmanyam, 1994, Risk aversion, imperfect competition, and long-lived information, *Economics Letters* 44, 181–90.

Huang, Chi-Fu, and Robert H. Litzenberger, 1998, *Foundations for Financial Economics* (Prentice Hall, Englewood Cliffs, NJ).

Huang, R. D., 1996, Dealer versus auction markets: A paired comparison of execution costs on NASDAQ and the NYSE, *Journal of Financial Economics* 41, 313–57.

Huberman, G., and W. Stanzl, 2004, Price manipulation and quasi-arbitrage, *Econometrica* 72, 1247–75.

Ingersoll, Jonathan E. Jr., 1987, *Theory of Financial Decision Making* (Rowman and Littlefield, Lanham, MD).

Irvine, Paul J., Marc L. Lipson and Andy Puckett, 2006, Tipping. *Review of Financial Studies* forthcoming.

Jones, Charles M., Gautam Kaul, and Marc L. Lipson, 1994, Transactions, volume, and volatility, *Review of Financial Studies* 7, 631–51.

Kagel, John H., Chung Kim, and Donald Moser, 1996, Fairness in ultimatum games with asymmetric information and asymmetric payoffs, *Games and Economic Behavior* 13, 100–110.

Karlin, Samuel, and Howard M. Taylor, 1975, *A First Course in Stochastic Processes* (Academic Press, New York).

Keim, Donald B., and Ananth Madhavan, 1995, Anatomy of the trading process: Empirical evidence on the behavior of institutional traders, *Journal of Financial Economics* 37(3), 371–98.

Keim, Donald B., and Ananth Madhavan, 1996, The upstairs market for block trades: Analysis and measurement of price effects, *Review of Financial Studies* 9, 1–36.

Keim, Donald B., and Ananth Madhavan, 1997, Transactions costs and investment style: An inter-exchange analysis of institutional equity trades, *Journal of Financial Economics* 46, 265–92.

Kempf, Alexander, and Olaf Korn, 1999, Market depth and order size, *Journal of Financial Markets* 2, 29–48.

Klemperer, Paul, 2004, *Auctions: Theory and Practice* (Princeton University Press, Princeton, NJ).

Kotz, Samuel, N. Balakrishnan, and Norman L. Johnson, 2000, *Continuous Multivariate Distributions, Volume 1: Models and Applications,* 2nd ed. (John Wiley, New York).

Krishna, Vijay, 2002, *Auction Theory* (Academic Press, San Diego).

Kumar, Praveen, and Duane Seppi, 1994, Limit and market orders with optimizing traders (Carnegie Mellon University).

Kurov, Alexander, and Dennis J. Lasser, 2004, Price dynamics in the regular and E-Mini futures markets, *Journal of Financial and Quantitative Analysis* 39, 365–84.

Kyle, Albert S., 1985, Continuous auctions and insider trading, *Econometrica* 53, 1315–36.

Lancaster, Tony, 1997, *The Econometric Analysis of Transition Data* (Cambridge University Press, Cambridge).

Lee, Charles M. C., 1993, Market integration and price execution for NYSE-listed securities, *Journal of Finance* 48, 1009–38.

Lee, Charles M. C., and Mark J. Ready, 1991, Inferring trade direction from intraday data, *Journal of Finance* 46, 733–46.

Lehmann, Bruce N. and David M. Modest, 1994, Trading and liquidity on the Tokyo Stock Exchange: A bird's eye view. *Journal of Finance* 49, 951–84.

Lehmann, Bruce N., 2002, Some desiderata for the measurement of price discovery across markets, *Journal of Financial Markets* 5, 259–76.

Levitt, Arthur, 1999, Remarks before the Bond Market Association, U.S. Securities and Exchange Commission, available online at http://www.sec.gov/news/speech/speecharchive/1999/spch268.htm.

Llorente, Guillermo, Roni Michaely, Gideon Saar, and Jiang Wang, 2002, Dynamic volume-return relation of individual stocks, *Review of Financial Studies* 15, 1005–47.

Lo, Andrew W., A. Craig MacKinlay, and June Zhang, 2002, Econometric models of limit order execution, *Journal of Financial Economics* 65, 31–71.

Lucchetti, Aaron, 2005, ESpeed yanks pricing initiative: electronic bond-trading firm alters platform after program sparked complaints about fees, *Wall Street Journal*, January 4, 2005, C, p. 1.

Lyons, Richard K., 2001, *The Microstructure Approach to Foreign Exchange Rates* (MIT Press, Cambridge, MA).

Macey, Jonathan R., and Maureen O'Hara, 1997, The law and economics of best execution, *Journal of Financial Intermediation* 6, 188–223.

Madhavan, Ananth, 2000, Market microstructure: A survey, *Journal of Financial Markets* 3, 205–58.

Madhavan, Ananth, and Minder Cheng, 1997, In search of liquidity: Block trades in the upstairs and downstairs markets, *Review of Financial Studies* 10(1) 175–203.

Madhavan, Ananth, Matthew Richardson, and Mark Roomans, 1997, Why do security prices change?, *Review of Financial Studies* 10, 1035–64.

Madhavan, Ananth, and Seymour Smidt, 1991, A Bayesian model of intraday specialist pricing, *Journal of Financial Economics* 30, 99–134.

Madhavan, Ananth, and Seymour Smidt, 1993, An analysis of changes in specialist inventories and quotations, *Journal of Finance* 48, 1595–628.

Madhavan, Ananth, and George Sofianos, 1998, An empirical analysis of NYSE specialist trading, *Journal of Financial Economics* 48, 189–210.

Maguire, Francis, 1998. Life's problems ... and solutions, *Futures* 27, September, 82–84.

Mathstatica, 2005, available online at http://www.mathstatica.com/spot_the_error/.

Mendelson, H., and T. I. Tunca, 2004, Strategic trading, liquidity, and information acquisition, *Review of Financial Studies* 17, 295–337.

Merton, Robert, 1980, On estimating the expected rate of return on the market, *Journal of Financial Economics* 8, 323–62.

Milgrom, Paul, 2004, *Putting Auction Theory to Work* (Cambridge University Press, Cambridge).

Morse, Andrew, 2005, Tokyo Exchange chief quits; Move follows technology blunders, may slow pace of reforms, *Wall Street Journal*, December 21, C, p. 14.

Neal, Robert, and Simon M. Wheatley, 1998, Adverse selection and bid-ask spreads: Evidence from closed-end funds, *Journal of Financial Markets* 1, 121–49.

New York Stock Exchange, 2005, *Constitution and Rules.*

Niederhoffer, Victor, and M. F. M. Osborne, 1966, Market making and reversal on the stock exchange, *Journal of the American Statistical Association* 61, 897–916.

Odders-White, Elizabeth R., 2000, On the occurrence and consequences of inaccurate trade classification, *Journal of Financial Markets* 3, 259–86.

O'Hara, Maureen, 1995, *Market Microstructure Theory* (Blackwell, Cambridge, MA).

Parlour, Christine A., 1998, Price dynamics in limit order markets, *Review of Financial Studies* 11, 789–816.

Perold, Andre, 1988, The implementation shortfall: Paper vs. reality, *Journal of Portfolio Management* 14, 4–9.

Peterson, Mark A., 2003, Order preferencing and market quality on US equity exchanges, *Review of Financial Studies* 16, 385–415.

Peterson, Mark A., and Erik R. Sirri, 2002, Order submission strategy and the curious case of marketable limit orders, *Journal of Financial and Quantitative Analysis* 37, 221–41.

Piwowar, Michael S., and Li Wei, 2005, The sensitivity of effective spread estimates to trade-quote matching algorithms (New York Stock Exchange).

Reiss, Peter C., and Ingrid M. Werner, 1998, Does risk-sharing motivate interdealer trading?, *Journal of Finance* 53, 1657–703.

Renaldo, Angelo, 2002, Transaction costs on the Swiss stock exchange, *Financial Markets and Portfolio Management* 16, 53–68.

Renaldo, Angelo, 2004, Order aggressiveness in limit order book markets, *Journal of Financial Markets* 7, 53–74.

Rock, Kevin, 1990, The specialist's order book and price anomalies (Graduate School of Business, Harvard University).

Roll, Richard, 1984, A simple implicit measure of the effective bid-ask spread in an efficient market, *Journal of Finance* 39, 1127–39.

Ronen, Tavy, 1998, Trading structure and overnight information: A natural experiment from the Tel-Aviv Stock Exchange, *Journal of Banking and Finance* 22, 489–512.

Ross, Sheldon M., 1996, *Stochastic Processes* (John Wiley, New York).

Roth, Alvin E., 1995, Bargaining experiments, in John H. Kagel, and Alvin E. Roth, eds., *The Handbook of Experimental Economics* (Princeton University Press, Princeton, NJ).

Roth, Alvin E., and Axel Ockenfels, 2002, Last-minute bidding and the rules for ending second-price auctions: Evidence from eBay and Amazon auctions on the internet, *American Economic Review* 92, 1093–103.

Rubinstein, Ariel, 1982, Perfect equilibrium in a bargaining model, *Econometrica* 50, 97–110.

Rust, John, John H. Miller, and Richard Palmer, 1993. Behavior of trading automata in a computerized double auction market, in Daniel Friedman, and John Rust, eds., *The Double Auction Market Institutions, Theories and Evidence, Proceedings Volume XIV, Santa Fe Institute* (Addison-Wesley, Reading, MA).

Saar, Gideon, 1998, Information and the pricing of assets when orders arrive one at a time (Johnson School, Cornell University).

Saar, Gideon, and Lei Yu, 2002. Information asymmetry about the firm and the permanent price impact of trades: Is there a connection? (Finance Department, Stern School, NYU).

Sandas, Patrik, 2001, Adverse selection and competitive market making: evidence from a pure limit order book, *Review of Financial Studies* 14, 705–34.

Sargent, Thomas J., 1979, *Macroeconomic Theory* (Academic Press, New York).

Seppi, Duane J., 1990, Equilibrium block trading and asymmetric information, *Journal of Finance* 45, 73–94.

Seppi, Duane J., 1997, Liquidity provision with limit orders and a strategic specialist, *Review of Financial Studies* 10, 103–50.

Shephard, Neil, 2005, *Stochastic Volatility* (Oxford University Press, Oxford); esp. General introduction.

Smith, Jeffrey W., 2000, Market vs. limit order submission behavior at a Nasdaq market maker, (National Association of Securities Dealers (NASD), NASD Economic Research).

Smith, Jeffrey W., James P. Selway III, and D. Timothy McCormick, 1998, The Nasdaq stock market: historical background and current operation (Nasdaq working paper 98-01).

Spiegel, Matthew, and Avanidhar Subrahmanyam, 1992, Informed speculation and hedging in a noncompetitive securities market, *Review of Financial Studies* 5, 307–29.

Stewart, James B., 1992, *Den of Thieves* (Simon and Schuster, New York).

Stoll, Hans R., 1978, The supply of dealer services in securities markets, *Journal of Finance* 33, 1133–51.

Stoll, Hans R., and Christoph Schenzler, 2002, Measuring market quality: the relation between quoted and effective spreads (Owen School of Management, Vanderbilt University).

Subrahmanyam, Avanidhar, 1991, Risk aversion, market liquidity, and price efficiency, *Review of Financial Studies* 4, 416–41.

Subrahmanyam, Avanidhar, 1991, A theory of trading in stock index futures, *Review of Financial Studies* 4, 17–51.

Teweles, Richard J., and Bradley, Edward S., 1998, *The Stock Market,* 7th ed. (John Wiley, New York).

Thaler, Richard H., 1988, Anomalies: The ultimatum game, *Journal of Economic Perspectives* 2, 195–206.

Tsay, Ruey S., 2002, *Analysis of Financial Time Series* (John Wiley, New York).

U.S. Securities and Exchange Commission, 1963, Special Study of the Securities Markets, U.S. Government Printing Office, via the Securities and Exchange Commission Historical Society, available online at http://www.sechistorical.org/collection/papers/1960/1963_SS_Sec_Markets/.

U.S. Securities and Exchange Commission, 1996, Final rule: Order execution obligations (Release No. 34-37619A; File No. S7-30-95). *CFR 17 Part 240*, available online at http://www.sec.gov/rules/final/37619a.txt

U.S. Securities and Exchange Commission, 1996a, Final rule: Order execution obligations, available online at http://www.sec.gov/rules/final/37619a.txt

U.S. Securities and Exchange Commission, 1996b, Report Persuant to Section 21(a) of the Securities Exchange Act of 1934 Regarding the NASD and the NASDAQ Market, available online at http://www.sec.gov/litigation/investreport/nasdaq21a.htm.

U.S. Securities and Exchange Commission, 1998, Final rule: Regulation of exchanges and alternative trading systems (Release No. 34-40760; File No. S7-12-98), available online at http://www.sec.gov/rules/final/34-40760.txt

U.S. Securities and Exchange Commission, 2000, Notice of Filing of Proposed Rule Change to Rescind Exchange Rule 390 (Release No. 34-42450; File No. SR-NYSE-99-48), available online at http://www.sec.gov/rules/sro/ny9948o.htm.

U.S. Securities and Exchange Commission, 2001, Frequently Asked Questions About Rule 11Ac1-5, Division of Market Regulation, Staff Legal Bulleting No. 12R (Revised), available at http://www.sec.gov/interps/legal/slbim12a.htm.

U.S. Securities and Exchange Commission, 2003, Rhino Advisors and Thomas Badian Settle Claims and Agree to Pay Jointly a $1 Million Penalty, Litigation Release No. 18003, available online at http://www.sec.gov/litigation/litreleases/lr18003.htm.

U.S. Securities and Exchange Commission, 2004a, Regulation NMS (Proposing Release No. 34-49325; February 26, 2004), available online at http://www.sec.gov/rules/proposed/34-49325.htm.

U.S. Securities and Exchange Commission, 2004b, Securities and Exchange Commission v. Moises Saba Masri, et al., SEC charges Moises Saba and Albert Sutton with fraud, Litigation Release No. 18593, available online at http://www.sec.gov/litigation/litreleases/lr18593.htm.

U.S. Securities and Exchange Commission, 2005, Regulation NMS (Final Rule Release No. 34-51808; June 9, 2005), available online at http://www.sec.gov/rules/final/34-51808.pdf.

Venkataraman, Kumar, 2001, Automated vs. floor trading: An analysis of execution costs on the Paris and New York Exchanges, *Journal of Finance* 56, 1445–85.

Viswanathan, S., and James J.D. Wang, 2004, Inter-dealer trading in financial markets, *Journal of Business* 77, 987–1040.

Watson, Mark W., 1986, Univariate detrending methods with stochastic trends, *Journal of Monetary Economics* 18, 49–75.

Werner, Ingrid M., 2003, Execution quality for institutional orders routed to Nasdaq dealers before and after decimals (Dice Center Working Paper, Ohio State University).

White, Halbert, 2001, *Asymptotic Theory for Econometricians* (rev. ed.) (Academic Press, Orlando).

Yao, Jian, 1997, Market making in the interbank foreign exchange market (Stern School of Business, New York University).

Index